Elections and Voters in Britain

CONTEMPORARY POLITICAL STUDIES SERIES

Series Editor: John Benyon, *University of Leicester*

Published

DAVID BROUGHTON
Public Opinion and Political Polling in Britain

CLYDE CHITTY
Education Policy in Britain

MICHAEL CONNOLLY
Politics and Policy Making in Northern Ireland

DAVID DENVER
Elections and Voters in Britain

JUSTIN FISHER
British Political Parties

ROBERT GARNER
Environmental Politics: Britain, Europe and the Global Environment; 2nd edn

ANDREW GEDDES
The European Union and British Politics

WYN GRANT
Pressure Groups and British Politics

WYN GRANT
Economic Policy in Britain

DEREK HEATER and GEOFFREY BERRIDGE
Introduction to International Politics

DILYS M. HILL
Urban Policy and Politics in Britain

ROBERT LEACH
Political Ideology in Britain

ROBERT LEACH and JANIE PERCY-SMITH
Local Governance in Britain

PETER MADGWICK
British Government: The Central Executive Territory

ANDREW MASSEY and ROBERT PYPER
Public Management and Modernisation in Britain

PHILIP NORTON
Parliament and British Politics

MALCOLM PUNNETT
Selecting the Party Leader

ROBERT PYPER
The British Civil Service

Forthcoming

RAYMOND KUHN
Politics and the Media in Britain

Elections and Voters in Britain

Second Edition

DAVID DENVER

palgrave
macmillan

First edition 2003
Second edition 2007

Published by
PALGRAVE MACMILLAN
Houndmills, Basingstoke, Hampshire RG21 6XS and
175 Fifth Avenue, New York, N.Y. 10010
Companies and representatives throughout the world

PALGRAVE MACMILLAN is the global academic imprint of the Palgrave Macmillan division of St. Martin's Press, LLC and of Palgrave Macmillan Ltd. Macmillan® is a registered trademark in the United States, United Kingdom and other countries. Palgrave is a registered trademark in the European Union and other countries.

ISBN-13: 978-0-230-00158-9   hardback
ISBN-10: 0-230-00158-0   hardback
ISBN-13: 978-0-230-00159-6   paperback
ISBN-10: 0-230-00159-9   paperback

This book is printed on paper suitable for recycling and made from fully managed and sustained forest sources.

A catalogue record for this book is available from the British Library.

A catalog record for this book is available from the Library of Congress.

10	9	8	7	6	5	4	3	2	1
16	15	14	13	12	11	10	09	08	07

Printed and bound in China

Contents

List of Figures

List of Tables

Preface to the Second Edition

As I note towards the end of this book, 'One of the pleasures – and, occasionally, frustrations – of studying elections is that they keep happening.' Since the first edition of the book was published, another general election has come and gone and another major book based on the British Election Study (BES) has been published: the evocatively titled *Political Choice in Britain* (Clarke *et al.*, 2004). In a review of that book (Denver, 2005) I suggested that while it is not for the statistically faint-hearted it 'will undoubtedly be the starting point for much future research on British electoral behaviour'.

In this edition, therefore, I have updated the material to take account of the ideas and data presented by Clarke *et al.*, especially in relation to what they call 'valence politics', which refers to the evaluations and judgements that they see as underpinning and explaining the party choices made by voters in contemporary British elections. In addition, results and survey data from the 2005 elections have been incorporated into the discussion as well as relevant tables and figures.

As noted in the Preface to the first edition, this book is not primarily for colleagues actively researching and writing about elections. Although I hope that they find it a useful overview which they could recommend to their students, specialists in electoral analysis will already know, more or less, most of what is written in the following pages. Rather, my intention here has been to summarize and simplify the work of these colleagues for non-specialists and students in both schools and universities (as well as, one hopes, people who just happen to be interested in elections). One consequence of this focus is that I have tried to keep tables as clear and uncluttered as possible. In many cases this has meant not showing in tables the raw numbers on which calculations are based. This would be unforgivable in a research paper, of course, but seems, on balance, to be a sensible strategy in this case.

As before, I have included a glossary of statistical terms and items appearing in the glossary are printed in bold when they first appear in the text. The explanations, and the descriptions of various statistical measures and techniques in the text, are intended to be non-technical, an attempt to enable readers to understand why various techniques are used and what the results can tell us.

Everyone writing about electoral behaviour in Britain has to acknowledge a debt to the successive teams which, from 1963 onwards, have undertaken the burden of directing the BES surveys. In particular, the team involved in 2001 and 2005 (David Sanders, Paul Whiteley, Harold Clarke and Marianne Stewart) deserve special thanks for making the survey data available to colleagues with unprecedented speed. The release of the 2005 data was so prompt that, had I not been acting as Head of my Department, I could have completed this book rather sooner than has proved possible.

At a personal level, I am grateful for the patience shown by my publisher, Steven Kennedy. Iain MacAllister read the entire typescript of the first edition and made many helpful suggestions while Damon Berridge (Applied Statistics, Lancaster University) gave advice and reassurance concerning the more complicated statistical issues.

DAVID DENVER

1
Studying British Elections

The British general election of 1950 was the first 'normal' general election after the Second World War. Due to the war, the previous election in 1945 was the first to be held for ten years and it had taken place while the war with Japan was still in progress. Many electors were still serving overseas with the armed forces, with about three million being registered as 'service voters'. By 1950 things had settled down and the election of that year is the most appropriate point of departure when surveying electoral developments in Britain over the post-war period.

A simple comparison of the results in 1950 with those of the most recent election (2005) illustrates some of the major changes that have occurred during these years (see Table 1.1). These data suggest that in many respects there were very marked differences – as might be expected – between the

Table 1.1   Results of the 1950 and 2005 general elections in Great Britain

	1950			2005		
	% of votes	*Candidates*	*Seats*	*% of votes*	*Candidates*	*Seats*
Conservative	43.0	607	288	33.2	627	197
Labour	46.8	612	315	36.2	627	355
Liberal (Democrats)	9.3	475	9	22.7	626	62
SNP	0.03	3	0	1.6	59	6
Plaid Cymru	0.06	7	0	0.7	40	3
Communist	0.3	100	0	0.0	6	0
Others	0.5	41	1	5.8	1,464	4
Turnout	84.1%			61.4%		

Note: The figures shown exclude Northern Ireland. For 2005, votes and seats won exclude the South Staffordshire constituency where the election was postponed due to the death of a candidate. The Speaker was not opposed by the Conservatives or Liberal Democrats and is counted as an 'other'.

Sources: Data from Rallings and Thrasher (2000); author's calculations (2005 election).

1

general election held in the middle of the twentieth century and the one that took place in the first decade of the twenty-first. Indeed, the only similarities relate to the position of the Conservative and Labour parties. In both elections they were the largest parties in terms of share of the votes obtained and seats won. Even so, their dominance was not nearly as overwhelming in 2005 as it had been in 1950. In the earlier election, together they obtained 89.8 per cent of the votes and 98.4 per cent of the seats; by 2005 they had declined to 69.4 per cent of the votes and 88.0 per cent of the seats. As will be seen later, it was the operation of the electoral system which ensured that the decline in seats won was much smaller than the decline in votes.

It is the changes between 1950 and 2005 that are more striking, however. First, the old Liberal Party emerged from the 1950 election with less than 10 per cent of the votes and only nine seats. By 2005 they had been transformed into the Liberal Democrats, more than doubled their vote share and won 62 seats, giving them their largest number of Members of Parliament (MPs) since 1923. Second, in Scotland and Wales the part played in elections by the nationalist parties was much more significant in 2005 than it was in 1950. In the early 1950s the Scottish National Party (SNP) and Plaid Cymru were generally regarded as rather eccentric parties, supported by eccentric individuals and on the fringes of politics. Few candidates were put forward in 1950 and, within Scotland, the SNP won just 0.4 per cent of the votes, while in Wales Plaid Cymru took 1.2 per cent. In 2005, however, both contested all seats in their respective countries; the SNP won 17.7 per cent of the Scottish vote while 12.6 per cent of Welsh voters opted for Plaid. Although these were somewhat disappointing results, both parties are now major players in the electoral and political game in their respective countries.

Third, there has been a massive increase in the number and variety of 'others' participating as candidates in British elections. In 1950 there were 100 candidates representing the Communist Party (who totalled more than 90,000 votes) but in 2005 there were just six 'Communist Party of Britain' candidates who managed only 1,124 votes between them. The Communists have been more than replaced, however, by new parties. In 2005 there were 496 United Kingdom Independence Party (UKIP) candidates, 203 representing the Green Party, 119 for the British National Party (BNP), 58 for the Scottish Socialist Party and almost 600 others representing a bewildering variety of other parties and groups, or simply themselves. Why has there been this explosion in the number of candidates from small parties? One reason is that the deposit required for candidacy (retained by the authorities if the candidate does not obtain 5 per cent of the votes in the relevant constituency) is no longer a serious barrier. In 1950 the deposit required was £150. This was equivalent to about £3,250 in 2005 but in fact the deposit in

2005 was only £500. Moreover, small parties and some individuals have realized that the deposit buys a lot of publicity. Every nominated candidate is entitled to a free postal delivery to every household in the relevant constituency; 50 candidates nominated nationwide guarantees that party a free national radio and television broadcast.

Finally, the figures in the table show that the turnout of electors in 2005 was much lower – by almost 25 percentage points – than in 1950, even although there was a small increase over the 2001 figure. It should be noted, however, that the figures for 1950 and 2005 are not exactly comparable. The voting age was lowered from 21 to 18 just before the 1970 general election so that the 2005 percentage turnout is based on a much larger electorate, containing a much larger proportion of young people (a group which has a poor turnout record) than the 1950 figure. Nonetheless, the declining turnout in general elections has provoked much discussion in recent years and is a subject to which I return in the next chapter.

To younger people, the election of 1950 probably seems like ancient history but it firmly established the broad pattern of two-party politics that was to dominate in Britain for most of the rest of the century, and it acts as a sort of benchmark against which later developments can be measured. The 1950 election is also important to students of voting behaviour since it was in that election that the first-ever election survey of British voters was carried out. Before discussing this and subsequent surveys, however, it is worth considering why we should study elections.

Why study elections?

One good reason for studying elections is that they are fun events. In the first half of the nineteenth century, part of the fun involved the voters getting roaring drunk at the candidates' expense (being 'treated', as this was known), pelting them with rotten fruit and brawling in the street with opponents. The practice of candidates treating voters was effectively ended by the Second Reform Act of 1867 which greatly enlarged the electorate. There were now simply too many voters to treat. In addition, in 1872 the Ballot Act made voting secret (previously voters had to declare their choice in public), so that candidates could no longer check that the voters they had treated actually voted for them. Finally, in 1883, the Corrupt Practices Act outlawed treating (much to the disappointment of many voters, one suspects). Despite this, elections continued to be a form of public entertainment until well into the twentieth century. In 1922 a crowd of 10,000 assembled to hear the declaration of the general election result in Dundee and was rewarded with the news that the sitting member, Winston Churchill, had been defeated by a Prohibitionist (in a city notorious for drunkenness).

Popular enthusiasm does not reach those standards today but elections continue to be enjoyed by all sorts of people. Candidates and party workers often experience a sense of exhilaration during campaigns; people in the media are caught up in the excitement of reporting a major national event; television presenters get to use all sorts of computer gadgetry; pollsters, analysts and pundits find themselves in great demand. Even the mass of ordinary voters who now largely 'spectate' on election campaigns appear to enjoy the 'horse race', some of them betting on the outcome and many watching campaign reports and party broadcasts on television. Election night parties are not uncommon.

Studying elections is also fun. Some people collect stamps, some are train spotters, others pore over cricket statistics in *Wisden*. But there are also 'election buffs' around the country who collect, collate and analyse election results. Part of the fascination is the sheer mass of information available. In British general elections there are results for 646 (UK) constituencies to be looked at, but in addition there are elections to the European Parliament, the Scottish Parliament, and the Welsh and Northern Ireland Assemblies as well as local council elections involving many thousands of wards and electoral divisions. Election results are also fascinating because they are numerical in form and numbers can be analysed endlessly. Voting figures can be aggregated, averaged, correlated, graphed and used to construct maps. Some academic studies of electoral behaviour take statistical manipulation so far that they are well-nigh incomprehensible to all but a few specialists, but most require only a basic understanding of some common statistical measures and techniques.

The fact that elections yield masses of quantitative data amenable to statistical analysis, together with the rapid development of computers and appropriate software, partly explains the huge growth in the academic literature focusing on elections over the past 40 years or so. There's more to it than that, however. Elections are studied because they are important. Most people would agree that it is the existence of free, competitive elections which distinguishes political systems that we normally call 'democratic' from others. Different versions of democratic theory attach different weights to elections and assign them different functions, but all see elections as central to democracy.

In traditional democratic theory, elections give sovereignty or ultimate power to the citizens. It is through elections that the citizen participates in the political process and ultimately determines the personnel and policies of governments. Only a government which is elected by the people is a legitimate government. Other democratic theorists view elections as only one among a number of channels of citizen influence, stressing the indirect nature of influence through the electoral process, and an influential version of democratic theory suggests that elections simply allow citizens a choice between competing elites. The existence of free elections remains, nonetheless, the essential difference between democratic and non-democratic states. In the 1990s, the extension of voting rights to black people in South Africa and the introduction of free competitive elections into the ex-Communist states of Eastern Europe were widely praised as extending democracy.

Exactly how and how much elections affect what governments do is, then, a matter of some debate. At a minimum, however, it is clear that they provide a peaceful way of changing governments (and this is not unimportant given the number of governments around the world that are removed by violence). Elections are also the means by which the great mass of citizens can participate directly in the political process, and in Britain millions of citizens do participate in this way. For most, voting is the only overtly political action which is regularly undertaken. Finally, elections make governments accountable to the electorate, at least once every five years in Britain. Voters can pass judgement on the government and either keep it in office or replace it.

Undeniably, even given the relatively poor turnouts in the 2001 and 2005, general elections are major national events which precipitate greatly increased political activity, discussion, interest and media coverage. On election night, the attention of a substantial portion of the nation is at least partly engaged by the election. Next day, the front pages of all newspapers are entirely devoted to election news. During the 2005 election, television channels dedicated to news provided almost round-the-clock campaign coverage: well over-the-top for most electors but certainly a feast for election 'junkies'.

These would be reasons enough for studying elections but it is also clear that elections do make a difference to the policies pursued by governments and hence to the lives of most people. There might be some debate about how much difference it makes when one party rather than another wins an election, and it is certainly true that governments of any party are constrained by external events over which they have little control. Nonetheless, it seems to strain credulity to suggest, for example, that the Conservative victory in the 1979 general election had little effect on, say, the status and role of trade unions in Britain or that the results of the 1997 election had nothing to do with the subsequent implementation of devolution to Scotland and Wales. Elections are so central to politics that, as David Butler (1998, p. 454) observed, 'History used to be marked off by the dates of Kings . . . Now it is marked by the dates of [general] elections.'

Elections, then, are central to democracy, occasion mass political behaviour, determine who governs and thus affect the lives of all of us. By studying them we seek to deepen our understanding of how a key process of democracy operates, to discover how citizens make their voting decisions and to explain election outcomes.

Studying elections

Unsurprisingly, given their importance and fascination, there is a vast literature dealing with elections and voting in Britain, including a specialized journal (*Journal of Elections, Public Opinion and Parties*). This literature covers every conceivable aspect of elections, but here I focus on the two main ways in which voting has been studied: by means of sample surveys and by analysing election results themselves.

Surveys of the electorate

Sample surveys are commonly used – by a variety of agencies in a variety of fields – to collect information about individuals. They provide, therefore, **individual-level data**. On the basis of the sample figures, generalizations can be made, within limits, about the population from which the sample was taken. Lay people frequently express astonishment or disbelief when it is pointed out that on the basis of a sample of around 2,000 voters generalizations can be made about the whole British electorate. Without going into sampling theory, however, it is the case that this can be done with some accuracy and surveys are among the most important tools of empirical social science.

Academic survey studies of voting behaviour were pioneered in the 1940s in the United States but, as noted above, the first-ever academic survey relating to voting behaviour in Britain was carried out at the time of the 1950 election. This was a local study: some 850 voters in the constituency of Greenwich were interviewed before, during and after the election. Partly because of the rudimentary nature of the technology available to analyse survey returns (there were no computers in those days), the book reporting the results of this study was not published until six years later (Benney, Gray and Pear, 1956). Although the topics covered have remained central concerns for electoral analysts – the role of social class and policy opinions, voters' attention to the local and national campaigns, vote switching, and so on – the report was very much an exploratory and mapping operation and the analysis was confined to what would now be regarded as the elementary technique of **cross-tabulation**.

Further local surveys followed in the 1950s – in Bristol (Milne and Mackenzie, 1954, 1958), Glossop (Birch, 1959) and Newcastle under Lyme (Bealey, Blondel and McCann, 1965) – but the next major development came in 1963. In that year, the first national survey study of the British electorate was undertaken under the direction of David Butler and Donald Stokes. Although 1963 was not an election year (the survey was one of two focusing on the 1964 election), this proved to be the first of a series of national surveys carried out at every general election since 1964 under the auspices of the British Election Study (BES). Butler and Stokes themselves covered the 1964, 1966 and 1970 elections. A team from the University of Essex took over for the elections of 1974 (two) and 1979. From 1983 until 1997 Anthony Heath, Roger Jowell and John Curtice were the principal investigators, while in 2001 and 2005 the baton passed to David Sanders and Paul Whiteley at Essex University and two election specialists from the United States (Harold Clarke and Marianne Stewart). These surveys have resulted in a number of major works on voting in Britain and hundreds, possibly thousands, of book chapters, scholarly articles and papers. The major BES reports on the elections from 1964 to 2001 are by Butler and Stokes (1969, 1974), Sarlvik and Crewe (1983), Heath *et al.* (1985, 1991, 1994, 2001), Evans and Norris (1999) and Clarke *et al.* (2004). In addition, an invaluable compendium of the main results of the surveys conducted between 1963 and 1992 can be found in Crewe, Fox and Day (1995).

Detailed and complex national surveys of the kind now undertaken by the BES, which involve asking respondents lots of questions in different survey 'waves', are expensive, however, and there are many examples of more limited surveys. Researchers have surveyed voters in particular localities and also specific groups of voters such as women, 'affluent workers', young people and members of ethnic minority groups. Others have focused on particular topics, such as voting in local elections or the impact of media coverage on political attitudes.

Other important sources of survey data about individual voters are the regular public opinion polls and election-day 'exit' polls (which involve interviewing voters as they leave the polling station after having voted and are regularly commissioned by the main terrestrial television channels at by-elections and general elections). Poll results are frequently used by commentators and electoral analysts (see, for example, Rose and McAllister, 1986, 1990; Worcester and Mortimore, 1999, 2001; Worcester, Mortimore and Baines, 2005). In addition, researchers sometimes 'piggy-back' on polls by paying them to ask specific questions in their regular monthly surveys (see, for example, Bartle, 2001; Clarke, Stewart and Whiteley, 2001).

The general public usually pay attention to political polls only at election time, when they achieve high visibility by giving almost daily figures for the voting intentions of the electorate. Polls have, indeed, become an important and controversial feature of modern election campaigns (see Chapter 6). In fact, the leading political pollsters (ICM, MORI and YouGov) monitor the opinions of the electorate on a regular basis, producing monthly reports which, in addition to current voting intention figures, record details of the voters' perceptions of party leaders, government performance, current issues and much else (see www.icmresearch.co.uk, www.mori.com, www.yougov.com).

Polling firms are commercial organizations, of course, and carry out political polls on behalf of clients (mainly newspapers and television). Their clients are not particularly interested in obtaining the kind of detailed information about voting choice and the factors affecting it that academics require. Poll interviews tend, therefore, to be much shorter than interviews for major academic surveys. They are mostly conducted by telephone (or, in YouGov's case, via the Internet) and the information sought from voters, in addition to their political opinions, is normally confined to a few obvious attributes such as age, education, sex and occupation. Nonetheless, polls constitute a valuable source of individual data. They provide regular monthly data and their results are analysed and published very rapidly. These days, almost as soon as an election is over commentators are using poll results to analyse voting patterns. In contrast, in the past it has taken many months, if not years, for reports on major academic surveys to become available.

The reliability and accuracy of survey results vary with the type and size of sample used. As a rule of thumb, however, in reputable studies it is usually highly probable (95 per cent certain) that a sample figure will be within about two points either way of the true figure for the population as a whole. For example, in MORI's aggregated election polls for the 2005 election it is reported that 28 per cent of 18–24 year olds who voted chose the Conservatives. It is highly probable, therefore, that among all 18–24 year olds the proportion voting Conservative was between 26 and 30 per cent (that is, 28 per cent plus or minus two points). The important point to note is that figures derived from surveys should not be regarded as being precise. They are *estimates* of the true situation among the population being studied. Put another way, surveys are liable to sampling error (a fact which authors sometimes forget when they report survey results with great precision). For this reason, when presenting data based on sample surveys it is sensible to round the figures to whole numbers rather than report them to one decimal place, as is sometimes done.

Surveys are also liable to other sources of error. Questions may be ambiguous or unclear, lead respondents to give particular answers, be incomprehensible to the respondent or be interpreted in a way that was not intended by the questionnaire designer. Mistakes may be made by interviewers in recording answers, whether by hand or on lap-top computers. Even so, sample surveys are generally reliable and powerful research tools. They have become an indispensable part of electoral analysis and have played a crucial role in advancing our understanding of electoral behaviour.

Analysing election results

A quite different approach to studying voting is to analyse election results themselves. This approach has a much longer pedigree than the use of surveys. There is, for example, a famous analysis of the relationship between votes and seats won in British elections dating from 1905 (Edgeworth, 1905) and the literature on proportional representation suggests that there certainly were election 'buffs' in the nineteenth century, poring over their figures by candlelight (see Hart, 1992). In the modern era, this approach has been sustained by the series of 'Nuffield Studies' of British general elections (so-called because of their association with Nuffield College, Oxford). Begun in 1945, the series has provided a contemporary account of the campaign in every election since then and also an analysis of the election results. The full list of Nuffield studies since 1950 is McCallum and Readman (1947); Nicholas (1951); Butler (1952, 1955); Butler and Rose (1960); Butler and King (1965, 1966); Butler and Pinto-Duschinsky (1971); Butler and Kavanagh (1974, 1975, 1980, 1984, 1988, 1992, 1997, 2002) and Kavanagh and Butler (2005).

A simple first step in this sort of analysis is to fill in the gap between 1950 and 2005 in order to assess trends in party support. The relevant data are shown in Table 1.2 and the parties' shares of the votes are graphed in Figure 1.1. Obviously, the picture is rather more complicated than that suggested by looking at only the first and last elections in the series.

After 1951 Labour's support in general elections fell steadily (with a slight reversal of the trend in the mid-1960s) to just 28.3 per cent in 1983. There was something of a recovery in 1987 and 1992 and a clear victory in 1997. In 2001 and, more significantly, in 2005, Labour's vote share declined again. Although Labour won the 2005 election, the party's vote share was smaller than it had achieved in every election between 1950 and 1979.

Table 1.2 Party shares of votes in general elections, 1950–2005 (Great Britain, %)

	1950	1951	1955	1959	1964	1966	1970	Feb. 1974	Oct. 1974	1979	1983	1987	1992	1997	2001	2005
Conservative	43.0	47.8	49.3	48.8	42.9	41.4	46.2	38.8	36.7	44.9	43.5	43.3	42.8	31.5	32.7	33.2
Labour	46.8	49.4	47.4	44.6	44.8	48.8	43.9	38.0	40.2	37.8	28.3	31.5	35.2	44.3	42.0	36.2
Liberal (Democrats)	9.3	2.6	2.8	6.0	11.4	8.6	7.6	19.8	18.8	14.1	26.0	23.1	18.3	17.2	18.8	22.7
Others	0.9	0.2	0.5	0.6	0.9	1.1	2.3	3.4	4.3	3.2	2.2	2.1	3.7	7.0	6.5	8.0
Con.–Lab. swing		+1.1	+1.8	+1.7	–3.1	–2.8	+4.9	–0.8	–2.2	+5.3	+4.1	–1.7	–2.1	–10.2	+1.8	+3.2
Standard deviation of swing		1.7	1.9*	2.3	2.4	1.7	2.1	2.9*	1.5	3.1	3.0*	3.2	2.8	3.4*	2.6	2.4
Pedersen Index		7.4	2.0	3.3	6.7	4.3	6.0	13.3	2.7	8.4	11.8	3.2	5.3	12.4	2.3	5.9

Notes: The figures for the Liberals in 1983 and 1987 are for the 'Alliance' between the Liberals and the Social Democratic Party (SDP). Standard deviation of swing figures for elections in which there were comprehensive boundary revisions are asterisked. In these cases, except for 1955, constituency swings are based on estimates of voting in the preceding election. The standard deviation for 1955 is calculated on the basis of seats in which there was no major boundary change (N = 442).

Sources: Data from Rallings and Thrasher (2000); Electoral Commission (2001b). Swing, standard deviation and Pedersen Index statistics were calculated from the original data.

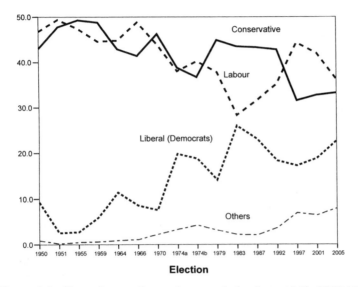

Figure 1.1   Party shares of votes in general elections, 1950–2005 (Great Britain)

Despite easily outpolling Labour in the 1980s and early 1990s, Conservative support was also on a downward trend over the period as a whole. However, the 1997 election was an unparalleled catastrophe for the party and since then it has failed to make much headway. The 1950 election marked almost the last gasp of the old Liberal Party and during the 1950s it was nearly eliminated as a serious force in electoral politics. Under Jo Grimond (party leader 1956–67) the abyss was avoided, however, and in February 1974 their share of the British vote increased sharply to almost 20 per cent. The formation of the Social Democratic Party (SDP) in 1981 revolutionized the politics of the centre and, in 1983, the 'Alliance' between the Liberals and the SDP almost pipped Labour for second place. In 1988 the two parties merged to form what we now know as the Liberal Democrats. In the four elections since then, support for the Liberal Democrats has been relatively steady, with signs of improvement in the last three elections, and the party is now a much more serious contender for votes than the Liberals were at the start of the period. Perhaps the most obvious message of Figure 1.1, however, is the fragmentation that has occurred in British electoral politics. Up to 1970 the two big parties were the main players on the stage with the rest being confined to bit parts. From 1974, however, when the Liberals took a leap forward, it would clearly be a mistake to think of elections in terms of a simple two-party system. In addition, the share of votes going to 'others' has steadily increased since 1987.

We can take the analysis of trends in election results a stage further by looking at 'swing' figures. Swing is a measure of the net change in support for two parties in a pair of elections. It was developed by David Butler, is simple to calculate and is defined as follows:

$$\frac{(C_2 - C_1) + (L_1 - L_2)}{2}$$

In this formula, C_1 is the percentage share of the total vote obtained by the Conservatives at the first election and C_2 the percentage at the second; L_1 is Labour's share at the first election and L_2 Labour's percentage at the second. The statistic produced by this formula is known as 'Butler' or 'traditional' swing. By convention the parties are put in the order shown and the effect of this is that a positive figure denotes a swing to the Conservatives and a negative figure a swing to Labour. The parties could appear in any order, however, and any two parties could be substituted for Conservative and Labour. A variant known as 'two-party' or 'Steed' swing (having been devised by Michael Steed) is also commonly used. Here the formula is exactly as above but, when calculating the percentage vote for the two parties concerned, votes for all other parties are excluded, so that the two parties' shares of the vote always total 100 per cent.

Table 1.2 shows the Butler Conservative–Labour swing between successive elections and is calculated on the basis of the national distribution of votes. The last point means that the swing shown is the 'overall' or 'national' swing. This needs to be distinguished from the **mean** swing, which is sometimes used in analysis and refers to the average of swings in individual constituencies (which is usually slightly different from the overall figure). Swings between the parties were very small in the 1950s but more variable thereafter. A new post-war record was set in 1979 with a swing of 5.3 per cent to the Conservatives, but this was dwarfed by the massive swing to Labour (10.2 per cent) in 1997.

The table also shows the **standard deviation** of constituency swings. This gives an indication of the extent to which swing varied across constituencies in each election: whether it was broadly similar (lower score) or varied a good deal (higher score). The figures up to October 1974 suggest that swings tended to be similar across the country: the average standard deviation is 2.1 for that period. From 1979 there was usually greater variation in swings as the standard deviation was 3.0 or more in four of the seven elections and the average was 2.9.

In the past, swing was a widely used and very useful measure of electoral change. It provided a simple summary of the extent of change and was used to compare inter-election movements in different parts of the country and different constituencies. In addition, before general elections psephologists could work out the swing needed for any constituency to change hands. Thus, if in a particular constituency the Conservatives had 48 per cent and Labour 44 per cent of the votes at the preceding election, then a swing to Labour of anything over 2 per cent would mean a Labour gain. Since swing tended to be in the same direction and of the same magnitude over the country as a whole, accurate estimates could be made of the number of seats that would change hands given a particular national swing, and of the swing needed for a party to win or lose a majority of seats in the House of Commons. Indeed, once the results in a relatively small number of seats had been declared a reasonable estimate of the national swing could be made, and the final result of the election could be predicted with some confidence, even to the extent of identifying which seats would change hands. As Crewe (1985a, pp. 101–3) put it: 'To know the swing in Cornwall was to know, within a percentage point or two, the swing in the Highlands; to know the results of the first three constituencies to declare on election night was to know not only which party had won – but by how many seats.' The last point is something of an exaggeration but it is a pardonable one. Significant deviations from the national trend used to be relatively rare.

In the context of more recent elections swing is rather less useful. This is partly because swings between elections have become less uniform across constituencies than they used to be but it is also the case that swing was developed in a situation in which elections were essentially contests between two parties only. Since 1974 patterns of party competition have been more complex and swing cannot tell us about relative change between three parties. There have been attempts to devise three-way swing figures (Miller, 1981) but these are complicated to calculate and lack the elegance and simplicity of traditional swing. The commonest way of measuring aggregate or net electoral change nowadays is simply to use the changes in each party's percentage share of the vote. There is, however, a relatively simple measure of overall electoral change called the 'Pedersen Index'. This was designed to measure the amount of electoral volatility revealed by election results and it is calculated by summing the changes in each party's share of the vote in successive elections and dividing by two. The relevant index scores for elections since 1950 are shown in Table 1.2. The figure for 1951 is relatively large, reflecting the steep decline in Liberal support, but thereafter the index suggests only moderate levels of change until February 1974, which saw the biggest turnover in votes of any post-war election. There was also high volatility in 1983 (due to the impact of the Liberal–SDP Alliance) and 1997 (when Labour won its first election in more than twenty years), but 2001 showed little net change and 2005 only moderate change.

Until the late 1960s, the analysis of aggregate election statistics was normally confined to the election results themselves (as in the statistical appendices to the Nuffield studies). There were very few examples of analysis systematically relating the distribution of party support or turnout in constituencies to their socio-economic characteristics. The reason for this was that it was not until the sample census of 1966 that census data were made available on a constituency basis. This was continued in subsequent censuses and has given rise to a flourishing industry in the aggregate analysis of election data. This sort of analysis can involve more complicated statistical methods, however, and I will consider some examples in later chapters.

Aggregate and survey data compared

Election results are a form of **aggregate data**: that is, data which relate to an aggregate or collectivity such as a constituency, region or country. We know, for example, that in the Lancaster and Wyre constituency at the 2005 general election there was a 64.5 per cent turnout and the distribution of votes was 42.8 per cent Conservative, 34.8 per cent Labour, 16.2 per cent Liberal Democrat, 4.4 per cent Green and 1.9 per cent UKIP. This result was obtained by totting up, or aggregating, the number of people who voted and the party that they voted for. From the final result we do not know whether or how any individual voted but we do know something about the collectivity of voters in the constituency. Other examples of aggregate data are the percentage of council tenants in a ward, the number of people aged 65 and over in a constituency, the percentage of manual workers in the North of England, and the change in Labour's share of the vote between 2001 and 2005 over the country as a whole. It is an important feature of aggregate data that they cannot be used to infer anything about the behaviour or characteristics of individuals; for that, survey data are required.

This point is well illustrated by returning to the topic of swing. As pointed out above, swing is a summary measure of net electoral change based on aggregate data (namely, election results). It does not tell us anything about how individuals behave but rather describes the net effect of the changes in individuals' voting behaviour between two elections. This can be easily understood if we distinguish the different components of electoral change. Whether over the country as a whole or in individual constituencies or wards (assuming no boundary changes) the differences between two consecutive election results are produced by four sorts of change.

1 *Switching between major parties* (conventionally the Conservatives and Labour). Some people who voted Labour in the first election will vote Conservative in the second, and vice versa. Clearly the outcome of the second election will only be affected if there is some imbalance in these switches.

2 *Minor party traffic.* Here again switching parties is involved but this time from minor parties (such as the Liberal Democrats, Greens, SNP) to one of the major parties, and vice versa. (There may also be some movement between different minor parties but this will not affect the swing calculation.) As with major-party switching, there will be some self-cancelling effect but an imbalance will affect the election outcome.

3 *Non-voting traffic.* Some people who did not vote in the first election will vote in the second; others who voted first time round fail to do so the second time. Clearly, if it is the case that one party's previous supporters stay away from the polls in larger numbers, or if previous non-voters flock to one of the parties, then this will affect the result.

4 *The physical replacement of the electorate.* Every year (although the number fluctuates a bit), around 750,000 people in Britain turn 18 and therefore become eligible to vote, while about 600,000 people die. If one party gets a disproportionate share of the new voters, or if the supporters of one party are dying off in greater numbers, this will affect election outcomes. Immigration to and emigration from the country or a particular constituency can have a similar effect. Population movement can change the character of a constituency or, more quickly, a ward over time.

Aggregate measures of electoral change, such as swing or changes in the parties' shares of the vote, simply summarize the effects of all of these ebbs and flows. For more detailed information about the various components of change we have to turn to individual-level data produced by surveys.

Ideally, a survey study designed to analyse electoral change would interview a sample of voters after one election and then re-interview the same 'panel' after a second election. It is well established that many voters do not accurately recall which party they voted for some years previously and the use of a panel minimizes the chances of this. Panel surveys have their own problems, however, in that they suffer from 'attrition' as many respondents drop out and the sample becomes unrepresentative; and even this approach is unable to measure the impact of the physical replacement of the electorate. It is, of course, not possible to re-interview people who have died or emigrated between the two elections, and it is difficult to identify respondents who are too young to vote in the first election but who reach voting age by the time of the second.

Nonetheless, when a survey obtains the reported votes of respondents at two successive elections the components of electoral change can be investigated by constructing a two-way table showing exactly what people did at the two elections concerned. A table of this kind is sometimes called an 'election transition matrix' or, more simply, a 'flow of the vote' table; Table 1.3 is an example of this based on survey respondents in 2005 recalling their vote in 2001. (Fuller examples of election transition matrices for earlier elections, including estimates of the population entering and leaving the electorate, are given in Butler and Stokes, 1974, ch. 12; Sarlvik and Crewe, 1983, ch. 2; and Heath *et al.*, 1991, ch. 2.) The table shows how survey data can provide information about the various elements of electoral change which cannot be derived from election results alone.

As in most elections, major-party switching between 2001 and 2005 was relatively rare. Only 4 per cent of 2001 Conservative voters switched to Labour compared with 7 per cent of 2001 Labour voters going in the opposite direction. Nonetheless, this represents a considerable gain by the Conservatives especially since there were many more Labour voters in 2001 (see *N*s at the foot of the table). Liberal Democrat traffic also harmed Labour. While about the same proportions moved from the Liberal Democrats to both Labour and the Conservatives (9 per cent), 12 per cent of former Labour voters defected to the Liberal Democrats compared with only 7 per cent of former Conservatives. The effect of non-voting traffic is more difficult to judge. Labour gained more previous non-voters than the other major parties (17 per cent) but also lost more to abstention (16 per cent). We have no information about the 2001 voting behaviour of people who died before the 2005 election was held, of course, but looking at those who came

Table 1.3   The 'flow of the vote' between 2001 and 2005 (%)

2005 vote	2001 vote					
	Too young	Did not vote	Conservative	Labour	Liberal Democrat	Other
Did not vote	44	58	13	16	12	21
Conservative	7	13	74	7	9	15
Labour	23	17	4	61	9	8
Liberal Democrat	22	9	7	12	65	17
Other	4	3	2	4	4	40
(*N*)	(267)	(756)	(864)	(1,411)	(412)	(155)

Source: Data from British Election Study (BES) 2005.

of voting age in that period it can be seen that a large minority of them did not vote in 2005 (44 per cent) and that Labour and the Liberal Democrats were roughly equal in popularity among those who voted, with the Conservatives trailing in third place. Taking all respondents together (N = 3,865), 59 per cent voted for the same party or did not vote in both elections. Major party switching involved 3 per cent, minor party traffic (including the Liberal Democrats) 11 per cent and non-voting traffic 19 per cent, while new voters comprised 7 per cent. In 2005, therefore, it was the movement of people between voting and non-voting that was the largest contributor to the net swing of 3.2 per cent from Labour to the Conservatives.

Clearly, then, aggregate measures of change between elections, while important and necessary, are limited. A fuller understanding of electoral change requires the kind of detailed information about individuals that only surveys can provide. Nonetheless, both aggregate and survey data are extensively used in electoral analysis and both have advantages and drawbacks. The advantages of using aggregate data are as follows.

1   If it is confined to publicly available data, analysing aggregate data is cheap. Whereas it costs many thousands of pounds to employ a firm to undertake a major national survey of the British electorate – and even a modest local survey is expensive – anyone can consult a newspaper, go to a library or access an appropriate website and collect election results, census data and other information. Armed only with a calculator (or, more likely, a personal computer), and a knowledge of some elementary statistical techniques, anyone can embark on analysing all of this freely-available data.

2   Aggregate data such as election results reflect real behaviour, or what voters actually did, while surveys only report what voters *say* they have done. There is sometimes a disjunction between these. Surveys always find, for instance, that more people claim to have voted in an election than actually did, according to the election returns.

3   Aggregate data usually refer to the total population being studied and are therefore not susceptible to sampling error in the way that survey data are. Whereas we know from election results the precise percentage of the electorate which voted Conservative, a survey would enable us only to estimate the percentage which did (or intended to).

4   Aggregate data are almost always **interval-scale** or **continuous data** and the most powerful statistical techniques can therefore be applied to them.

5   Whereas survey studies of electoral behaviour are of relatively recent origin, lots of relevant aggregate data – in particular, election results –

are available going back to the nineteenth century. This has enabled modern techniques to be applied to elections in the distant past (see, for example, Field, 1997; Miller, 1977).

On the other hand, surveys also have certain important advantages:

1 When using aggregate data the analyst is usually restricted to material that has been collected and published by official bodies. Until an appropriate question was included in the 2001 census, for example, there were no reliable figures showing the distribution of different religions or Christian denominations across constituencies (except in Northern Ireland). In surveys, on the other hand, the investigator can ask respondents for any information that seems appropriate.
2 More precisely, aggregate statistics refer only to the objective characteristics and behaviour of a population. It is only by using surveys that the knowledge, beliefs, attitudes and opinions of voters can be discovered.
3 Individual data collected by survey permit analysis of individuals rather than collectivities. I have already commented on the importance of this with respect to electoral change, but it is of more general significance in electoral analysis. Without surveys we would not know which groups vote for which parties and in what proportions, how opinions relate to party choice, and so on. Theories about why people vote the way they do would remain highly speculative.

Theories of voting

Despite the impression that is sometimes given, the study of elections and voting behaviour is not just about collecting facts and 'number crunching' on the basis of complicated statistical analysis. As in all social sciences, facts have to be selected, collected, ordered, analysed and interpreted. For that, theory is required. I have never yet seen a survey study of voting which asked respondents what colour their eyes are, for the simple reason that there is no theory suggesting that eye colour may affect a person's choice of party. Theories give guidance as to which facts should be collected and how they should be organized, interpreted and explained.

   In electoral analysis there is an assortment of theories at different levels of generality. At a simple level, someone might have a theory that married people are more likely to vote because they are more likely to conform to socially-approved behaviour. This is better described as a hypothesis and it could be tested by asking a sample of electors whether they were married and whether they voted. If the expected association is found, the hypothesis provides the explanation. At a slightly more general level, there are various theories which seek to explain why older people tend to be more likely to vote Conservative than younger people, the changing pattern of party choice among women, the effect of newspapers on opinions and so on. These will be considered in later chapters. Here, however, I introduce three even more general theories which have strongly influenced how voting in Britain has been understood and explained, and which inform much of the rest of the book.

'Social determinism'

The first theory or model suggests that voting is largely a product of the social situation of the voter. The authors of the first-ever survey study of voting behaviour in the USA, *The People's Choice* (Lazarsfeld, Berelson and Gaudet, 1968, first edition 1944), had intended to focus upon short-term factors affecting voting choice in the Presidential election of 1940 – the book was subtitled 'How The Voter Makes Up His Mind in a Presidential Campaign' – but in the course of their research they became more impressed by the importance of social characteristics such as class, religion and race in structuring party choice. Lazarsfeld and his colleagues discovered that they could predict a person's vote with considerable accuracy from knowledge of just a few social characteristics. They concluded (p. 27) that 'a person thinks, politically, as he is socially. Social characteristics determine political preference.'

Describing relationships between various social and demographic characteristics and party choice is not in itself very useful, however. It would certainly be interesting if it were found that left-handed people with brown eyes tended to vote in a distinctive way, but it seems unlikely that knowing this will advance our understanding of what motivates voters. What is required is some theory that explains why there *should be* a link between specific social or personal characteristics and voting. We need an answer to the question: 'Why are some social differences associated with political differences whereas others are not?'

In 1948, the authors of *The People's Choice* carried out a second study and, in *Voting* (Berelson, Lazarsfeld and McPhee, 1954), they extended and reinforced their original argument. In particular, they provided an answer to the above question by suggesting (p. 75) that for a social difference to be translated into a political cleavage three conditions need to be fulfilled:

(a) initial social differentiation such that the consequences of political policy are materially or symbolically different for different groups;
(b) conditions of transmittibility from generation to generation; and
(c) conditions of physical and social proximity providing for continued in-group contact in succeeding generations.

The first condition requires that the social groups concerned must have differing material or symbolic interests which are affected by government policy. Thus council tenants and owner-occupiers might have different interests with regard to housing policy. Policy in areas such as abortion or embryo research might not directly affect many people but could be said to be of symbolic importance to some groups (such as Roman Catholics and others). On the other hand, 'groups' such as the left-handed or the brown-eyed are not normally treated differently from the rest of the population in matters of public policy and do not fulfil the first condition. The second and third conditions relate to the processes by which social and political divisions are maintained and reinforced.

We have here, then, what might be termed an 'interests plus socialization' theory or model. Different social groups have different interests and hence different needs. They tend, therefore, to vote for different parties which they perceive as representing these interests. Awareness of a group's distinctiveness and of group–party links is sustained by regular contact with fellow group members in the family, among peers and in the community.

This is an appealing and apparently simple model but it is not without difficulties. Very briefly, four problems with the model are set out below:

1 *Overlapping group memberships.* Everyone belongs to a variety of social groups and the theory offers no clues as to which will be decisive in determining an individual's party support, and why.
2 *Group interests.* It is not self-evident that a large and relatively heterogeneous group of people – such as those belonging to the same class, religious denomination or geographical region – will have the same interests. Who decides what the group's interests are, and in what sense can political parties be said to represent the interests of such diverse groups?
3 *Deviants.* How does the model account for the (often large) minorities who do not conform to group voting norms, such as middle-class Labour supporters in the 1950s or ethnic minority Conservatives in the 1990s?
4 *Political parties.* The theory tends to give the impression that party choice is a sort of spontaneous effect of social location and ignores the active role that political parties play in mobilizing and structuring the electorate.

Despite criticisms of this kind, some form of 'social determinism' under-pinned by the idea of 'interests plus socialization' has played a large part in voting research in Britain. In more recent writing, however, the emphasis has shifted from the interests of groups to group identities: the subjective sense of belonging to a distinctive group (being Scottish, for example) which voters may have (see Norris, 1997a).

The Michigan model and Butler and Stokes

A second major American influence on British voting studies derives from a book called *The American Voter* (Campbell *et al.,* 1960). In this famous study, Campbell and his colleagues developed a model or theory of voting behaviour that has come to be known as the 'Michigan model', since the original research was directed from the University of Michigan. Like the 'social determinism' model, the Michigan model suggests that long-term factors are most important in determining party choice, but there is no simple step from social location to voting behaviour. Rather, the social position that an individual occupies affects the kinds of influences that he or she will encounter in interacting with family, friends, neighbours, work colleagues and so on. As a consequence of these interactions – especially within the family – the individual acquires a *party identification*. This means a sense of attachment to a party, a feeling of commitment to it, being a supporter of the party and not just someone who happens to vote for the party from time to time.

When an election comes along, there is an interaction between a voter's long-term party identification and various short-term influences, such as current political issues, campaign events, the personalities of party leaders or candidates and, in the British case, the tactical situation in the local constituency, to produce a vote decision. The Michigan team were at pains to emphasize, however, that it is the long-term factors which are usually decisive. Indeed, a person's party identification will influence how he or she interprets and evaluates issues, party leaders and so on.

The concept of party identification (also referred to as 'party identity' or 'partisanship') is central to the Michigan model and worth exploring in a little more detail. It is analogous to national identity. Most of us think of ourselves as English, Scottish, Welsh, British or whatever (perhaps even as European when the Ryder Cup golf match is being played). Similarly, party identity involves people thinking of themselves as Conservatives, Labour supporters, Liberal Democrats and so on. Another analogy, borrowed from marketing, sees party identification as akin to 'brand loyalty'. Just as consumers frequently have a long-lasting preference for a particular make of car, brand of toothpaste or breakfast cereal, so voters develop a loyalty to a party. It is important to grasp that identifying with a party is not the same as voting for it; indeed, it is possible to identify with one party and vote for a different one. For example, in recent years a good deal of attention has been given to the idea of tactical voting, which involves voters who might identify with one party voting for another one because their own party has no chance of winning in the constituency concerned. A Labour supporter living in Bath, for example, might decide to vote Liberal Democrat while still remaining basically a Labour supporter.

There are three clear differences between party identification and voting:

1   Party identification is psychological, while voting is behavioural. This means that identification exists in people's heads; we cannot observe it directly. Voting, however, is a definite action – putting a cross on a piece of paper in the case of British elections – and, in principle, it is observable (although normally done in secret).
2   Voting is time-specific, while party identification is not. Voting can only take place at an election (and general elections occur relatively infrequently in Britain), whereas identification is ongoing and continuous. There does not need to be an election in the offing for people to consider themselves supporters of a party.
3   Party identification varies in intensity, while voting does not. Some people will be very strong party supporters, while others will be not very strong or just weak supporters. All votes count equally, however, whether the voter marks the ballot with a large bold black cross or a tiny faint one.

Conceptually, then, party identification is distinct from voting. This means that it can be used to help explain party choice in an election, as in the Michigan model. According to the theory, party identification serves important functions for the individual, including simplifying the task of understanding the complex world of politics. Once someone decides (or has learned) who are the 'goodies' and who the 'baddies' in the party battle, there is no need to pay great attention to the details of political debate, and no need to bother with the details of party policies or election manifestos. Identification acts as a sort of psychological filter or prism through which political messages pass to the individual; it provides a framework within which political events are understood and evaluated.

When party identification is widespread, it has important effects on the political system as a whole. Most obviously it provides an element of stability and continuity. If people identify with a party they are not likely to shoot off in all directions at successive elections (just as people who identify themselves as Everton supporters don't suddenly switch their affections to Liverpool or Manchester United). Rather, they will have a 'normal' vote which, in most cases, will remain stable from election to election and across different types of election.

The way in which party identification has been measured in Britain (although not the concept itself) has come under considerable criticism in recent years (see Bartle, 2001), but the idea is central to the model of party choice in Britain that was developed by Butler and Stokes (1969, 1974) in their pioneering survey studies. Simplifying drastically, the picture that Butler and Stokes drew of the British voter at this time was as shown in Figure 1.2. The starting point of the model is the class and party of voters' parents and it is underpinned by the theory of political socialization, which suggests that families are particularly important in transmitting political attitudes and beliefs to succeeding generations. Butler and Stokes saw party identification as being inherited to a large extent through the family and leading almost automatically to support for one party or another in elections.

Voting as rational choice

One of the most striking aspects of the two theories considered so far is that they make little reference to voters' opinions about the policies or performance of parties. Although the Michigan model does include 'issue orientation' and 'candidate orientation' as short-term influences on party choice,

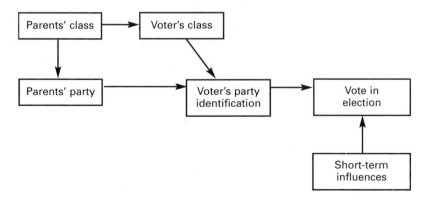

Figure 1.2   Butler–Stokes model of party choice (individual voters)

their role is very much downplayed. The two models are largely concerned with voting as a function of social and psychological processes. A quite different broad approach stems from rational choice theory (see McLean, 1982). In its modern form rational choice theory derives from economics but it has been applied in a variety of ways in a large number of fields. In economics, the starting point of the theory is to make an assumption that economic actors (whether firms or individuals as consumers) act rationally: that is, before deciding on a course of action (such as buying a particular product) they weigh up the costs and benefits of the various alternatives and they will take the decision which maximizes the benefits and minimizes the costs to themselves. On the basis of this assumption, economic behaviour can be successfully predicted.

When applied to political activity, this elegant and simple idea – and propositions deduced from its by logical reasoning – has been fruitful in yielding insights in a number of areas, including the behaviour of parties, pressure groups, politicians and voters. As with consumers, it can be hypothesized that voters weigh up the pros and cons of voting for different parties (or of voting at all) and opt for the course of action which they think will bring them the greatest benefit. This apparently simple suggestion has importantly influenced recent electoral analysis, spawning a variety of more specific approaches to understanding party choice – such as issue voting, economic voting and valence voting – which focus on the judgements made by voters and which will be explained and discussed in later chapters.

To summarize this section, then, theories or models are required to provide frameworks within which appropriate data can be collected and understood and also to provide explanations for the empirical relationships that are discovered. Having outlined the most influential general theories of voting behaviour here I will discuss them again – offering some evaluation of their relative usefulness – in the final chapter. Before examining patterns of party choice, however, it is important to discuss another decision that electors have to make (whether to vote at all) which logically must precede a decision about which party to vote for. The next chapter, therefore, is concerned with turnout in elections.

2
Turnout: Why People Vote (or Don't)

Electoral turnout is a **variable**. The level of turnout varies from country to country and within Britain it varies from one type of election to another and from one election to the next. In any one election turnout varies across constituencies or wards and it also varies from person to person: some people vote and some don't. Variations across different types of election in Britain between 2001 and 2005 are illustrated in Table 2.1.

Interpretation is complicated by the fact that different elections are sometimes held on the same day (the European Parliament and some English local elections in 2004, for example) and by the use of compulsory postal voting for some elections in some areas in some years. Nonetheless, it is apparent that different types of election do not attract the same level of interest on the part of the electorate. The lowest turnout shown was for English local elections in 2002 (32.8 per cent). Previously, the wooden spoon for turnout has consistently been held by the European Parliament elections, but in 2004 the decision to hold local elections on the same day as the European election and to have compulsory postal voting in three English regions clearly made a

Table 2.1   Turnout in British elections, 2001–5 (%)

Election	Turnout
General election (GB) 2001	59.1
Local elections (England) 2002	32.8
Local elections (England) 2003	33.7
Scottish Parliament 2003	49.4
Welsh Assembly election 2003	38.2
Local elections (England) 2004	40.2
European Parliament election (GB) 2004	38.2
London Mayor election 2004	35.9
Mean in six Parliamentary by-elections 2001–4	39.6
General election (GB) 2005	61.4

Sources: Various. For local elections see the *Local Elections Handbook* series by C. Rallings and M. Thrasher.

difference to turnout. In Scotland, where there were no local elections and no postal voting, the figure was closer to normal at 30.8 per cent. Turnout in the Scottish Parliament election of 2003 was close to 50 per cent, but more than ten points lower in the Welsh Assembly elections of the same year. The two general elections at the start and end of the period saw the highest turnouts, even though participation in these was poor by historical standards.

The electorate, then, differentiates between different levels and types of elections. In general these variations can be explained by the importance that is attached to the body being elected, which is sometimes referred to as the 'salience' of the election concerned (Franklin, 1996). Thus the European Parliament is seen as remote (its activities being virtually unreported in the British media) and there is a good deal of antipathy to the EU in general. Local councils have steadily lost powers to the central government and voters could be forgiven for thinking that it doesn't really make an enormous difference whichever party controls their local government. By-elections return a Member of Parliament for the constituency concerned but do not determine who forms the government or becomes Prime Minister. The Scottish Parliament has extensive powers, however, and that is reflected in the relatively high turnout, while the Welsh Assembly is more restricted (and setting it up was much more controversial) and, in line with that, elections to it attract a much smaller proportion of the electorate. Despite devolution, general elections are still seen by the voters as the most important elections; as suggested in Chapter 1 they are major national events. Although the idea was first developed in relation to European elections, all elections in Britain other than general elections can be described as 'second-order' elections (Reif and Schmitt, 1980): not a great deal appears to be at stake, they attract much less media coverage, and the parties do not campaign very strongly. In general elections, on the other hand, there is saturation media coverage, the parties mount intense national and local campaigns and the electorate usually think it important who wins. These are 'first-order' elections, and electors are keener to turn out and vote in them.

There have been three main theoretical approaches to explaining variations in the propensity of people to vote in elections (see Franklin, 1996). The first concentrates on the social locations and circumstances of voters. As we shall see, different social groups tend to have different turnout rates, and these differences can be explained in a variety of ways. The second focuses on the connections between parties and voters, and is concerned with how parties mobilize voters and the impact of voters' identification with parties. The third derives from rational choice theory, especially the work of Anthony Downs (1957). This directs attention to the costs and benefits of voting and suggests that voters act instrumentally. Turnout will be higher when there are more incentives to vote and costs are kept at a minimum. Where the incentives are less strong and/or costs are higher, turnout will be lower. The patterns shown in Table 2.1, for example, suggest that voters are more willing to turn out when they believe the relevant elections to be more important. Although these three approaches do not exhaust possible lines of explanation, they provide valuable frameworks within which to discuss turnout variations in Britain.

Turnout variations over time

Before discussing the turnout trends in Britain, it is worth remembering what it is that turnout figures measure. When comparing turnout across different countries – and British turnout has not been very high in an international context (see Crewe, 1981a; Franklin, 2002) – it is important to remember that rules about registration and voting vary and this affects the interpretation of comparative figures. In the USA, for example, registering to vote is a fairly complex process, and in Australia voting is compulsory. In Britain, official turnout figures report the percentage of people whose names are on the electoral register who put a ballot paper into the ballot box (or vote by post). Compiling the electoral register is the responsibility of local authorities. Until recently, the list of eligible electors was drawn up every October, usually on the basis of information supplied to the local authority on forms distributed to every household, institution or other place where voters might live. Although it was drawn up in October, the register did not come into operation until the following February, and then it remained in force for a year.

Even when it was first compiled the register could not possibly be 100 per cent accurate. People were accidentally missed off (most commonly young people who would become 18 before the register lapsed); others were included who should not have been; yet others were registered in two places (students, for example, were often registered at their homes and at their college or university). When it came into force, the register was already four months out of date – people would have died, moved or emigrated – and it continued to decay during the year for which it was in force. Official turnout figures do not take account of the ageing of the electoral register but some electoral analysts have tried to do so. Rose (1974, p. 494), for example, calculated that the 'real' national turnout figure could be obtained by dividing the reported percentage turnout by 100 plus 2.4 (to take account of those not registered less those registered twice) minus 0.82 for each month from the compilation of the register to the date of the election (to take account of those who have died or moved away in the intervening period), expressing the result as a percentage.

In February 2001, however, a new system of 'rolling registration' was adopted. There is now no fixed date of registration; instead, once the initial register is drawn up (still in October) people can apply to be included and, if eligible, their names will be added up to a short time before an election. It is not clear, however, whether local authorities have made any provisions for deleting names. The net effect was that at the time of the 2005 general election, before returning officers reported to the Electoral Commission, there was considerable uncertainty about the precise numbers of people on the register in individual constituencies and hence about the precise turnout.

The Rose formula for adjustment is probably not now as accurate as it was originally but Table 2.2 shows adjusted figures, as well as the overall 'raw' turnout in general elections in Britain since 1950. Again it should be remembered that turnout levels are not exactly comparable over the whole period, since in 1970 the voting age was lowered from 21 to 18 and this added some three million young people to the register. The unadjusted figures show that turnout was very high in 1950 and 1951 but then was always between 70 and 80 per cent until 2001, when it slumped to below 60 per cent with a slight recovery in 2005. The adjusted figures suggest that, once the age of the register is taken into account, turnout was actually greater than the 'raw' figures imply, although the trend over time is similar. The trend can be seen more clearly in Figure 2.1, which plots the adjusted turnouts – measured on the *y*-axis (vertical line) – against the number of years after 1950 that each election was held as measured on the *x*-axis (horizontal line). Simply looking at the figure suggests that four of the first five elections had relatively high turnouts, the next eight showed no real trend, while in the last three (1997 to 2005) the trend has been sharply downwards.

Table 2.2   Turnout in British general elections, 1950–2005 (%)

Election	Turnout	Adjusted	Election	Turnout	Adjusted
1950 ·	84.1	84.8	Oct. 1974	73.0	78.9
1951	82.6	90.0	1979	76.2	79.5
1955	76.9	79.6	1983	72.7	76.5
1959	79.0	85.4	1987	75.5	79.5
1964	77.2	83.4	1992	77.9	79.9
1966	76.1	78.7	1997	71.5	74.0
1970	71.9	75.7	2001	59.1	61.8
Feb. 1974	79.1	80.5	2005	61.4	63.5

Note: For details of the 'adjustment' made, see text.

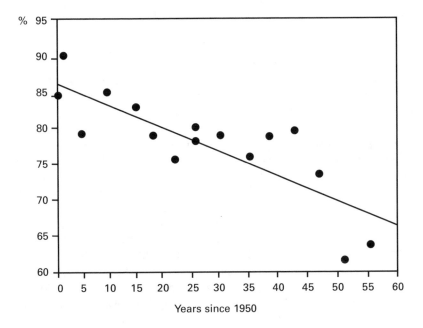

Figure 2.1   Turnout (adjusted) in Great Britain, 1950–2005

The point of using 'years since 1950' on the *x*-axis (rather than just each election in turn) is that this measure is a **continuous variable** with scores on an interval scale. When we have two continuous variables (turnout is scored as a percentage) we can undertake some further interesting and informative analysis of the relationship between them. As a first step, a line has been drawn (by the relevant computer package) through the points. This is the 'best-fitting' line derived from **regression analysis**. Without going into the details of how the line is derived, it is apparent that it slopes down from left to right, indicating that turnouts have tended to fall over the period. The line can be described by a simple regression equation as follows: turnout = 86.8 − 0.34 (years). Thus, with a constant (starting point) of 86.2 per cent, turnout declined on average by about 0.3 per cent for every year that passed. Every regression equation has an associated ***r*-squared statistic (r^2)** which indicates the proportion of the **variation** in the **dependent variable** (in this case, turnout) that is 'explained' or 'accounted for' by variations in the **independent variable** (in this case, years since 1950). For this equation r^2 is 0.646, meaning that 64.6 per cent of the variation in turnout in these 16 elections can be explained simply by the fact that there was a downward trend over time.

Research on turnout variations over time has suggested that they can be at least partly explained by the closeness (or expected closeness) of the election concerned, together with the extent to which the parties were perceived as offering significantly different choices (Heath and Taylor, 1999; Clarke *et al.*, 2004). This is in line with rational choice theory. There would appear to be more incentive for people to vote if they think that an election is likely to be close rather than a foregone conclusion, and if they believe that the winning party will bring in policies that are significantly different from those that the losing party would have pursued. These suggestions help to explain deviations from the trend shown in Figure 2.1. In three elections turnout was clearly higher than would be expected on the basis of the general trend: 1951, 1987 and 1992. The result in the first was very close, while polls also predicted a close-run thing in 1992. In 1987 an unusually large proportion of BES respondents (84 per cent) perceived 'a good deal of difference' between the parties. Lower than expected turnouts occurred in 1970 (the first election after the lowering of the voting age) and 2001 (when both causes of low turnout were in operation: many voters believed that the result was a foregone conclusion and that there were no major policy or ideological differences between the parties). The result in 2005 was predicted to be closer (at least in terms of votes) and this probably explains the slight recovery in turnout. (For a more detailed and complex analysis of turnout trends over time, see Clarke *et al.*, 2004, pp. 261–74.)

Turnout variations across constituencies

In any general election turnout varies markedly across constituencies. In the 2001 election, for example, excluding Northern Ireland, it ranged from 72.3 per cent (Winchester) to 34.1 per cent (Liverpool Riverside). In 2005, Liverpool Riverside took the wooden spoon for the third consecutive election (41.5 per cent) while Dorset West (76.4 per cent) had the highest figure. Turnout was 70 per cent or greater in 34 British constituencies while in 36 it was below 50 per cent. A more general indication of the extent of variations in constituency turnouts is given by the standard deviation, and the figures suggest that such variation has been increasing in recent elections. The standard deviations of turnout in the last five elections have been as follows: 1987 – 4.5, 1992 – 5.2, 1997 – 5.6, 2001 – 6.4, 2005 – 6.4.

Clearly, variations such as this require explanation and investigations of the topic have drawn attention to four main sorts of explanatory factor: the practicalities of voting, the social composition of constituencies, the local electoral context and what, for want of a better term, might be called 'cultural norms'. The method of analysis most frequently used to investigate the problem is to try to account for variations in the dependent variable (constituency turnout) by reference to a series of independent variables, employing **correlation coefficients** and **multiple regression analysis** (see, for example, Denver and Hands, 1997b).

A particularly clear example of a simple practical matter affecting constituency turnouts occurred at the 1992 election. The election took place during a university vacation and, since most students had returned home, constituencies with large resident student populations recorded turnouts which were much lower than usual (see Curtice and Steed, 1992, p. 347). Practical considerations also relate to the accuracy of the electoral registers on which turnout calculations are based. If the registers in some constituencies are more inaccurate than in others – due to including more people who have moved away from the area or have died – then they will report lower turnouts; very low turnouts tend to be found in inner-city constituencies, for example. These tend to be areas in which there are large floating populations and it seems likely that the low reported turnout figures are in part a consequence of electoral register inaccuracy. Denver and Halfacree (1992b) tackled this problem more generally, arguing that in areas of high out-migration electoral registers will become more inaccurate more quickly than in areas of more stable population. They used regression analysis to demonstrate that the level of out-migration from a constituency does indeed have a significant negative effect on recorded turnout levels. People who move to a new area can apply to vote by post in their former constituency, of course, but these days it is easier for those who are keen to vote to get their names added to the register in their new constituency.

The fact that the social composition of constituencies is associated with varying levels of turnout is well established. In one of the first published analyses of British census and election data, Crewe and Payne (1971) showed that, as far back as the 1970 election, turnout in England was higher in seats with more professional and managerial workers, more owner-occupiers, a better standard of housing, more retired people and more people employed in agriculture. It was lower, on the other hand, where there were more households without a car, poorer housing and more ethnic minority immigrants. This type of analysis is hampered by the fact that censuses (which provide details of the social composition of constituencies) are held only once every ten years. As a result, the social composition data can be somewhat out-of-date when applied to an election which is some distance in time from the census date. On the other hand, most constituencies do not change in character all that quickly and there is little dispute about the nature and strength of the relationships between turnout and the social characteristics of constituencies. Table 2.3 illustrates the standard pattern, showing for the 1983 and 2005 elections the simple correlation coefficients measuring the association between nine indicators of the social composition of constituencies and turnout. As explained in the glossary, correlation coefficients indicate whether a relationship between two variables is positive or negative, and also how strong the association is. The closer the figure is to zero, the weaker the relationship; the closer to 1, the stronger the relationship.

All of these coefficients are **statistically significant** – they indicate relationships which are too strong to have occurred by chance – and two features of the data are immediately striking. First, despite being separated by more than 20 years, the pattern of relationships is identical in the two elections. Variables that correlated positively with turnout (as the proportion with the given characteristic increases, so does turnout) in 1983 also did so in 2005; those that were negative in 1983 (as the proportion increases turnout declines) were also negative in 2005. In other words, although turnout was much lower in the 2005 election, the *pattern of variation across constituencies* was much as it had been 22 years before. Second, most of the coefficients were larger for 2005 than they were in 1983. This means that in the 2005 election there was a clearer and more consistent difference in turnout between the different sorts of constituencies. The country was more clearly divided into relatively low-turnout and relatively high-turnout constituencies, and the two were very different in social terms.

Table 2.3   Correlates of constituency turnout, 1983 and 2005

	1983	2005
% Professional and managerial workers	0.33	0.54
% Manual workers	−0.23	−0.57
% Owner–occupiers	0.52	0.71
% Council tenants	−0.34	−0.66
% Private tenants	−0.37	−0.17
% Ethnic minority	−0.51	−0.40
% Households with no car	−0.63	−0.80
% Employed in agriculture	0.31	0.44
Persons per hectare	−0.66	−0.55
Previous marginality	0.27	0.72
(*N*)	(633)	(627)

Notes: For 1983, the scores on the social composition variables derive from the 1981 census, while for 2005 they are taken from the census of 2001. In 1983, what is described here as the percentage of the population belonging to ethnic minorities was actually the percentage born in the New Commonwealth and Pakistan. 'Previous marginality' is 100 minus the winning party's percentage majority in the preceding election.

It is important to emphasize with respect to these figures that they tell us nothing about the behaviour of individuals, only about *constituencies*. Thus we cannot infer from the strong positive correlation between the proportion of owner-occupiers in a constituency and turnout that owner-occupiers as a group vote in greater proportions than others. Just because the proportion of households without a car is negatively related to constituency turnout does not of itself tell us that people without cars are less likely to vote. Both *may* be true but, from aggregate data, we can only draw conclusions about collectivities (constituencies in this case) and not about the individuals who comprise them. To do the latter is to commit what is known as the 'ecological fallacy'. In addition, it is important to note that correlation coefficients tell us exactly what the word 'correlation' implies and no more. They tell us the extent to which two variables are co-related or associated (whether they increase and decrease in value together or whether, as one goes up, the other goes down). They cannot tell us whether variations in one *cause* the variations in the other; imputing causal relationships between variables is a matter for theory rather than statistical manipulation.

It is easy to hypothesize how different aspects of the electoral context might cause variations in constituency turnouts. It could be suggested, for example, that the more candidates there are the greater will be the turnout, since the choice before the voters will be more extensive and they are less likely to be able to use the excuse that there was no one that they wanted to vote for. Also, more candidates would presumably mean more local campaigning, and this could heighten awareness of (and interest in) the election. In fact this hypothesis, which is an aspect of the mobilization theory mentioned above, is not supported by the data. In 2005 there was a weak negative relationship between the number of candidates and turnout (a correlation coefficient of -0.13): the more candidates in a constituency, the lower was the turnout, on the whole.

Another aspect of the electoral context has been consistently found to have an important influence on constituency turnouts, however, and that is the marginality or 'safeness' of the seat. As with the closeness of the national contest, a simple application of rational choice theory would suggest that electors would be more inclined to go to the polls in places where the contest is likely to be close than in places that are rock-solid for one party or another. It is also the case that parties campaign harder in constituencies where the result may be in doubt than in those where they have no chance or expect to cruise to victory without much effort, so that there are elements of mobilization also involved. Previous analyses of this question have shown that the level of marginality has usually been strongly associated with constituency turnout, even when other variables are taken into account (Denver and

Hands, 1974, 1985, 1997b; Pattie and Johnston, 1998; Denver, Hands and MacAllister, 2003). Table 2.3 shows the correlations between previous marginality and turnout in 1983 and 2005. In both cases the coefficients are positive: the more marginal the seat, the higher the turnout. Again, however, the relationship was much stronger in 2005 than it was in 1983. Figures for the intervening elections do not suggest a steady trend in the strength of this relationship but, for reasons that are not immediately apparent, the correlation between marginality and turnout became markedly more pronounced in 2001 (coefficient 0.70) and then reached a record level in 2005 (0.72). This may be because voters are now much more aware of the distinction between marginal and safe (or hopeless) seats. Alternatively (and perhaps more likely), it could be a consequence of the increased tendency of parties to concentrate campaigning resources and effort in more marginal seats while running much less intense campaigns elsewhere.

We can take the analysis of turnout variation across constituencies a step further by using **multivariate analysis**. The data in Table 2.3 are important and interesting, but they show the strength of the association between a series of variables and turnout separately (this is called **bivariate analysis** as it involves looking at only two variables at a time). The problem is that the various measures of social composition are themselves highly inter-correlated. Thus, constituencies in which a large proportion of households have no car tend also to have larger proportions of ethnic minority voters, local authority tenants and manual workers, as well as a higher population density (persons per hectare). By using multiple regression (regression analysis with more than one independent variable), we can sort out which variables are the most important influences on turnout, see whether a partic-ular variable remains significant when all others are held constant and eval-uate how successfully combinations of variables explain turnout variations. On the basis of all the variables shown in Table 2.3, the 'best' multiple regression equation (that is, the one that includes all significant independent variables) predicting turnout across all British constituencies in 2005 is as follows:

$$\% \text{ turnout} = 61.0 + 0.13\,(M) - 0.05\,(PPH) + 0.77\,(AG) + 0.10\,(OO) - 0.18\,(PR) - 0.29(\text{MW})$$

$$r^2 = 0.780$$

(M = previous marginality; PPH = persons per hectare; AG = % employed in agriculture; OO = % owner occupiers; PR = % private tenants; MW = % manual workers)

'Predicting', as used in this context, has nothing to do with the future; it simply means calculating what a constituency's turnout should have been on the basis of its scores on the variables concerned, given the overall relationships identified by the analysis. As with simple regression, the r-squared statistic tells us how much of the variation in turnout is explained by this combination of variables (78 per cent in this case). So, turnout across constituencies varied a good deal in 2005 but we can account for over three-quarters of that variation – three quarters of the variation is 'explained' – by variations in marginality and five indicators of the social characteristics of constituencies.

This means, of course, that some variation remains unexplained. When all of the above factors are taken into account there remain a number of constituencies in which turnout is clearly higher or lower than expected. It is at this point that 'cultural norms' often come into play as a sort of residual explanation. In the 1950s and 1960s, for example, it was plain that coal-mining areas had much higher turnouts than would be expected on the basis of the social and political characteristics of the constituencies concerned. That is no longer the case (not surprisingly, given that we now have only ex-coal-mining areas). Indeed, examination of the most 'deviant' constituencies in 2005 suggests no real patterns. Factors peculiar to the constituencies concerned would be required to explain why, for example, Blaenau Gwent and Leicester East top the list of seats with higher than expected turnout.

The same sort of unexpected deviations are found at ward level in local elections. A study of turnout patterns in English county council and metro-politan borough elections during the 1980s (Rallings and Thrasher, 1990) produced results closely resembling those found for general elections. Turnout was lower in wards of low socio-economic status and was positively related to the marginality of the ward. As with constituency studies, however, Rallings and Thrasher found that even the 'best' combination of political and socio-economic variables left some turnout variation unexplained, with some individual wards regularly returning much higher or lower turnouts than expected. They conclude that: 'one is reluctantly driven almost to a cultural explanation of why turnout in Todmorden should be consistently 15 per cent above the average for Calderdale' (p. 89). Similar results have been reported from a more recent analysis of ward turnouts in Scotland (Denver and Hands, 2004).

Survey studies of non-voting

When we focus attention on the varying propensity of individuals to vote or not, rational choice theory suggests an arresting conclusion: it is irrational to vote. As has already been seen, the starting point of this approach is to assume that the individual weighs up the costs and benefits before deciding on a course of action and the argument then proceeds by logical deduction. It is clear that voting involves the individual in some costs (the time taken getting to the polls, for example, or the effort required to find out about the candidates). On the other hand, any benefit is not immediately apparent. The chances of an individual's vote making any difference to a constituency result, let alone the result of the election as a whole, are infinitesimal. The chances that one vote will result in the voter's preferred party becoming the government and eventually benefiting the voter are so remote that they are hardly worth considering. Voting, therefore, is irrational and the question that should be posed is not why some people don't vote but why anyone does! As we have seen, however, most electors do vote in general elections. This implies either that the costs involved are so small that they do not deter on the scale that rational choice theory would suggest, or that voters have reasons for voting that are not purely instrumental (see McLean, 1982, ch. 4). I will return to this question at the end of the discussion.

As explained in Chapter 1, in order to study variations in turnout at the level of individual voters – to find out who votes and who doesn't, and why – we need to turn to survey data. This is not as straightforward as it may appear. In the first place (at least up until 2001) large majorities of electors do vote in general elections, so that sample surveys tend to have relatively few non-voting respondents and this inhibits analysis. Second, the problem is compounded by the fact that post-election surveys regularly find that more people claim to have voted than actually did so. In part this is because people who are willing to answer survey questions about politics are also more likely to have voted because they are more interested in politics. Partly, also, it is because (as explained above) official turnout figures take no account of the fact that some people on the electoral register will have died or moved away and these, of course, will not be contacted by a survey. In addition, voting is a culturally-valued activity – the good citizen goes to the polls – and it appears that some people are unwilling, or perhaps ashamed, to admit that they failed to vote. By comparing official records with survey responses in a pioneering piece of research, Swaddle and Heath (1989) established that among respondents to the 1987 BES survey who had not in fact voted according to official records, about a quarter claimed to have done so.

In order to overcome the problem of small numbers, the first substantial individual-level study of non-voting in Britain used the combined results of BES surveys at the four general elections between 1966 and October 1974 (Crewe, Fox and Alt, 1977). Crewe and colleagues found, first of all, that in this period very few people were consistent non-voters. Only 1 per cent of their respondents who were eligible abstained in all four elections. Someone who did not vote in one election was quite likely to vote in the one after, or the one after that. This phenomenon was linked to the reasons people give for failing to vote, which were overwhelmingly 'accidental' or 'apathetic'. People said that they were away on polling day, or ill, or simply forgot. Very few were deliberate abstainers in the sense of refusing to vote on principle. In both respects, however, things have changed a bit. As seen in Chapter 1 (Table 1.3), a majority of non-voters in 2001 also did not vote in 2005 (amounting to 12 per cent of those eligible on both occasions). A larger core of persistent non-voters seems to be developing. In addition, when asked why they failed to vote, only a minority (47 per cent) indicated that they were prevented by circumstances. Others were simply not interested (21 per cent), thought that the outcome was not in doubt (9 per cent) or were hostile to the parties and politicians (16 per cent). Persistent non-voting is, then, much more common than it used to be and non-voters appear less likely to feel rather ashamed of it.

The second major conclusion of the study by Crewe, Fox and Alt was something of a surprise. They investigated the effects of a series of social variables on propensity to vote and found that, contrary to common assumptions, most seemed to have little effect. Working-class people were as likely to vote as the middle classes, women as likely as men, the poorly educated as likely as the highly educated, and so on. Only four inter-connected social factors were associated with poor turnout: being young (the most important), being unmarried, living in privately rented accommodation and being residentially mobile. Crewe, Fox and Alt explain higher levels of non-voting by these groups in terms of isolation from personal and community networks, which are characteristic of stable communities and which encourage conformity with the norm of voting.

In a later analysis, Swaddle and Heath (1989) sought to overcome the problem of respondents overreporting voting by getting access to the official electoral registers used by polling officials to mark off the names of people as they actually voted in the 1987 election. They were, therefore, able to tell which of their respondents had really voted, irrespective of what they told interviewers. This procedure has been followed in all subsequent BES surveys and has enabled analysis of 'genuine', as opposed to 'admitted', non-voters. Nonetheless, studies relating non-voting on this basis to social characteristics have generally confirmed the results originally reported by Crewe and his colleagues, although in some cases class and income have also been found to affect voting levels, with manual workers and poorer people having lower turnouts.

Table 2.4 shows the turnout of various social groups in the 2005 election.

Apart from the simple 'flow-of-the-vote' table (Table 1.3) shown in Chapter 1, this is the first example in this book of a table based on cross-tabulations and it is worth making a few explanatory comments about this very common method of analysing and presenting data. Continuous variables enable each case to be given a specific score. Where cases can only be assigned to a category (male/female, say, or Conservative/Labour/Liberal Democrat) and not given a score, the variables concerned are known as **categoric variables**. The most common method of analysing categoric variables is cross-tabulation. Having assigned cases (usually survey respondents) to the categories of one variable (in this case, voted or didn't vote), they are then categorized on the basis of another (for example, occupational class). This would produce, in this example, six categories and these would constitute the cells of a table. Normally the independent variable (class) is shown along the top and constitutes the columns of the table, while the dependent variable (voted or not) is arranged down the side, constituting the rows, and the numbers in each column are converted to percentages totalling 100 for each column.

Table 2.4   Turnout of social groups in 2005

	%		%
Sex		*Housing*	
Men	61	Owner-occupiers	69
Women	62	Renters	44
Marital Status		*Highest education qualification*	
Married	69	None	57
Live with partner	46	Occupational qualification	60
Separated/divorced	53	GCSE (or equivalent)	56
Widowed	75	A level (or equivalent)	61
Single/never married	48	Professional qualification	76
		Degree	74
Occupation		*Income*	
Professional and managerial	73	Lowest third	56
Other non-manual	62	Middle third	63
Manual	54	Top third	67
Age			
18–24	34		
25–34	43		
35–44	58		
45–54	63		
55–64	73		
65+	76		

Source: Data from BES 2005 cross-section survey. The original data have been weighted to reflect the actual turnout in the election.

Theoretically, additional variables can be added, but one of the problems of cross-tabulation is that as extra variables are incorporated the number of table cells multiplies very quickly. If the respondents classified by class and vote were further divided into six age groups, for example, the resulting table would contain 36 cells. Not only would such a table be difficult to read but at least some of the cells would inevitably contain a rather small number of cases, making the figures unreliable.

Another problem when analysing survey data in this way is that the figures derived are, of course, estimates based on a sample of the electorate. If we find differences in behaviour or in attitudes between different categories of respondents, it is important to know whether these differences are significant. We can do this by carrying out a test of statistical significance. Easily the most common test used for cross-tabulations is the **chi-squared test**. This calculates the probability that a difference found among survey respondents reflects a real difference among the population that was sampled. Nowadays, the necessary calculations are produced by suitable computer packages and all that we need to understand is what the results mean. Authors frequently simply report that what they have found is 'significant at the 95 per cent level', or '$p < 0.05$'. This means that there is only a 5 per cent chance, or a probability of less than 0.05 (a very small probability), that the difference found in the sample does *not* reflect a difference in the population as a whole. In other words, the difference found is statistically significant; it is not due to chance. In subsequent tables details about statistical significance will not normally be given, but will be referred to in the text where appropriate.

Table 2.4 summarizes a series of separate cross-tabulations relating to whether or not respondents voted in the 2005 election. Marital status, occupational class, age, housing tenure and income level are clearly associated with variations in turnout (and the differences found are all statistically significant) but, confirming recent experience, there were no significant differences between men and women. As in previous elections, married people were more likely to vote than those who lived with a partner without being married, were separated or divorced, or were single. This may be because married people are more likely to conform to society's norms or – more tendentiously – because they are more likely to take their responsibilities seriously, but there could be other reasons. In terms of marital status, widowed people had the best turnout of all. This is related to age since older voters are also more likely to have been widowed. Middle-class groups voted more heavily than the working class, the better off more than the worse off, owner-occupiers more than renters and those with a university degree or professional qualification more than those without. Paralleling the results of the constituency analysis, the survey data reveal that, contrary to what was found in the 1960s, there is now a clear division in levels of turnout between relatively well-off, well-educated professional middle classes on the one hand and the less well-educated manual working class on the other. This may have something to do with the translation of the Labour party into New Labour or the particular circumstances of the 2005 election, but if it persists it is a worrying development for politicians of all parties.

Perhaps the most striking figures in the table, however, are those for age. The turnout of the youngest voters was only 34 per cent but this increased steadily with age and reached 76 per cent among those aged 65 and above. A simple, practical explanation for the heavy turnout of the oldest group is that it might just be a consequence of the fact that, being retired, they have more time to go to the polling station. At a more general level, however, it is widely suggested that as people get older they become more involved in the political process, acquire a greater sense of responsibility and are more likely to view voting as a civic duty. In the course of a full analysis of trends in turnout to 2001, Clarke *et al.* (2004, ch. 8) show that younger people – 'the Thatcher and Blair generation' – have a much weaker sense of civic duty than their elders and are much less likely to think that non-voting is a serious neglect of a citizen's responsibilities. Moreover, this is not something that they seem to be 'growing out of', as it were, and for that reason we are unlikely to see a return to pre-2001 turnout levels for the foreseeable future.

In their original article, Crewe and his colleagues also investigated the impact of political interest and motivation on non-voting. Much of this sort of analysis comes close to tautology. To discover that people who are more interested in and knowledgeable about politics and who discuss politics more than average tend to vote in greater numbers is hardly surprising. However, one individual-level 'political' variable has been consistently found to have a strong effect on turnout levels, and that is strength of party identification. This is linked to the approach which sees turnout as being related to the extent to which citizens are mobilized by parties. Butler and Stokes (1974, p. 40) reported that in the early 1960s some 64 per cent of very strong identifiers voted in local elections, compared with 54 per cent of fairly strong identifiers and only 39 per cent of not very strong identifiers. Figures from the analysis by Crewe, Fox and Alt (1977), together with data from the last four BES surveys, are given in Table 2.5 and the pattern is very clear. The stronger a person's party identification, the more likely they are to vote. This is not difficult to understand; people who are strong party support-ers clearly have more incentive to go out and vote for their party than those who have only a mild preference for one party or another, or are indifferent. The figures also show that the turnout of people with no party identification

Table 2.5   Turnout by strength of party identification (%)

	Very strong	Fairly strong	Not very strong	No party identification
Regular voters (1966–74)	84	74	54	–
Voted 1992	92	90	80	58
Voted 1997	89	87	73	51
Voted 2001	81	72	50	28
Voted 2005	82	73	59	36

Notes: The first row shows the percentages who voted in all four general elections from 1966 to October 1974; – = data not provided.

Sources: Data from Crewe, Fox and Alt (1977); and BES 1992, 1997, 2001, 2005 cross-section surveys.

has been very much poorer than that of even 'not very strong' identifiers. Moreover, the decline in turnout over the period is steepest among non-identifiers and slightest among 'very strong' identifiers. The problem is, as we shall see in later chapters, that there are now fewer strong identifiers than there used to be.

The data in Tables 2.4 and 2.5 show associations between voting and a variety of social and political characteristics separately. As already mentioned, however, some of the characteristics are themselves inter-related. Age relates to marital status and to strength of party identification, for example; class, housing tenure and income are also likely to overlap. What we really want to know, therefore, is whether differences in marital status, for example, would continue to be important if we also took account of age, and so on. Producing more detailed cross-tabulations to do this would not be very helpful, since a table combining voting versus non-voting, marital status and age group would contain some 60 cells, and adding a simplified three-category income variable would increase that to 180 cells. A table of this size would be difficult to present, never mind interpret.

During the last ten years, however, new techniques have found their way into mainstream electoral analysis which enable us to assess the impact of categoric variables in a way that is analogous to using multiple regression analysis with interval-scale variables. The best-known of these is **binary logistic regression**. This enables us to assess the impact of individual independent variables on a dependent variable while holding all the other independent variables in the analysis constant, and also provides measures of the combined effect of the included variables. The mathematics involved are as terrifying as the name of the technique suggests, but students of voting behaviour only need some (approximate) understanding of what it does and what the results tell us.

The dependent variable can only have two values or categories (such as 'voted' and 'did not vote'), and a category of each independent variable has to be used as a reference for that variable. The results tell us whether, and by how much, respondents in each category of each independent variable differ from the reference category in terms of the dependent variable (in this case, whether they voted or not) while holding all of the other independent variables constant. That sounds very complicated, but an example will help to clarify what is meant.

Table 2.6 presents the results of two logistic regressions with voting versus non-voting as the dependent variable. The first (column *A*) analyses the effects of all the social variables already discussed. The figures shown for each category are **odds ratios**, which indicate how more or less likely someone in the category was to vote in the election than someone in the reference category, while controlling for the other included variables. A ratio of less than 1 indicates that people in that category were less likely to vote, while a ratio greater than 1 shows that they were more likely to do so. Thus, those aged 65 and over were more than nine times (9.49) more likely to turn out than those aged 18–24. The analysis shows that sex, occupation and some categories of marital status (being widowed or single) made no significant difference to turnout levels when all characteristics are considered together: as suggested above, these categories overlap to a great extent with age so that, when we take account of the latter, widowed or single people show no distinct pattern. On the other hand, the older voters were the more they differed from the youngest age group, taking everything else into account. Electors with any educational qualification were more likely to vote than those without, but people with a degree showed the biggest difference, while those renting their homes were less likely to turn out than owner-occupiers even when other characteristics are taken into account.

The output from the relevant SPSS (Statistical Package for the Social Sciences) programme also provides a number of statistics to enable evaluation of each analysis. Some of these are incomprehensible to all but statisticians (and, perhaps, the odd psephologist) but some are easy to interpret and are shown in the table. The **Nagelkerke r^2** (named after the person who devised it and sometimes called a 'pseudo' r^2) gives an estimate of the proportion of variation in the dependent variable (voting versus non-voting) that is explained or accounted for by the variables in the analysis (in this case, 19.8 per cent). Second, the proportion of respondents correctly predicted to be, or classified as, voters or non-voters on the basis of the characteristics included can be calculated. Of course, we would get a good many

Table 2.6   Logistic regression analyses of voting versus non-voting in 2005

	A	B
Sex (Reference = male)		
Female	1.07	1.09
Marital Status (Reference = married)		
Living with partner	**0.72**	**0.66**
Separated/divorced	**0.69**	**0.67**
Widowed	1.37	1.24
Single/never married	0.96	0.96
Occupation (Reference = prof. & managerial)		
Other non-manual	1.01	1.05
Manual	0.88	0.85
Age (Reference = 18–24)		
Aged 25–34	**1.52**	**1.62**
Aged 35–44	**3.41**	**3.43**
Aged 45–54	**4.00**	**3.78**
Aged 55–64	**7.61**	**6.85**
Aged 65+	**9.49**	**7.72**
Housing tenure (Reference = owner-occupier)		
Renter	**0.57**	**0.56**
Education qualification (Reference = none)		
Occupational qualification	**1.83**	**1.95**
GCSE equivalent	**1.66**	**1.77**
A-level equivalent	**2.71**	**2.72**
Professional qualification	**2.37**	**2.35**
Degree	**3.17**	**3.34**
Income (Reference = lowest third)		
Middle third	**1.28**	**1.27**
Top third	**1.31**	1.27
Strength of party identification (Reference = none)		
Very strong	–	**6.61**
Fairly strong	–	**3.96**
Not very strong	–	**2.06**
Nagelkerke r^2	0.198	0.270
% Correctly classified (original)	62.8	62.8
% Correctly classified (equation)	70.1	72.1
% Correctly classified (change)	+7.3	+9.3
(*N*)	(3,036)	(3,029)

Notes: Significant odds ratios ($p < 0.05$) are shown in bold.

of these predictions right by simply assigning everyone to the largest category (voters), and this is shown as the 'original' classification (62.8 per cent). The influence of the variables analysed can be gauged by the extent to which knowing how respondents are categorized on each of them improves our ability to classify them correctly. Here the improvement is 7.3 per cent.

In column *B* strength of party identification is added to the analysis. Very strong identifiers were more than six times as likely to vote as those with no identification. Even fairly strong and not very strong identifiers were significantly more likely to go to the polls than non-identifiers. There are only minor changes in respect of the other variables once strength of identification is taken into account. It can be seen that only one of the income categories is now significantly different from the reference group. On the other hand, age, housing tenure and level of education continue to have a significant independent effect. Adding party identification increases the variation explained to 27.0 per cent (r^2) and also improves the ability of the model to classify people correctly as voters or non-voters.

There is no doubt that logistic regression analysis looks and sounds daunting, and it is certainly not as easy to undertake or understand as simple cross-tabulations. Nonetheless, it has major advantages over the latter in that it enables electoral analysts to examine the combined impact of a large number of categoric variables on voting, and to assess the effect of specific variables while controlling for a large number of others. It seems likely that the use of the technique will become more common in electoral analysis and it is important, therefore, that those interested in the subject are able to understand the meaning of the results that it produces.

The significance of party identification in the preceding analysis helps to answer the question raised by rational choice theory: why do people vote when the costs outweigh the benefits? Back in the 1960s, Butler and Stokes (1969, pp. 36–7) suggested that while rational choice theory assumes that people vote for *instrumental* reasons only (to achieve some end such as helping to elect a particular candidate), many actually vote for *expressive* reasons. Strong party identifiers vote to express their support for their party. Butler and Stokes go on to show that others have *normative* reasons for voting: they see it as a civic obligation, a duty for citizens. BES respondents in 2005 clearly exemplified the latter since 60 per cent agreed that they would feel very guilty if they didn't vote, 69 per cent thought that not voting was a serious neglect of their duty and 77 per cent agreed that it was a citizen's duty to vote (*N* close to 4,000 in all cases). Not surprisingly, people agreeing with these sentiments were much more likely to vote than those who did not. For example, turnout was 74 per cent (*N* = 2,981) among those

Table 2.7   Party identification of non-voters (%)

	1992	1997	2001	2005
None	15	18	31	34
Conservative	41	21	16	19
Labour	30	46	40	33
Lib. Dem.	10	10	7	8
Other	4	5	5	6
(N)	(398)	(495)	(876)	(1,003)

Source: Data from BES cross-section surveys.

who agreed that it is a citizen's duty to vote and 21 per cent among those who did not agree ($N = 590$).

Finally, it is worth looking briefly at the consequences of variations in individual turnout. Does one party consistently suffer as a result of the patterns that have been described? Aggregate turnout figures can be interpreted as suggesting that Labour suffers if turnout is poor and benefits if the turnout is high. As we have seen, turnout tends to be lower in poorer, more working-class constituencies, and these would be expected to be strongly Labour areas. Indeed, in 2005, mean turnout in seats won by Labour was 58.1 per cent ($N = 355$) compared with 65.5 per cent in those won by the Conservatives ($N = 197$) and 65.0 per cent in Liberal Democrat seats ($N = 62$). Survey data cast doubt on this interpretation, however. Although recent BES surveys have not asked non-voters which party they *would have* supported if they had voted, we can use party identification as an indicator of how they would have voted and Table 2.7 shows the relevant data for the last four elections. The Liberal Democrats consistently do worse among non-voters than among people who actually voted, but at each election the party that won the election also 'won' among non-voters. As Labour's share of the vote in elections has fallen since 1997 so has its support among non-voters. The pattern of individual turnout does not, then, appear to favour either the Conservatives or Labour in a consistent way.

Conclusion: what is to be done about low turnout?

All three of the theoretical approaches to participation in elections have found some supportive evidence in the preceding discussion. Some social characteristics (especially age) affect the propensity to vote and, if strong party identification is understood as an aspect of the mobilization of the electorate, then that too is clearly important. There is also evidence that the level of voting is affected by instrumental considerations relating to the costs and benefits of turning out. Participation is greater in more marginal seats and lower in second-order elections, for example. In addition, however, voting can also be an expression of support for a party or can simply be a matter of fulfilling one's duty as a citizen.

In this list I have not mentioned the actual process of voting: the fact that most people have to go to a polling station on a Thursday between 7 a.m. and 10 p.m. and mark a ballot paper. Nonetheless, that is the area on which the authorities have concentrated when considering what might be done to improve turnout. In other words, the focus has been on the costs rather than the benefits of voting. In the first place, opportunities for postal voting have been greatly increased in recent elections. Previously, anyone wanting a postal vote had to have a reason, such as being ill or absent on business. Now, however, anyone can have a postal vote simply by applying for it. Indeed the government has gone further by making postal voting compulsory in some regions at the 2004 European elections (and in the North East referendum on a regional assembly) while various local authorities have done the same in local elections. In general, easier (or compulsory) postal voting appears to boost turnout a little, although there is evidence from local elections that the effect fades as voters become accustomed to it in successive elections. On the other hand, fears have been expressed that extended postal voting gives greater opportunities for fraud and corruption in elections. These fears appeared vindicated just before the 2005 general election when a highly-publicized court case found evidence of serious corruption in Birmingham local elections with the presiding judge declaring that there had been activities that would 'disgrace a banana republic' (*Daily Telegraph*, 5 April 2005). In the light of this and other cases, there has been something of a reaction against compulsory voting by post but claiming a postal ballot is likely to remain much easier than it used to be.

There has been a variety of other experiments with the process of voting in local elections which have involved, among other things, locating polling stations in places such as supermarkets, keeping polling stations open for a few days and allowing voting via the Internet, telephone, or text messages. These have been largely a waste of time. As previously suggested, the costs of voting for most people are trivial and so we must look elsewhere for explanations of decreased turnout in recent elections. In addition to a decline in the sense of civic duty among younger voters, two further causes are structural and political (see Bartle, 2002).

As will be seen in Chapter 7, the first-past-the-post electoral system makes voting rather pointless in seats that are safe for one of the parties, and also leads parties to focus their local campaigns on a small number of 'target' seats. It is arguable that the electorate now has a clearer appreciation of how the system works and that, despite the less than encouraging experience of the 1999 European Parliament elections, a change to a system in which more votes count is needed in order to encourage more people to the polls. In addition, declining turnout has been paralleled by a decline in the intensity of party identification and an increase in the proportions of voters who don't see great ideological differences between the main parties. Both of these are, at least in part, consequences of deliberate strategies pursued by the parties (see Crewe, 2002). After 1997, for example, New Labour clearly moved to the political centre by adopting what were, in many people's eyes, Conservative policies and doing little to enthuse their core vote. After the election of David Cameron as Conservative leader in late 2005, he too seemed concerned to reposition the party towards the centre rather than emphasizing differences between the two main parties. It is clearly in parties' interests to try to occupy the centre ground, since that is where most voters are positioned, so that distinguishing them on ideological grounds is likely to continue to be difficult. For that reason, the decline in the strength of party identification is unlikely to be reversed and this may result in future turnouts continuing to be relatively low. On the other hand, if future elections are thought likely to be close, and/or a greater ideological gap opens up between the parties, then the upturn in participation experienced in 2005 could be repeated.

3

Party Choice in the Era of Alignment, 1950–70

The investigation and understanding of British electoral behaviour in the 1950s and 1960s was strongly influenced by two of the theories introduced in Chapter 1. The first survey studies focused mainly on the social underpinnings of party choice. In doing so, they were not only following the lead given by early American voting studies but also treading the same path as an emerging comparative literature on party systems, best exemplified by the work of Lipset and Rokkan (1967), which argued that the various party systems in Europe were the product of the major social cleavages within the country concerned. In the first British studies based on national surveys, Butler and Stokes (1969, 1974) introduced a more subtle model, which combined both the social influences on party choice and the effects of socialization in producing a psychological attachment to a party among voters: a party identification. Figure 1.2 showed how this model applied to an individual voter; Figure 3.1 gives a (much simplified) representation of how the electorate as a whole was seen.

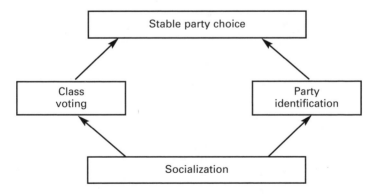

Figure 3.1   The Butler–Stokes model of party choice (electorate as a whole)

48

'Socialization' refers to the process of largely informal learning that almost everyone experiences throughout their lives as a consequence of interactions within families and with friends, neighbours, colleagues and so on. It is particularly important, however, in childhood when people are socialised by their families: they learn what is right and wrong, for example, and pick up what their parents' attitudes are on a whole variety of subjects, including politics. According to Butler and Stokes, most people learned to associate the different parties with classes (Labour was for the working class, the Conservatives for the middle class), and most also adopted their parents' party. We can speak, then, of the electorate being 'aligned' in two main ways. First, there was a class alignment: people in different classes aligned themselves with different parties. Second, there was a 'partisan alignment' in that individuals aligned themselves with a party by thinking of themselves as supporters of it. Broadly speaking, the electorate was divided into two large blocs which provided reliable and stable voting support for the Conservative and Labour parties. The inter-connected phenomena of class and partisan alignment were the twin pillars, as it were, which supported and sustained stable party support on the part of individual voters and a stable two-party system overall. In what follows I will first concentrate on the social correlates of party choice in this period before turning to patterns of party identification.

Class and party

Although a number of social divisions could be hypothesized as fulfilling the conditions required for party differentiation laid down by Berelson, Lazarsfeld and McPhee (1954; see Chapter 1), in fact it was social class that was consistently found to be the most important influence on party choice in Britain. In general, about two-thirds of working-class voters were found to support the Labour Party and upwards of four-fifths of the 'solid' middle class voted Conservative. Writing in 1967, Peter Pulzer concluded, in a much-quoted sentence, that 'Class is the basis of British party politics; all else is embellishment and detail' (1967, p. 98). Similarly, on the basis of figures such as those given in Table 3.1, Butler and Stokes concluded (1974, p. 77):

> Our findings on the strength of links between class and partisanship in Britain echo broadly those of every other opinion poll or voting study . . . there were strong enough cross-currents in each class for partisanship not to have been determined entirely by class. Yet its pre-eminent role can hardly be questioned.

Table 3.1　Vote in 1964 by occupational class (row percentages)

	Conservative	Labour	Liberal	(N)
Higher managerial/professional/ administrative	73	16	11	(91)
Lower managerial/professional/ administrative	68	18	14	(139)
Skilled/supervisory non-manual	59	24	17	(231)
Lower non-manual	54	28	18	(131)
Skilled manual	29	62	9	(564)
Other manual	25	69	6	(350)

Note: These data are based on the occupation of the 'head of household'.
Source: Data from BES 1964 cross-section survey.

In comparative terms, Britain was considered to exemplify the archetypal class-based party system (Alford, 1964).

Butler and Stokes (1974, pp. 81–94) investigated in more detail how voters perceived the link between class and party, and they suggested three possibilities. First, voters could view the party struggle as reflecting opposing class interests: a case of 'us versus them'. One party promotes 'our' interests; the other is concerned to do 'us' down. Second, parties could be seen as simply representing class interests without any implication that these interests are necessarily in conflict. Voters are clear that their party represents their class but display no hostility to, or even concern about, the other class or party. Third, the link could be 'normative', which is to say that voters are simply aware that most people in their class vote for the relevant party; it is simply 'our' party and supporting the party is the class norm, an expression of identity with the relevant class. Butler and Stokes found that working-class Labour voters were more inclined to think of parties in terms of class interests (39 per cent in terms of opposing class interests and 47 per cent in terms of the simple representation of class interests). Only 5 per cent were 'normative' class voters, and the remainder did not think in class terms at all. In contrast, 65 per cent of middle-class Conservative supporters did not think of the parties in class terms and only small minorities (13 per cent, 12 per cent and 10 per cent respectively) subscribed to each of the three views previously outlined. The differences between the two groups reflected the different ways in which the parties portrayed themselves. Labour campaigned as the party for the working class while the Conservatives generally eschewed class rhetoric, claiming to be the party of the nation as a whole, at least partly because they could not win elections without a good proportion of working-class votes.

Defining and measuring social class

Despite its central position in voting behaviour theory, the concept of class is slippery and difficult to define precisely. It is even more difficult to measure or 'operationalize' in empirical research.

When we say that a person is 'middle class' or 'working class' (to the extent that people still use these terms) we often have a variety of things in mind: wealth, income, occupation, education, accent, 'style of life', and so on. So how is a person's class to be determined? Generally, voting researchers, as well as opinion pollsters and market researchers, have opted for occupation as a short-hand indicator of class. This can be justified on the grounds that most people have traditionally described different classes in terms of different occupations (see Butler and Stokes, 1974, p. 70) but it also gives rise to other problems. How many classes are there? Which occupations belong to which classes? The classes of bank managers and unskilled labourers may be fairly obvious, but what about typists, policemen or foremen on building sites? Is a self-employed plumber in a different class from a plumber who is employed by a large firm? Another set of problems relates to the categorization of women: should employed married women be classified according to their own job or the job of their husbands (the reasoning being that the husband used to be thought of as the 'head of the household' and thus determines the whole family's status)? And what about married women who are full-time housewives and mothers?

Clearly, the definition and measurement of this most basic social variable is fraught with difficulty. Indeed, as we shall see in Chapter 4, the very definition of class came to be an important element in the debate over trends in class voting which dominated discussion among academics in the field during the 1980s. Various classification systems have been employed, including 17 socio-economic groups and five social classes used in past censuses and a seven-fold scheme devised by Butler and Stokes. Perhaps the best-known scheme is that used by opinion pollsters, which allocates voters to one of six main occupational groups whose names have become familiar to poll-watchers. These are shown below:

A   Higher professional, managerial and administrative
B   Intermediate professional, managerial and administrative
C1   Supervisory, clerical and other non-manual
C2   Skilled manual
D   Semi- and unskilled manual
E   Residual, casual workers, people reliant on state benefits

Whatever the original classification system, voting researchers frequently collapse categories into just two groups, non-manual workers (in the market research case, ABC1) and manual workers (C2DE). This is partly for purely practical reasons. If a survey uses a six-fold categorization, the number of respondents in each class will be smaller than with a dichotomous scheme and detailed analysis will be inhibited. Partly, also, the reality is that most people used to think of – and talk about – the British class structure in terms of a basic division between a middle and a working class. Nevertheless, it should be borne in mind that the manual/non-manual distinction is a very rough and ready approximation to what we mean when we talk about social class, and in some cases finer distinctions are used.

The party choice of manual and non-manual workers at the elections of 1964, 1966 and 1970 are shown in Table 3.2. Using this simplified, dichotomous indicator of class certainly dampens class differences somewhat as compared with the figures given in Table 3.1. Nonetheless, the differences between the two broad occupational groups are clear enough. More than 60 per cent of non-manual workers voted Conservative in each election; a clear majority of manual workers always voted Labour.

Thus far, we have talked about measuring class in objective terms: people are categorized in terms of their occupation. Arguably a better way to detect the influence of class on voting is to concentrate on how people allocate themselves to a class. This is sometimes called 'self-assessed' or 'subjective' class (or 'class identity'), and defining class in this way usually produces stronger associations with party choice. In 1966, for example, 57 per cent of BES respondents readily placed themselves in a class (without prompting). Those who described themselves as middle class ($N = 267$)

Table 3.2   Occupational class and party choice, 1964, 1966 and 1970 (%)

	1964		1966		1970	
	Non-manual	Manual	Non-manual	Manual	Non-manual	Manual
Conservative	62	28	61	25	63	33
Labour	22	64	26	69	26	58
Liberal	15	8	13	5	9	7
Other	1	*	*	*	2	2
(N)	(595)	(877)	(595)	(947)	(566)	(856)

Note: These data are based on the occupation of the 'head of household'. * = less than 1 per cent.
Source: Data from BES 1964–70, cross-section surveys.

voted 66 per cent Conservative and 22 per cent Labour; self-described work-ing-class respondents ($N = 621$) voted 75 per cent Labour and 20 per cent Conservative.

Other social influences on voting

Although class was the dominant source of party alignment in Britain in the 1950s and 1960s, other social and demographic characteristics were also consistently found to be associated with party choice. Two preliminary points about these relationships should be noted. First, the importance of class as a determinant of voting was such that, for any other variable to be shown to affect party choice, it had to continue to have an effect when class was 'controlled'. That is, the variable in question would need to make a difference to party choice *within* at least one of the different classes. There would be little point in getting excited over a finding that most Roman Catholics voted Labour, for example, if it were also the case that most Roman Catholics were working class. Second, while the job of establishing the existence of relationships between social attributes and party choice, whether at any single election or over a period of time, is relatively straight-forward, explaining them is not. Voting researchers might agree about which groups tended to vote for which parties but that does not mean that they are in agreement about why they did so. Although a variety of social characteristics were associated with party choice in the era of aligned voting, many of them – including housing tenure and education – were clearly class-related. I concentrate here on the three most interesting characteristics which were not obviously a function of class position: age, sex and religion.

Age

There is a well-known aphorism, the origins of which are obscure, which goes something like this: 'If you're not a radical at 20 you've no heart; if you're not a conservative at 60 you've no head.' The precise ages referred to vary somewhat but the general sentiment of this piece of folk-wisdom is clear enough and it found empirical support from voting studies in the 1950s and 1960s. Academic surveys and opinion polls regularly found that younger people, especially the youngest age group in the electorate, were more inclined to vote Labour while older voters favoured the Conservatives.

A typical set of figures is shown in Table 3.3, which relates to the 1970 election (the first after the voting age was lowered to 18). The top row refers

Table 3.3   Age and vote (percentage Conservative) in the 1970 election

	Aged 18–24	Aged 25–34	Aged 35–44	Aged 45–54	Aged 55–64	Aged 65+
All	37	43	41	42	52	55
Non-manual	52	58	62	69	71	69
Manual	28	32	28	25	38	46

Note: Occupation refers to the 'head of household'.
Source: Data from BES 1970 cross-section survey.

to all voters and shows that although the overall trend is not linear – the percentage of Conservative voters does not increase in steps across every age group – the youngest age group is clearly the least Conservative and there is a sharp increase in Conservative support among the over-55s. The second row is restricted to non-manual workers and here the trend is even clearer: there is a steady rise in Conservative voting as age increases. In the third row (manual workers) it is the 45–54 year old age group which gives the least support to the Conservatives but, once again, the oldest people are most Conservative. Overall, then, there is an age effect within each class and we can conclude that there is a clear association between age and party choice; what is not clear is why this should be so.

Two main explanations have been proposed. The first involves what is called a 'life-cycle' effect and is essentially the explanation implicit in the aphorism quoted above. Young people tend to be idealistic and to favour social and political change. As they grow older, however, people acquire more responsibilities (such as a family of their own), more of a stake in society (such as property), more commitments (a mortgage) and become more aware of the difficulties associated with rapid social change. They thus become more cautious and conservative in outlook.

The second explanation concentrates on political generations or 'cohorts'. In this view, it is not so much a person's chronological age that is important as when he or she was young and beginning to experience politics. As each generation enters the electorate it is influenced by currently decisive political events – the Vietnam War in the 1960s, for example, or the 'winter of discontent' in 1978/9 – or, more broadly, 'the nature of the times' such as the apparent dominance of 'Thatcherite' values in the 1980s. Thus, the group aged 45–54 in 1970 would have been aged 15–24 in 1940. They would have first been eligible to vote in 1945 when, after a long hard war, feeling in the country was strongly pro-Labour; their political attitudes and behaviour would continue to be influenced by this early experience for a long time afterwards. This interpretation certainly finds some support – at least among manual workers – in the data in Table 3.3. In a similar way, the idea of political generations could be used to explain the strength of Conservative support among older people in Britain in the 1950s and 1960s since anyone aged over 60 in, say, 1964 would have come of voting age in the 1920s or before, when Labour was a relatively new party. Their earliest influences, therefore, were unlikely to have been in a pro-Labour direction.

Sex

As with age, a person's sex is not usually too difficult to discover and classify. It is not immediately clear that the differences between men and women create groups which meet the criteria for a politically-relevant social cleavage as defined by Berelson, Lazarsfeld and McPhee, although it could be argued that the consequences of political policy are different for each. Nonetheless, in the 1950s and 1960s there was a regular pattern to party choice: men were less likely to vote Conservative and more likely to vote Labour than women. As Pulzer (1967, p. 107) put it: 'There is overwhelming evidence that women are more Conservatively inclined than men ... sex is the one factor which indubitably counter-balances class trends: working-class women are more right-wing than working-class men, middle-class women are more right-wing than middle-class men.' Table 3.4, based on BES data for the 1966 election, illustrates this claim. Whereas 36 per cent of men voted Conservative in that election, 41 per cent of women did so and the difference persisted among people from both non-manual and manual families. It is possible, however, that the apparent difference in party choice

Table 3.4   Sex and vote (percentage Conservative) in the 1966 election

	Men	Women
All	36	41
Non-manual	59	62
Manual	23	27
Aged 18–45	33	36
Aged 45–64	39	44
Aged 65+	40	46

Note: Occupation refers to the 'head of household'.
Source: Data from BES 1966 cross-section survey.

between men and women is misleading. Since women tend to live longer than men, the difference may actually be a product of the age difference that has already been identified. The table also shows, therefore, support for the Conservatives on the part of males and females within three age groups. Again, the differences persist (and, looking at the column figures, these data also show that age differences persist when controlling for sex). It should be said, however, that even by 1966 the differences between men and women were relatively small, and those shown in the table were not quite great enough to reach statistical significance.

Nonetheless, there is no shortage of hypotheses to explain the greater Conservatism of women in this period. It can be argued, for instance, that at this time women were more home-centred than men. While men went out to work, women stayed at home to look after children and attend to other domestic duties. This insulated them from industrial conflicts and wider community pressures. If this is correct then we should expect to find the 'gender gap' narrowing as more and more women entered the work-force from the 1970s onwards. Other explanations would not predict an erosion of the differences between men and women. It could be suggested, for example, that women are more likely than men to be attached to, and be transmitters of, traditional values relating to religion and the family and this makes them more conservative. It has even been suggested that women are more socially aspiring than men, which is why they tend also to have more 'genteel', less strongly regional accents.

Religion

As used in this context, 'religion' is a shorthand. Christianity is a religion, as is Islam or Hinduism. In the context of voting in the United Kingdom, however, what is usually being referred to is adherence (or not) to a Christian denomination, such as the Church of England, the Methodists and so on. Members of non-Christian religions constituted only a very small percentage of the electorate in the period to which this chapter refers.

Religious or denominational divisions, stretching back to the Reformation, were identified by Lipset and Rokkan (1967) as one of the key sources of social cleavage giving rise to party divisions. In many Western European states, including Germany and the Netherlands, the Protestant–Catholic divide remains an important influence on party choice, while in predominantly Catholic countries (such as France) there is a tradition of party division over the role of the Church.

In Britain in the late nineteenth and early twentieth centuries, religion played a major role in party politics and in determining party support. In those days, the Church of England could fairly be described as 'the Tory Party at prayer' while the Liberal Party was strongly supported by Nonconformists. Religious issues, such as support for Church of England schools from the rates (local taxes) or the question of the disestablishment of the Anglican Church in Wales, excited much political passion. The divide spilled over into other issues, however, including licensing laws, with the temperance/Nonconformist/Liberal forces opposing the brewers/Anglican/Tory nexus. In this period, too, the Conservatives vigorously opposed Irish Home Rule and supported Ulster Protestants in attempting to preserve the union and, eventually, in forcing the partition of Ireland in 1922.

Although these events were in the distant past, even in the 1960s Butler and Stokes (1969, pp. 124–34) found that religion had a 'political legacy'. Before looking at the data, however, it is worth considering the meaning of survey-derived data about religious affiliation. The following incident is recorded in Butler and Stokes's (1969, p. 125) discussion of religious affiliation and party choice:

> One of our interviewers recorded a colloquy with a respondent who said 'none' in answer to her initial question about religious affiliation. She then inquired, on her own initiative, whether she ought to put him down as 'atheist' or 'agnostic'. The respondent thereupon asked to be told the difference between the two . . . After hearing her account, the respondent said, 'You had better put me down as Church of England.'

This illustrates very well the difficulty of classifying voters according to religious denomination and of analysing the relationship between religion and party choice. The respondent presumably *was* put down as Church of England and incorporated into the analysis on that basis. Indeed, in their three election surveys only around 3 per cent of Butler and Stokes's respondents were classed as having no religion. In what was, even then, a largely secular, non-churchgoing society this seems odd, and it is not clear in these circumstances what it means to say that someone 'belongs' to one religious denomination or another. Difficulties also arise in combining different denominations for analysis (there are so many of them that this is usually necessary) especially in relation to Scottish Protestants (since the established Church in Scotland is Presbyterian).

Nonetheless, the first part of Table 3.5 is based on the Butler–Stokes classification of religious affiliation and shows the relationships between this and party in 1964. Anglicans and Scottish Protestants (mostly Church of Scotland) were more likely to support the Conservative Party than were Nonconformists or, especially, Roman Catholics, and the differences are

Table 3.5 Religious affiliation and party choice (percentage Conservative) in the 1964 election

	Anglican/ C. of E.	Scottish Protestant	Nonconformist	Roman Catholic	None
All	46	45	35	26	–
Non-manual	67	66	54	48	–
Manual	32	29	20	14	–
Attenders					
All	50	52	35	27	39
Non-manual	68	73	49	52	60
Manual	35	32	20	14	26

Notes: In the first part of the table too few respondents were categorized as 'None' to give meaningful results; in the second part of the table respondents who attended church only once per year or less are classified as 'none'.
Source: BES 1964 cross-section survey.

statistically significant. Although there are clear class differences within each denomination, there are also differences between denominations within each of the classes. Thus, middle-class Nonconformists and Catholics were less likely to be Conservative voters than Anglicans, and the same is true among the working class. In the second part of the table only those who attended church more than once a year are classified as belonging to the denomination, while those who attended less often (or never) are classed as having no affiliation (together with those initially classified as such). Not unexpectedly, the figures show that, for the most part, the differences between denominations are now larger than before (both overall and within classes), while the Conservatives were also relatively weak among voters with no religious attachment. By the 1950s and 1960s, therefore, although the influence of religious affiliation on political party choice had declined as compared with the early years of the century, it was still in evidence (and was, of course, of paramount importance in Northern Ireland).

Explanations of the continuing association between religion and party in Britain have tended to focus on the fact that the Church of England, as the established church, is identified with the social and political establishment, while religious dissent goes hand-in-hand with political dissent. In addition, religious attachments at this time did not change a great deal from generation to generation, and the parents or grandparents of many voters in the 1960s would have been voting in the early part of the century when the connections between religion and politics were more direct. Many Nonconformists, for example, would have inherited an anti-Conservative tradition. Similarly,

Catholics in Britain are to a considerable extent descendants of Irish immigrants and, for them, the role of the Conservatives (known for a long time as the Conservative and Unionist Party) in the struggles over Irish home rule continued to play a large part in their political thinking. As this point illustrates, the influence of religion on party choice in the 1950s and 1960s was very much a legacy of past struggles, and Butler and Stokes were convinced that it was a legacy that was steadily disappearing.

The combined effect of social characteristics

Over the years, voting studies have investigated and provided information on the influence on party choice of a large number of social variables, including housing tenure, trade union membership, income, level of education, urban–rural differences, car ownership and so on. To a large extent, however, these can be seen as variations on the main themes provided by the most important socio-demographic characteristics of class, age, sex and religion (together with region, to be considered in a later chapter), the significance of which was established in the era of aligned voting. It is worth noting that I have not mentioned race or ethnicity in this context; this is because what are now known as the ethnic minorities constituted a tiny fraction of the electorate during this period and little attention was paid to their voting behaviour until relatively recently.

Examining the associations between party choice by means of a series of cross-tabulations produces interesting and important results. As discussed in the previous chapter, however, if we want to assess the relative impact of an independent variable while holding others constant, or to assess the overall impact of a set of independent variables, then the limitations of cross-tabulation analysis (to which Butler and Stokes and all previous survey reports were largely restricted) quickly become obvious. As the data have been presented so far, party choice has usually involved four categories (although I have simplified presentation in some cases by presenting figures for Conservative voting only), class has involved two, age has involved six, sex two and religion five. A table cross-tabulating all of these variables would consist of no fewer than 480 cells ($4 \times 2 \times 6 \times 2 \times 5$). One more variable with three categories (English, Scottish, Welsh, say) would push the number up to 1,440!

As explained in the previous discussion (Chapter 2), one answer to the problem is to use binary logistic regression analysis, and Table 3.6 shows logistic regressions of Conservative and Labour voting in the 1964 election. (For guidance in interpreting the results of the analyses, see the discussion in the previous chapter.) The first column compares Conservative voters with

Table 3.6   Logistic regression analyses of Conservative and Labour voting
in 1964

	Conservative versus others	Labour versus others	Labour versus Conservative
Class (Reference = Professional and managerial)			
Intermediate non-manual	**0.63**	**1.38**	**1.46**
Manual	**0.20**	**6.52**	**6.99**
Age (Reference = 18–34)			
Aged 35–44	**0.61**	1.30	**1.53**
Aged 45–54	1.17	0.89	0.87
Aged 55–64	**1.54**	0.71	**0.65**
Aged 65+	1.31	0.90	0.86
Sex (Reference = male)			
Female	1.19	0.96	0.88
Religion (Reference = Anglican)			
None	**0.72**	**1.80**	**1.63**
Roman Catholic	**0.41**	**2.56**	**2.69**
Nonconformist	**0.41**	**1.86**	**2.21**
Scottish Protestant	1.08	1.17	0.98
Tenure (Reference = Owner-occupier)			
Rents from council	**0.34**	**3.59**	**3.79**
Rents privately	**0.61**	**2.15**	**2.01**
Nagelkerke r^2	0.252	0.320	0.339
% Correctly classified (original)	58.5	52.7	53.3
% Correctly classified (equation)	70.1	71.7	73.1
% Correctly classified (change)	+11.6	+19.0	+19.8
(*N*)	(1,456)	(1,450)	(1,288)

Note: Significant odds ratios ($p < 0.05$) are shown in bold.
Source: Data from BES 1964 cross-section survey.

all others, the second compares Labour voters with all others and the third
directly compares Labour and Conservative voters. Recall that the coefficients shown (odds ratios) show how more (odds ratio greater than one) or
less (odds ratio less than one) likely someone in the category is to vote
Conservative/Labour – as opposed to the other party or parties being
compared – than someone in the reference category, while controlling for
other included variables.

In all three analyses class makes a significant difference: intermediate non-manual and, even more so, manual workers were less likely to vote Conservative and more likely to vote Labour, even when all the other variables were taken into account. Manual workers were almost seven times (6.99) more likely to vote Labour rather than Conservative. Age does not have a consistent effect once the other variables are taken into account, although those aged 35–44 were less likely to vote Conservative and more likely to support Labour than the youngest age group, while the opposite was true of those aged 55–64. Religious denomination does have a consistent effect. Even after taking account of the other variables, people with no religious affiliation, Catholics and Nonconformists were significantly less likely to have voted Conservative and more likely to have voted Labour than Anglicans. Similarly, those renting their homes behaved in a different way from owner-occupiers. On the other hand, being male or female made no significant difference, once the other variables are taken into account.

The Nagelkerke r^2 statistics show that about 25 per cent (0.252) of the variation in Conservative versus non-Conservative voting is explained by the five variables, while for Labour versus non-Labour voting and Labour versus Conservative voting the respective proportions are 32 per cent and 34 per cent. As far as classifying respondents in terms of the dependent variables (Conservative versus others, and so on), knowing their class, age, sex, religion and housing tenure clearly made for marked improvements in the proportion correctly classified than would be the case if they were all assigned to the largest category. The improvements are greater when Labour voting is involved, indicating that – in line also with the r^2 figures – support for Labour was more easily predicted on the basis of these social characteristics than Conservative voting.

Partisan alignment

As indicated at the start of this chapter, the alignment between classes and parties was only one of the main features of voting in Britain in the 1950s and 1960s. There was also a 'partisan alignment' in the sense that electors identified themselves with a party. The standard BES survey question designed to elicit the kind of generalized psychological commitment implied by party identification is: 'Generally speaking, do you think of yourself as Conservative, Labour, Liberal Democrat or what?' Surveys at the three elections between 1964 and 1970 found that the overwhelming majority of voters – around 90 per cent – were willing to nominate a party that they supported and, of those, most nominated the Labour or Conservative parties (see Table 3.7).

Table 3.7   Party identification, 1964–70 (%)

	1964	1966	1970
With party identification	92	90	89
With Conservative or Labour identification	81	80	81
'Very strong' identifiers	43	43	41
'Very strong' Conservative or Labour identifiers	40	39	40

Source: Data from BES 1964–70 cross-section surveys.

It is possible that this survey question does not in fact tap the kind of enduring, deep-rooted commitment which is implied by the concept of party identification, but that voters respond by simply naming the party which they currently favour. This possibility was considered by, among others, Butler and Stokes (1974, pp. 39–47) and Crewe, Sarlvik and Alt (1977, pp. 139–42). Both investigations found that voters were much more likely to change their vote without changing identification than to change their identification without changing their vote. Both suggested, on this basis, that the question 'works' and that party identification really did exist amongst voters. Butler and Stokes concluded (1974, p. 47) that in the 1960s: 'millions of British electors remain anchored to one of the parties for very long periods of time. Indeed many electors have had the same party loyalties from the dawn of their political consciousness.' It is worth noting, however, that a much later analysis of the Butler and Stokes panel data (Clarke, Stewart and Whiteley, 2001) suggested that Butler and Stokes had exaggerated the stability of party identification. It was found that, over four interviews (1963, 1964, 1966 and 1970), only 61 per cent of respondents identified with the same party.

As a standard follow-up to the party identification question in election surveys, respondents are usually asked: 'How strongly (chosen party) do you generally feel – very strongly, fairly strongly, or not very strongly?' In the three surveys reported in Table 3.7, more than two-fifths of the electorate were prepared to describe themselves as 'very strong' party supporters, and almost all of these were Conservative or Labour identifiers.

Strength of party identification has important effects upon electoral behaviour. As seen in Chapter 2, stronger identifiers are more likely to turn out to vote and, in addition, they are more likely to vote for the party that they identify with, and to be stable in their party choice over time than are weaker identifiers. The latter are more likely to make their minds up about which party to vote for closer to election day itself, rather than well in advance of it, and to be more 'wobbly', in the sense of seriously considering

Table 3.8   Party identification in 1964 by parents' party preference (%)

	Both parents Conservative	Both parents Labour	Both parents Liberal	One parent Conservative other none	One parent Labour other none
Conservative	74	12	37	50	19
Labour	13	79	31	30	65
Liberal	6	6	28	12	11
Other/none	6	4	3	8	5
(*N*)	(320)	(309)	(102)	(76)	(107)

Source: Data from BES 1964 cross-section survey.

voting for a party other than their eventual choice. I shall return to these important differences in the next chapter.

What was the source of the party identification adopted by voters? As Figure 1.2 illustrated, Butler and Stokes argued that it was largely inherited through the family, and they supported this contention with evidence similar to that shown in Table 3.8. As can be seen, where both parents had supported a major party, three-quarters or more of Butler and Stokes's respondents identified with the same party; even if only one parent had supported a party, there was still a clear effect on the subsequent party identification of their children. Given that in 1964 the Liberals were very much a minority party, it is intriguing to note that almost a third (28 per cent) of respondents who remembered their parents being Liberal supporters themselves identified with the Liberals. Later critics have cast doubt on the way in which Butler and Stokes analysed and interpreted these data (see Rose and McAllister, 1990, pp. 46–8) – they excluded voters who didn't know or couldn't remember how their parents voted, for example – but they are consistent with the general model put forward by Butler and Stokes.

Consequences of aligned voting

The picture of the British electorate that was painted by voting studies of the 1950s and 1960s, then, was one of stability. Class and partisan alignment divided voters into two blocs which could be relied upon to turn out in election after election to support their party, and the extent and strength of commitment to the Conservative and Labour parties provided a basis for stability in electoral behaviour and for a two-party system that seemed secure. Indeed, it made little sense to think of voters as 'deciding' to vote for

one party or another in an election; in fact, the voter had a 'standing decision' or commitment to a party, and voting for it in elections was nearly
automatic. This generalized picture does not, of course, describe the voting
behaviour of every single elector. Not everyone supported their 'natural'
class party and there were, in fact, special studies of 'working-class Tories'
in the 1960s (Nordlinger, 1967; McKenzie and Silver, 1968). Some voters
did not identify with a party, and there were always 'floating' voters who
switched parties in successive elections. Nonetheless, stable party choice
was the watchword of analysts and this is reflected in election results up to
the 1970s (see Table 1.2 and Figure 1.1). Labour and the Conservatives
dominated elections in this period, their shares of the vote were fairly steady
and swings were relatively small. Net volatility as measured by the Pedersen
Index was highest in 1951 – mainly due to a collapse in Liberal support – but
thereafter was relatively modest.

This raises a problem, however. If voting behaviour was so stable, how
can we account for electoral change? In the short term, between pairs of
elections, if this model were accurate we would expect little change. If we
think in terms of an election transition matrix or 'flow-of-the-vote' table, the
majority of voters would fall in the cells on the diagonal from top left to
bottom right. Table 3.9 is not a flow-of-the-vote table but it summarizes
electoral change between three pairs of elections in the aligned voting
period. On each occasion about two-thirds of respondents were in these
cells, and most of those who were not drifted between voting and non-
voting, which is also consistent with the model. Only small minorities of
voters actually switched parties. Nonetheless, it was this switching at the
margins, together with the non-voting traffic, that accounted for short-term
electoral change. 'Floating' of this kind appeared, if anything, to be a

Table 3.9   Constancy and change between pairs of elections, 1959–70 (%)

	1959–64	1964–66	1966–70
Voted Conservative or Labour twice	51	55	47
Voted Liberal Democrat or minor party twice	2	4	3
Did not vote twice	11	15	16
Total constant	64	74	66
Switched between Conservative and Labour	5	3	5
Switched between major and minor parties	7	4	4
Switched between voting and non-voting	24	19	25
Total changed	36	26	34

Source: Data from relevant BES surveys.

response to rather vague short-term factors but, overall, floaters were less concerned and less knowledgeable about politics, less interested in the outcome of elections and less able to say why they had voted for a particular party than were those whose voting pattern was stable. Paradoxically, it was not the politically interested and knowledgeable voters who determined which party won elections – since they were largely committed and loyal party supporters – but those whose concern with political affairs was peripheral (see Milne and Mackenzie, 1958, p. 192; Butler and Stokes, 1969, p. 437).

According to the Butler–Stokes picture of the electorate, electoral change would be very slow and gradual, depending upon demographic trends (the differential fertility and mortality of the different classes, for instance), changes in the social structure and disruptions to patterns of socialization. Nonetheless, by the second edition of their book Butler and Stokes (1974, pp. 193–207) detected an 'ageing of the class alignment'. Changes in the nature, policies and propaganda of the parties, the emergence of a more affluent working class and a revolution in life-styles during the 1960s all contributed to a weakening of class–party links and an apparent increase in electoral volatility, especially among younger voters. As we shall see in the next chapter, however, these straws in the wind proved to be highly significant in elections after 1970, and expectations based on the broader model were unfulfilled.

4

Dealignment and its Consequences

In the previous chapter we saw that, in the 1950s and 1960s, the British electorate was portrayed as being aligned in two important ways: there was a
partisan alignment and a class alignment. Other social characteristics also
aligned with party but more weakly than class. Not surprisingly, the aligned
electorate sustained a stable two-party system. The Conservative and
Labour parties regularly won about nine out of every ten votes, and almost
all of the seats in the House of Commons, and thus they monopolized
government; electoral change was slow and small.

Even the most casual observer must have noticed, however, that from the
1970s onwards things were different. The party system has been far from
stable and electoral change has been swift and extensive. In general elections
the two-party duopoly in England has been eroded, at first by the Liberals,
then by the Liberals in alliance with the SDP and finally by the Liberal
Democrats. At the same time, in Scotland and Wales the nationalist parties
have become important and established features of the political landscape.
During these years electoral volatility rather than stability has been emphasized by election commentators. There was even a period in the late 1970s
when single-party government could not be sustained and a 'Lib–Lab' pact
was required to keep the Labour government in office. Clearly something
had gone wrong with the admittedly greatly-simplified model of a stable,
aligned electorate outlined in Chapter 3.

Having pictured the electorate as aligned, we can imagine that a process
of realignment could take place. Large sections of the electorate could stop
identifying with one party and start to identify with another; some social
group as a whole might switch its party allegiance. The most frequently cited
example of a realignment of this kind is the case of black voters in the United
States. Up to about 1928, when American blacks voted they usually
supported the Republican Party (on the perfectly reasonable grounds that
President Abraham Lincoln, who had been instrumental in abolishing slav-
ery, was a Republican). From 1928 onwards, however, blacks began to
switch to the Democratic Party, and today they are an overwhelmingly
Democratic group.

There is no similar example of realignment in modern British political history. What largely explains the electoral turmoil after 1970, however, is a sort of half-way house between alignment and realignment: namely, *dealignment*. This refers to a weakening of previously existing alignments. The word (which will not be found in a standard dictionary) appears to have been first used in the British context in a seminal article published in 1977 by Ivor Crewe and colleagues (Crewe, Sarlvik and Alt, 1977; see also Crewe, 1984), and class and partisan dealignment have been identified by numerous writers as the key processes underlying electoral behaviour over the last 30 years. It is not, of course, that voters woke up on New Year's Day in 1970 and decided to start dealigning themselves. Instead, the election of February 1974 was seen by commentators, including Crewe, Sarlvik and Alt, as marking a new departure and an appropriate point from which to date a marked change in British electoral behaviour (see also Franklin, 1985, ch. 7). Others suggest that dealignment began to affect Labour voters in the late 1960s and Conservative supporters between 1970 and 1974 (see Miller, Tagg and Britto, 1986).

Class dealignment

Presenting data showing the basic relationship between occupational class and party choice in the eleven elections from 1964 to 2001 would be rather cumbersome. For illustrative purposes, however, Table 4.1 shows the average figures for 1964 and 1966 (elections won by Labour) and those for 1997, 2001 and 2005 (also won by Labour). The proportion of non-manual workers who voted Conservative slumped from 62 per cent in the 1960s to only the mid-to-high 30s in the three most recent elections, while the proportion voting Labour increased. Among manual workers, the proportion voting Labour declined (especially in 2005) although there was also a fall in the proportions supporting the Conservatives. In both cases, the trends are partially explained by the increased level of support for the Liberal Democrats.

In order to make comparisons over time easier, voting researchers have devised a variety of summary measures of the relationship between class and party choice. The one that is perhaps most commonly used is known as the 'Alford Index' (since it was devised by a political scientist called Robert Alford: see Alford, 1964). This is calculated by simply subtracting Labour's percentage share of the vote among non-manual workers from its share among manual workers. Thus for 1997 (Table 4.1) the score is $(60 - 40) = 20$. A little thought will show that the index can vary between 0 (equal percent-

Table 4.1   Occupation and party choice, 1997–2005 (%)

	Mean 1964–6	1997	2001	2005
Non–manual				
Conservative	62	36	34	38
Labour	25	40	38	31
Liberal (Democrat)	12	19	23	24
(*N*)		(1,197)	(1,228)	(1,990)
Manual				
Conservative	29	19	20	21
Labour	64	60	61	49
Liberal (Democrat)	7	15	14	20
(*N*)		(891)	(833)	(800)

Notes: The columns do not total 100 because votes for 'others' are not shown.
Sources: Data from relevant BES surveys.

ages vote Labour in each class and there is, therefore, no class voting) and 100 (all manual workers vote Labour, but no non-manual workers do). By convention, it is Labour voting that is used as the basis for calculating the Alford Index but Conservative voting could just as easily be used (in which case, of course, we would subtract the percentage Conservative among manual workers from the percentage Conservative among non-manuals). The index is, then, a measure of the relative strength of a party in two classes and Table 4.2 shows calculations for both Labour and Conservative voting. In both cases there was a sharp fall in the index score in 1970 and the decline continued thereafter with the Labour index reaching a new low in 2005. On this measure, clearly, there has been a decline in class voting since 1970. Even in the most recent elections the index scores are greater than zero, however, indicating that there still remains some class basis to party choice.

A similar tale is told by the figures for 'absolute class voting'. These indicate the percentage of voters supporting their 'natural' class party; in other words, it is the number of non-manual workers voting Conservative plus the number of manual workers voting Labour, as a percentage of all voters. As can be seen, whereas at least three-fifths of voters supported the expected party in the 1960s, that fell to around half in the 1980s and less than half in 1997, 2001 and 2005. It should be borne in mind that these figures refer only to those who actually voted. If non-voters were included in the calculations then the figures for absolute class voting would be substantially smaller. Even among voters, however, by 2005 only around two-fifths voted as the

Table 4.2   Measures of class voting, 1964–2005

	1964	1966	1970	Feb. 1974	Oct. 1974	1979	1983	1987	1992	1997	2001	2005
Alford Index (Labour)	42	43	32	35	32	27	25	25	27	20	23	18
Alford Index (Conservative)	34	36	30	29	27	25	19	19	19	17	14	17
Absolute class voting	63	66	60	55	54	55	49	49	52	46	45	41
Odds ratios	6.4	6.5	4.3	5.7	4.8	3.7	3.8	3.6	3.4	2.8	2.7	2.9

Notes: In all cases scores are calculated from the relevant BES data. In line with the practice of the original investigators, the figures for 1964–70 are based on the occupation of the 'head of the household'. From 1974 to 1979 married women are coded according to the husband's occupation. From 1983 the occupation of the respondent is used in all cases.

class voting model would predict. It is hard to imagine stronger evidence that the class alignment in British electoral politics is now firmly consigned to history.

Finally, the table shows 'odds ratios'. This measure was used by Heath, Jowell and Curtice (1985) in their controversial attack on the class dealignment thesis and is designed to show the extent of relative, rather than absolute, class voting. The ratio used here is the odds of a person with a non-manual occupation voting Conservative rather than Labour, divided by the corresponding odds for a manual worker. Thus, using the data in Table 4.1, the odds of a non-manual worker voting Conservative rather than Labour in 2005 were 38:31, whereas for a manual worker they were 21:49. The odds ratio is, therefore, (38/31)/(21/49) = 2.9. The larger the odds ratio, the stronger is relative class voting. The use of odds ratios by Heath, Jowell and Curtice to describe trends in class voting was heavily criticized. Dunleavy (1987), for example, described the measure as, among other things, 'quite inappropriate', 'distorting', 'peculiar', eccentric' and 'virtually meaningless'. Crewe (1986, p. 626) argues that the odds ratio 'offers a spurious degree of precision and converts tiny ripples of movement – whether real or illusory – into dramatic tides of change'. Even so, the trend in odds ratios is similar to that of the other measures, reaching low points in the last three elections. A visual impression of the trend in class voting is given by Figure 4.1, which shows clearly how absolute class voting and the Alford Index of Labour voting have declined since 1964.

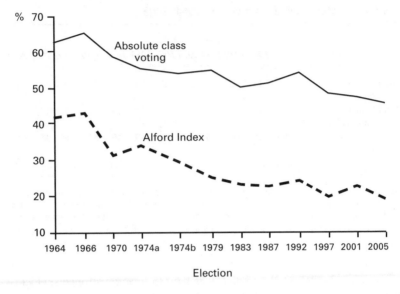

Figure 4.1   Class voting, 1964–2005

The debate over class dealignment

By the early 1980s the view that there was an ongoing class dealignment among voters was the orthodoxy among most electoral analysts. This position was taken by the leading academic specialists and was accepted by many political commentators and practising politicians. In 1985, however, Anthony Heath, Roger Jowell and John Curtice, who co-directed the British Election Study from 1983 to 1997, directly challenged the prevailing orthodoxy in their report on the 1983 election, *How Britain Votes* (Heath, Jowell and Curtice, 1985). Their conclusion, that there had been no class dealignment, was re-asserted in the BES study of the 1987 election (Heath *et al.,* 1991) and provoked furious debate.

The argument and analysis concerning class dealignment put forward by Heath, Jowell and Curtice can be summarized in three stages. First, they used a new way of allocating respondents to classes, rejecting the traditional manual/non-manual dichotomy as 'wholly inadequate for studying the social bases of politics' (1985, p. 13) and proposing a new scheme based on economic interests. Second, they argued that absolute class voting (the percentage of the electorate who support their 'natural' class party) is not a useful way of either thinking about or measuring the level of class voting.

What should be measured is the *relative* support for the parties in the different classes, and this is best done by looking at odds ratios. Third, when odds ratios measuring relative class voting from 1964 to 1983 in what they define as the 'salariat' and the 'working class' are examined, the figures suggest no progressive class dealignment but, rather, 'trendless fluctuation' in the extent of class voting. In their later work, *Understanding Political Change* (Heath *et al.,* 1991), the authors used a different analytical technique and slightly modified their previous position, conceding that there had been a sharp decline in class voting between 1964 and 1970. They maintained, however, that after 1970 there was no steady downward trend and again insisted that the pattern was one of 'trendless fluctuations' (at least up to 1987) in the level of class voting.

The argument that there had been no progressive class dealignment clearly represented a major challenge to the orthodox view about the changing relationship between class and party choice, and it was a challenge that did not go unanswered. *How Britain Votes,* in particular, was subjected to some very strong criticism (see especially Crewe, 1986; and Dunleavy, 1987) and a vigorous debate ensued. Each stage in Heath *et al.*'s argument was attacked with their use of odds ratios to measure class voting attracting particularly ferocious criticism, as already mentioned.

In any event, the controversy over class dealignment ended up as something of a damp squib. After 1987, it became clear that what was at issue between Heath *et al.* and their critics was largely a matter of definition, or 'semantics rather than substance' as Miller *et al.* put it (1990, p. 8). In addition, a re-analysis of the data from 1964 to 1997 by members of the BES team, using very advanced statistical techniques, ended up producing diagrams showing the trend in class voting as not very different from the trend in the simple Alford Index (Evans, Heath and Payne, 1999). Effectively, the class dealignment controversy was over and it was agreed all round that there had been a decline in class voting

Perhaps the final nail in the coffin of class voting was hammered in by Clarke *et al.* (2004, ch. 3) in the report of the BES study of the 2001 election. Referring to a variety of measures, they confirm the sharp decline in the influence of class since the 1960s and conclude firmly (p. 43) that 'over time, British voters have become less "tribal" – less class-driven – in their electoral choices'. Clarke *et al.* go further, however. They suggest, first, that even in the past the influence of class on party choice may have been exaggerated. Close inspection of the BES surveys reveals that around 50 per cent of respondents regularly failed to assign themselves to a class spontaneously and would only do so when prompted. This implies that the 'class tribes' may have been smaller than supposed and leads Clarke *et al.* to question whether an explanatory framework based on class identities can ever have been more than partially correct. Second, Clarke *et al.* find that no other social characteristic has replaced class as a basis for party choice. Taken together, social factors had less and less of an impact on party choice so that by 2001 explanations of voting based on what I have called 'social determinism' were of limited value. Preliminary analysis of the 2005 BES surveys (Clarke *et al.*, 2006) gave no reason to revise this conclusion.

Partisan dealignment

In Chapter 3, Table 3.7, we saw that in the 1960s most electors aligned themselves with parties in the sense of identifying with them. Table 4.3 compares the 1960s data with the relevant figures from the three most recent elections.

   The first row of the table shows the percentage of people volunteering a party identification and there has been a clear decline in the last two elections. Nonetheless, the great majority of voters still do identify with a party. The trend in all elections since 1964 is shown in Figure 4.2 and it is noticeable that a very slow downward drift was sharply reversed in 1992 – when the percentage of identifiers was greater than ever recorded by the BES – but was then resumed in 1997. This is probably explained by the fact that in the 1992 survey (and later ones) the positioning of the relevant questions in the BES questionnaires was altered and this had the effect of making it easier for respondents to report having a party identity. On another somewhat technical, but nonetheless important, point, it has been argued by Bartle (2001) that the standard survey question eliciting party identification causes the percentage of identifiers to be overestimated since it does not clearly indicate to respondents that it is an acceptable answer to say that they have no identification. Bartle himself (p. 13) experimented with a redesigned question put to voters in the monthly Gallup poll and found that, over a period of

Table 4.3   Party identification, 1997–2005 (%)

	Mean 1964–6	1997	2001	2005
Identify with a party	90	93	89	81
Very strong identifiers	42	16	13	10
Identify with Conservative or Labour	81	76	73	63
Very strongly Conservative or Labour	40	15	11	9

Source: Data from BES surveys.

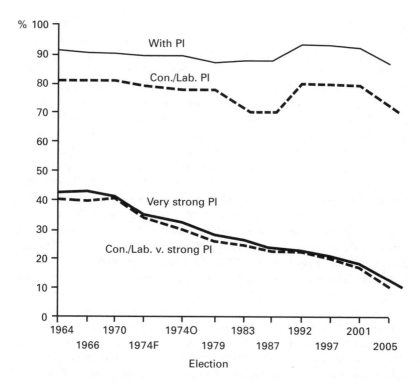

Note: 'PI' means party identification.

Figure 4.2   Party identification, 1964–2005

12 months in 1999–2000, the average proportion of respondents nominating a party identification was 68 per cent (significantly smaller than the proportions reported by the BES over the years).

In comparison with the trend in identification, the decline in the proportion of the electorate whose commitment to their party is 'very strong' is striking. Despite variations in the placement of the party identification question in the BES questionnaires, this has not fluctuated but has been on a relentless downward trend since the 1960s. The proportion of very strong identifiers in 2005 was less than a quarter of what it was at the start of the series.

The third and fourth rows of Table 4.3 refer specifically to identification with the Conservative and Labour parties. Although there are some fluctuations (Figure 4.2), there is a clearer decline in identification with the two main parties than in identification overall. This is not really surprising since, as compared with the 1960s, the Liberal Democrats and the nationalist parties have many more supporters. Again, however, the decline in the percentage describing themselves as 'very strong' Conservative or Labour supporters is clear. Having comprised 40 per cent of the electorate before 1970, 'very strong' Conservative or Labour identifiers totalled only 9 per cent in 2005. They are, indeed, now something of an endangered species. Figure 4.2 confirms that this is part of a long-term trend. It is worth emphasizing that this decline is not just a product of defections from the major parties: even among those who have remained loyal there has been a decrease in commitment. Among both Conservative and Labour party identifiers in 1964 and 1966 almost half (49 per cent in both cases) were 'very strong'. By 2005, among the much smaller band of identifiers with these parties, the 'very strong' proportions were 13 per cent for the Conservatives and 14 per cent for Labour. In the same period the proportion of Liberal/Liberal Democrat identifiers feeling 'very strongly' attached to their party fell from 31 per cent in 1964 to just 3 per cent in 2005.

On this evidence, then – and, unlike the question of class dealignment, there has been no significant disagreement over the evidence or its meaning – most people do still tend to align themselves psychologically with political parties, but they do so much less strongly than before (for a more detailed, discussion of trends in party identification see Crewe and Thomson, 1999). When it is remembered that stronger partisanship is associated with more stable voting and with an increased propensity to vote, the wide-ranging implications of this weakening of partisan alignment are clear. In addition, the predominance of the two major parties in this respect has been substantially reduced. This means that whereas the Conservatives and Labour both used to be able to rely on solid and consistent support from about 40 per cent of the voters, their core support is now very much smaller.

The causes of dealignment

It is fairly obvious that class dealignment and partisan dealignment are closely related. As Crewe (1984, p. 193) put it some time ago, 'it is easier to vote against one's class once party loyalties weaken, easier to abandon one's party once class loyalties wither'. Although the two can be distinguished conceptually, and some explanations are focused more clearly on one or other of them, there is such an overlap in practice that it seems sensible to outline the suggested causes of dealignment in general. It would be naive, of course, to expect that a phenomenon as complex as dealignment would have one simple cause; instead, it is a product of a series of interlocking developments. It is useful, however, to distinguish what might be described as 'bottom up' explanations and 'top down' explanations.

'Bottom up' explanations

By 'bottom up' I mean explanations which suggest that dealignment was produced by changes occurring, for a variety of reasons, among the voters themselves. Six explanations of this kind can be distinguished.

Changes in the occupational and industrial structures   Over the last 40 years the occupational and industrial structures of Britain have changed almost beyond recognition. Three features especially deserve to be noted in the context of dealignment. First, there has been a shift from manual to non-manual work. Census statistics show that in 1961 manual workers comprised 58 per cent of the work-force; by 1981 this had fallen to 45 per cent (the first time since records began that manual workers had become a minority of the work-force); by 1991 the figure was 42 per cent and a further decline has no doubt occurred since then. Although a reclassification of occupations for the 2001 census makes it difficult to give a figure, only just over 30 per cent of respondents to the 2005 BES survey had manual occupations. To some extent the growth in non-manual employment has been associated with inter-generational upward social mobility. Many people from working-class backgrounds now have professional and other non-manual occupations, and this has diluted the previously solid Conservative allegiance of the middle class. Second, there has been a shift from employment in manufacturing to the service sector. In 1961, roughly 38 per cent of employees worked in manufacturing and 47 per cent in services. By 2001 manufacturing was down to about 15 per cent and services (depending on the definition) to about 64 per cent. Indeed, more people worked in education, health and social work (18.6 per cent) than in manufacturing. Put simply, there are fewer factory workers around today and more social workers, hairdressers and 'consultants' of various kinds. Third, even within manufacturing there has been an especially sharp contraction in heavy industries such as coal-mining, steel and ship-building. These were traditionally male-dominated, highly-unionized industries with large plants, which tended to create distinctive and homogeneous working-class communities. In contrast, the emerging 'sunrise' industries are less heavily unionised and rarely located at the centre of established working-class communities. Taken together, it seems likely that these sorts of change have undermined the general level of class consciousness and class solidarity which underpinned the class–party relationship.

Cross-class locations Partly as a consequence of these developments, and partly as a result of the increased proportion of women in the work-force, more and more people are in 'cross-class' locations: that is, they individually have characteristics that traditionally would be ascribed to different classes. Thus, buying one's house used to be thought a middle-class attribute and, according to BES figures, in 1964 only 35 per cent of manual workers were owner-occupiers. By 2005, however, the figure (for the sharply reduced number of manual workers) was 57 per cent. On the other hand, trade-union membership (traditionally a characteristic of manual workers) has increased among white-collar employees. In 2005, BES data suggest that a greater proportion of non-manual workers were union or staff association members (19 per cent) than were manual workers (17 per cent). It is certainly the case that the University and College Union has very many more members than the National Union of Mineworkers! In addition, the growth of female employment (especially in non-manual jobs) has contributed to an increase in mixed-class families. Even by the 1970s over one-third of the growing number of households in which both husband and wife had jobs were 'mixed-class' in the sense that one partner had a non-manual job while the other was a manual worker. When the effects of inter-generational mobility are added to this, the result is that more than half of all extended families – grandparents, parents and children – are mixed in their class composition. Again, this reduces the potential for class solidarity in electoral behaviour.

Embourgeoisement In the early 1960s there was much agonizing in Labour circles over the fact that the party had lost three successive elections. Support seemed to be draining away and a popular explanation for this came to be known as the 'embourgeoisement thesis'. This suggested that the working class were becoming more affluent and hence more 'bourgeois' in their attitudes and behaviour, which extended to deserting their traditional Labour loyalties. The thesis was tested and largely rejected by Goldthorpe *et al.* (1968), but these authors detected a significant difference in the nature of the support given to Labour by affluent workers as compared with the traditional working class. Affluent workers voted Labour because they expected a Labour government to bring them direct benefits. Support was conditional and instrumental rather than 'solidaristic'. If Labour did not deliver the goods then their support would be withdrawn. The kinds of development that led people to speculate about the possibility of embourgeoisement at that time have continued apace ever since. Despite the persistence of pockets of poverty and the growth of a poor 'underclass' during the 1980s, manual workers on the whole have become even more affluent. More and more own their own homes and cars, go on foreign holidays, and so on; some have become shareholders. At least on the surface, differences between, say, skilled manual workers and lower non-manual groups – or even traditionally solid middle-class groups such as school teachers – are not all that obvious. If, as Goldthorpe *et al.* argued, support for the Labour Party among more affluent workers is more conditional and less 'solidaristic' than it was among traditional workers, and we ally this to the voters' dim view of the performance of the parties in office (see below), then it seems likely that the spread of affluence among the working class has created at least the potential for reduced working-class Labour voting.

Sectoral cleavages According to Patrick Dunleavy (1980), party choice after 1970 was still basically a product of social location. What happened, however, was that the old cleavage based on occupational class was replaced by two new cleavages. The first relates to sector of employment – whether the public or the private sector – and its importance is a consequence of the sharp growth in public-sector employment in Britain (at least up to the 1980s). In 1961, some 24 per cent of all employees worked for the state; by 1982 the figure was 31 per cent (Dunleavy and Husbands, 1985, p. 21). The second cleavage relates to sector of consumption. People who live in council houses, rely on public transport and depend on the National Health Service (NHS) for medical treatment need these services to be collectively provided. They are consumers in the public sector. In contrast, people who own their own homes, use cars rather than buses or trains and have their own medical insurance arrangements are consumers in the private sector. The groups created by these production and consumption cleavages are in different social locations and they have conflicting interests which are translated, according to Dunleavy, into differential voting behaviour. Those in the private sector favour the Conservatives; those in the public sector do not. Dunleavy's theory is not without its critics (see, especially, Franklin, 1985, ch. 2), and supporting evidence is stronger on the consumption than on the production side. Nonetheless, the sectoral cleavage approach helps to account for the growth in non-Conservative support among white-collar employees in the public sector (such as teachers and social workers), and it provides a solid theoretical basis for the differences in party choice found among different housing groups.

Fragmented working-class interests Ivor Crewe does not subscribe entirely to the sectoral cleavage thesis, but has put forward a somewhat similar argument at various times (see, for example, Crewe, 1984). He suggests that part of the explanation for class dealignment is the increased fragmentation of class (especially working-class) interests. Manual workers who are owner-occupiers or who work in the private sector have different interests from those who are council tenants or are public-sector workers. As the tax net has widened, even moderately well-off workers have different interests (lower taxes) from those who are poorer (higher taxes, increased welfare benefits). Workers living in the affluent and (in population terms) expanding South East are likely to want economic and industrial policies that are different from those favoured by people living in the North and Scotland. Workers who belong to powerful trade unions benefit from free, collective pay bargaining; those in weak unions or in none do not. Crewe uses these sorts of difference to distinguish a 'traditional' working class (manual workers who live in Scotland and the North, are council tenants, union members and public-sector employees) and a 'new' working class (manual workers who live in the South, are owner-occupiers, not union members and private-sector employees). The 'new' working class is increasingly dominant within the working class as a whole and its support for Labour is relatively weak.

Increased political awareness: education　　As noted in Chapter 1, one of the functions that identifying with a party served for the individual was that it simplified the complex political world. Identification supplied 'cues' to the voter about how to evaluate policies, personalities and the actions of governments. Thus a very strong Conservative would believe, almost without thinking, that Conservative policies on taxation or health or defence or anything else were 'good', and that Conservative leaders were 'best'; by definition the Labour Party and all its works were 'bad'. Strong Labour identifiers, of course, would take the opposite view. If, however, voters have become more politically aware simply because they are now better educated than they used to be, then they will have less need of such a psychological device to simplify the world. And it is certainly the case, in aggregate, that over the past 30 years the amount (if not necessarily the quality) of education that the electorate receives has steadily increased. The school-leaving age has been raised to 16; more and more pupils stay on at school beyond the minimum age (and more take A-level Politics); and a much greater proportion of 18 year olds now enter higher education than ever before. It is possible that as the general educational level has risen, so has the level of political sophistication and, as a result, emotionally-based attachments to political parties have declined in intensity.

　　There is some supporting evidence at the individual level for this proposition. In their seminal article on partisan dealignment, Crewe, Sarlvik and Alt (1977) found that the decline in strength of partisanship up to 1974 was most marked among those who had gone on to higher education and least marked among those who left school at the minimum age (pp. 166–7). This difference persists. Coming up to date, the 2005 BES data show that only 7.5 per cent of respondents with a university degree were 'very strong' party identifiers, compared with 14 per cent of those with no educational qualifications. By implication, then, as the electorate has slowly become more highly educated its dependence on the 'psychological crutch' afforded by party identification has decreased.

'Top down' explanations

By 'top down' explanations I mean explanations which focus on events (in particular, political events) at national level, and see these as the main causes of dealignment. Three explanations of this kind can be identified.

The performance of the parties   A fairly direct source of weakening party identification is the apparent lack of success that both major parties have had in office. Put minimally, neither has been a dazzling success. Governing a modern industrial society is a difficult and complex task and, no doubt, voters are overoptimistic about what governments can achieve and too quick to blame governments when things go wrong. Nevertheless, the series of disappointments, policy failures and U-turns that have marked government performances since the 1960s, together with the persistence of major problems facing the country, must surely have shaken any conviction voters might have had that 'their' party had all the answers. This was even true of the Blair government between 1997 and 2001. Although Labour was reelected in fine style, turnout was disastrously low and commentators were unanimous that the voters were far from enthusiastic about the government. Between 2001 and 2005, of course, the government ran into blizzards of criticism, not least from its own supporters.

Some evidence in support of this interpretation is given in Table 4.4 which shows, first, the average net satisfaction ratings for governments since 1951. Up to the mid-1960s all governments – despite periods of unpopularity – received positive ratings overall. The Labour government of 1966–70 plumbed new depths of unpopularity but thereafter, with the exception of Labour's first term under Tony Blair from 1997 to 2001 which just scraped into positive figures, the electorate was clearly dissatisfied with all governments and from 1979 (again excepting 1997–2001) all were more unpopular (spectacularly so in the case of the Conservatives from 1992–7) than those that had gone before. Figure 4.3 plots these data and the general downward trend in satisfaction is clear.

Table 4.4 Average net satisfaction ratings for governments and Prime Ministers

		Satisfaction with:	
Governments		*Prime Ministers*	
1951–5	9.9	Churchill 1951–5	12.6 (7)
1955–9	8.0	Eden 1955–7	28.1 (12)
1959–64	1.7	Macmillan 1957–63	18.7 (61)
1964–6	7.7	Douglas Home 1963–4	7.8 (9)
1966–70	−23.2	Wilson 1964–70	1.4 (64)
1970–4	−14.9	Heath 1970–4	−13.2 (41)
1974–9	−17.6	Wilson 1974–6	1.8 (23)
1979–83	−28.1	Callaghan 1976–9	7.5 (38)
1983–7	−26.6	Thatcher 1979–90	−14.6 (124)
1987–92	−27.5	Major 1990–7	−26.0 (74)
1992–7	−62.9	Blair 1997–2005	4.7 (89)
1997–2001	0.4		
2001–5	−25.4		

Notes: The figures to 1979 are based on Gallup data and thereafter on monthly polls by MORI. Gallup asked for approval/disapproval of the government record while the relevant MORI question concerns satisfaction with the way the government is running the country. The figures show the mean net score (positive minus negative responses) over the period in question. For Prime Ministers the number of separate observations is shown in brackets.
Sources: Data from King and Wybrow (2001); MORI website.

Satisfaction with the performance of Prime Ministers has also declined. People were significantly more satisfied overall than not with Winston Churchill, Anthony Eden and Harold Macmillan in the 1950s and early 1960s. Even Alec Douglas-Home in his short spell in office was positively rated and every Prime Minister since has done worse. There were, of course, times when the electorate was very happy with each of them and in this respect it is worth noting that over his first term (1997–2001) Tony Blair had strongly positive ratings (+22.0) but this fell to −14.7 for his second term (2001–5). Taking their periods in office as a whole, however, it has clearly become more difficult for Prime Ministers to keep the electorate content. If the data on Prime Ministers are plotted then it will be seen that the downward trend in satisfaction is even steeper than it is for governments.

The indications are, then, that the electorate has become more dissatisfied with the performances of governments and Prime Ministers. Much wider considerations than simply what parties have done when in office may underlie these trends. Some commentators have argued that, from the late

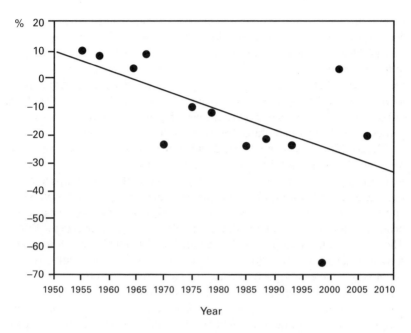

Figure 4.3   Net satisfaction with governments, 1951–2005

1960s, the electorate's expectations of government became unreasonably high; governments simply could not deliver what the voters expected and thus the latter were bound to be disappointed (see King, 1975). Others suggest that there has been a decline in deference among the electorate: people have become less trustful of, and willing to accept the authority of, government and political leaders (Beer, 1982). This relates to the argument about declining party identification, since identification itself implies a kind of deference to the authority of a political party.

Ideological disjuncture   Ivor Crewe (1985a, pp. 138–41) argues that a significant source of weakening identification with the Labour Party during the 1970s was the fact that a gap opened up between the opinions of Labour supporters and the policies and principles espoused by the party. Between 1964 and 1979, among the declining number of Labour identifiers, the percentages favouring each aspect of Labour's 'collectivist trinity' of public ownership, trade union power and increased spending on social welfare fell by more than 20 points. By 1979, according to Crewe, there was an 'ideological chasm' between the Labour Party and its supporters. Over an even longer period (1957–80), Martin Harrop (1982), using Gallup data, found a marked drop in the percentages of Labour voters who favoured restricting dividends and profits, cutting defence expenditure and abolishing the House of Lords. This problem became even more critical in the early 1980s as Labour lurched to the left, adopting a series of left-wing policies. This move was noticed by the electorate (half of the 1983 BES sample believed that Labour had moved to the left since 1979) and was unpopular. Almost half (47 per cent) of 1979 Labour supporters who thought that the party had moved left defected to other parties in 1983 (see Heath, Jowell and Curtice, 1985, pp. 146–50).

Clearly, if there is an increasing disjuncture between the basic tenets of a party and the opinions of its supporters (let alone its potential supporters) we would expect commitment to the party on the part of its supporters to become more and more strained. Labour, of course, recognized this problem and in the late 1980s embarked on a series of policy reviews designed to bring the party more in line with the attitudes of voters (see Shaw, 1994). The process culminated in the election of Tony Blair as Labour leader and the subsequent transformation of Labour into 'New Labour', with a whole set of new policies designed to make the party more attractive to the electorate. While this certainly worked wonders for Labour's popularity among voters in general, the new approach may have been less than rapturously received by at least some committed members and supporters, who had been attracted by the old ideology in the first place.

A similar argument can be applied to the Conservatives. Under Margaret Thatcher, the Conservatives clearly moved to the right during the 1980s. This undoubtedly pleased Conservative activists and the party was very successful in electoral terms, but the evidence suggests that the broader electorate was far from persuaded of the virtues of Thatcherism. Crewe (1988) shows that there was widespread opposition to a raft of Thatcherite principles and policies. By 1997, the policy of privatising public utilities – a key Thatcherite innovation which had been popular initially – was an albatross around the Major government's neck. The elections of 1997, 2001 and 2005 seemed to show that it was the Conservatives who were now out of touch with the electorate. The debate over what to do about this, and how to reconnect with the electorate, is still continuing in 2006 following the election of David Cameron as party leader.

The impact of television   Partisan and class dealignment have been closely paralleled by changes in the extent, nature and style of television coverage of politics. It was not until the 1960s that ownership of television sets became well-nigh universal in Britain, and in its relatively short history the reporting of politics on television has vastly increased in quantity and become qualitatively different.

Before the advent of television, radio coverage of elections had always been minimal. During the 1950 campaign, as Nicholas (1951, p. 126) notes, 'the BBC kept as aloof from the election as if it had been occurring on another planet'. After the election was called, 'virtually all mention of election politics disappeared from the British air', until the sober reading out of constituency results on election night. This tradition was initially carried over to television. During the 1955 campaign, for example, television news broadcasts made no references whatsoever to the election. The broadcasting authorities feared that if they covered the election they would be in breach of the laws regulating the conduct of elections. It was only in the 1960s that campaign reports of the kind we are now familiar with began to develop. Even outside campaign periods, television coverage of politics was initially limited and circumspect in the extreme. In the first half of the 1950s there was even a rule preventing discussion on television of matters that were about to be, or had recently been, debated in the House of Commons. When leading politicians deigned to be interviewed, they determined the questions to be asked and were treated in a highly deferential manner by interviewers.

The contrast with today could hardly be greater. Intense and detailed coverage of politics is available for those who want to watch it. Live coverage of debates in the House of Commons is now permitted and MPs rush from the House to comment on debates still in progress for the benefit of the television audience. During the 2001 and 2005 campaigns there was round-the-clock coverage on dedicated news channels. Set-piece interviews with the party leaders are practically an institutionalized part of election campaigns. Politicians of all parties are questioned aggressively and, indeed, if a party leader appears to have been given an 'easy ride' by an interviewer, complaints are loud and long. All of this may have increased the political knowledge and sophistication of the voters and thus indirectly weakened party commitment.

In more subtle ways the style of political television also helps to diminish the strength of partisanship. News reporting tends to assume that the viewer has a dispassionate interest in hearing all sides of the story (and is, in any event, required to provide balanced coverage). Moreover, in political discussion programmes, such as the popular *Question Time,* viewers seem to be encouraged to be like the chairman, aloof from party bickering. Partisans are projected as unreasonable ideologues and the viewer encouraged to recognize that party representatives on the panel are putting forward a one-sided point of view. In addition, in the 1950s very few voters would ever have seen party leaders in the flesh and they could, therefore, quite easily idealize them or else think of them as 'hate' figures. Now we see them every week on the box, and it is manifest that they are not gods or devils. Labour politicians are not, on the whole, dripping blood as they prepare to pillage the savings of the thrifty, and most Conservatives do not come over as grim-faced capitalists bent on grinding down the poor. Even entertainment shows serve to discourage voters from thinking that their party is something to be 'loved and trusted'. (Graham Wallas, 1910, described parties as 'something that can be loved and trusted and can be recognised at successive elections as the same thing that was loved and trusted before'.) Impressionists such as Rory Bremner poke fun at politicians, and programmes such as *Have I Got News For You* hold politicians of all parties up to ridicule.

It would be very difficult, if not impossible, to measure the effects of the messages transmitted to voters by the style of political television; by their nature they are diffuse and subtle. It would be surprising, however, if the clear decline in the strength of partisan commitment since the 1960s was unrelated to the ways in which politics and politicians have been projected by television.

*　　　*　　　*

As suggested above, none of these explanations by themselves account for class and partisan dealignment. There is, of course, no single explanation; instead, a variety of social changes at the 'bottom' has interacted with other (mainly political) developments at the 'top' to produce a weakening of the old alignment between class and party and to weaken voters' commitment to the major parties especially. As a consequence, the aligned electorate of the 1950s and 1960s has given way to a dealigned modern electorate that behaves in a very different way.

The consequences of dealignment: electoral volatility

A priori, one would expect the decline in the average strength of party identification among voters in Britain to have had important consequences. Strong party identification acted as a sort of psychological anchor in the sea of electoral politics. It provided an element of stability, and for very strong identifiers party choice at elections was almost automatic. When the anchor is removed, or becomes more weakly attached, voters are likely to be more open to persuasion, more indecisive about which party to vote for, and more likely to switch parties. The core of support upon which each party can rely is much diminished in size. The party system, rather than being set in stone, as it were, is more unstable; its foundations are less solid and secure. In short, partisan dealignment is likely to produce an electorate that is very different from that described by voting studies in the 1950s and 1960s.

Rather than basing their vote on tradition or a 'standing decision', they are likely to be influenced by short-term factors such as their perceptions of the competence of the parties or the quality of the party leaders. Rather than being stable and predictable so far as party choice is concerned, voters are likely to be volatile and unpredictable in their behaviour.

Defining and measuring electoral volatility is not straightforward, however. First of all, we have to distinguish between *net* and *overall* or *individual* volatility. The distinction is similar to that between swing and the 'flow of the vote' between elections (see Chapter 1). Net volatility usually refers to changes in the parties' shares of the votes at two successive elections (although it could also apply to the share of voting intentions received in successive opinion polls), while overall volatility refers to change on the part of individual voters and the total amount of changing that takes place in order to produce the net outcome. Thus, self-cancelling changes – some people switch from Conservative to Labour while others switch from Labour to the Conservatives – are part of overall volatility but would not affect net volatility if similar proportions went in each direction. Indeed, it is perfectly possible to imagine a situation in which there is no net volatility at all, while overall volatility is high.

Second, we can distinguish three different contexts giving rise to three types of volatility which can be labelled 'inter-election volatility', 'mid-term movements' and 'campaign swithering' (to use a descriptive Scots word, which means being indecisive or leaning one way and then another). Inter-election volatility relates to voter behaviour in successive elections. Those who switch parties are clearly behaving in a volatile way, but it is less clear whether those who move between voting and non-voting should also be classed as volatile. They may support the same party in both elections but simply have been prevented from voting for one reason or another. There are also opportunities to display volatility in the period between general elections. All electors can vote in European Parliament elections and local elections; the Scots, Welsh and Northern Irish in elections for devolved institutions; and a few in parliamentary by-elections. In addition, monthly opinion polls give estimates of how the electorate would vote if there were a general election 'tomorrow'. In these contexts we can register mid-term movements on the part of the electorate. Finally, during general election campaigns there are almost daily opinion polls and some panel surveys. These show that while some voters have their minds made up about which party to support when the campaign begins and never waver from that position, others are slow to decide, hesitant, or actually switch between parties. This sort of campaign 'swithering' represents another form of electoral volatility.

Inter-election volatility

I have already briefly discussed net inter-election volatility, as measured by the Pedersen Index, in Chapter 1 (see Table 1.2). Although there is no consistent upward trend – and indeed the 2001 election in these terms was exceptionally stable – it is significant that the three most volatile elections (February 1974, 1983 and 1997) all took place after the onset of dealignment. Nonetheless, the dealignment thesis does not necessarily imply that all elections will display high levels of net volatility. The net figure may conceal self-cancelling changes, or short-term factors may favour the same party in successive elections.

In order to measure overall or individual volatility in its different dimensions, survey data are required. It is well established, however, that when asked to recall their vote in an election held a few years previously, a significant proportion of survey respondents do not recall their vote accurately and tend to mis-remember in such a way as to make their past vote consistent with their current preference (see Himmelweit, Jaeger and Stockdale, 1978). This problem can be avoided by interviewing the same people at different points in time – this is called a panel survey – and asking how they voted (or intend to vote) at each point. Nonetheless, most of the major BES surveys have had to rely on recall of past vote in order to estimate the extent of inter-election volatility. Table 4.5 presents two measures of volatility for pairs of elections since 1959, as indicated by the BES surveys. The first column shows the percentages of those who voted in both elections who switched parties in successive elections. The figures are well below 20 per cent in the 1960s when party identification was strong. In the 1970s and early 1980s, however, as party identification weakened, the proportion of switchers was clearly larger (with the exception of the two elections in 1974 when there was only an eight-month gap between them). In 1987 and 1992 just under 20 per cent of voters switched, but in 1997 the figure rose to a quarter (the largest proportion recorded in the whole period) and it stayed at a relatively high level in both 2001 and 2005. The trend in the proportion of switchers is not perhaps as clear or as strong as might be expected on the basis of the party identification figures, but it is nonetheless certainly on an upward track. The mean figure for party switchers in the first three elections in the series is 14.7 per cent; in the last three the average is 23.7 per cent (almost a quarter of those who voted in each pair of elections).

The percentages in the second column are based on everyone eligible to vote at each pair of elections and, this time, 'switchers' include those moving from voting to non-voting and vice versa. Not unexpectedly, when non-voting is included in the calculation, volatility estimates are higher than

Table 4.5 Trends in inter-election volatility (%)

	Switched parties	Switched (incl. non-voters)
1959–64	18	35
1964–6	10	22
1966–70	16	34
1970–4 (Feb.)	24	42
1974 (Feb.)–1974 (Oct.)	16	28
1974 (Oct.)–1979	22	37
1979–83	23	40
1983–7	19	37
1987–92	19	34
1992–7	25	35
1997–2001	22	34
2001–5	24	37

Sources: Data from Heath, Jowell, Curtice with Taylor (1994, p. 281) and relevant BES surveys.

when only party switching is considered. Indeed, more detailed figures show that switching between the Conservative and Labour parties is always the least common form of inter-election volatility. Switching between major and minor parties is more frequent, while moving between voting and non-voting is usually the most common form of individual change between elections. When movement involving non-voting is included in the measure of volatility there is only a slight upward trend (although the story might be different if we could calculate both measures for elections in the 1950s). It is worth noting, however, that the wider definition of switching suggests that in all elections since 1979 more than a third of the electorate have changed their behaviour in one way or another as compared with the preceding one.

Mid-term movements

A cursory glance at the results of recent mid-term elections and of monthly opinion polls shows that they fluctuate wildly as compared with the preceding general election. The evidence from polls and parliamentary by-elections suggests that, in net terms, mid-term movements in party support became much more violent from the late 1960s onwards (see Crewe, 1985a, pp. 104–5; Norris, 1990), and this form of volatility remained at a high level through the 1990s and after. A striking example of a large mid-term movement occurred in the European Parliament elections of 1989 when the Green Party, having received just 0.3 per cent of the votes in the general election two years before, suddenly jumped up to 14.9 per cent, pushing the Liberal Democrats into fourth place. The Pedersen Index score for change between the two elections was 25.1. A similar feat was performed in the 2004 European elections by the UKIP which leapt from 1.5 per cent in the 2001 general election to 16.2 per cent (while the British National Party rose from 0.2 to 4.9 per cent) and the overall effect was a Pedersen Index score of 29.7. Another example is the Welsh Assembly election of 1999 when Plaid Cymru jumped from just under 10 per cent of the Welsh vote in the 1997 general election to more than 28 per cent. In this case, the relevant Pedersen Index score was 21.0. Further examples of such massive aggregate mid-term movements are easy to find.

For evidence of individual volatility in the mid-term we have to turn to panel surveys involving a mid-term wave. As part of a 1983–7 panel survey, Heath *et al.* (1991) also interviewed their sample in 1986. They found that whereas 71 per cent of these respondents voted the same way in both 1983 and 1987, only 61 per cent supported the same party on all three occasions (Heath *et al.*, 1991, p. 29). Similarly, using up to five interviews at different points between 1983 and 1987, and considering only support for the three major British parties, Miller *et al.* (1990, p. 33) estimated that only 55 per cent of voters maintained consistent support for one party during the early and mid-1980s. For strong party identifiers the figure was 71 per cent, for medium-strong identifiers 49 per cent, and for weak identifiers only 29 per cent. Although they had no comparable data for earlier periods, Miller *et al.* were in no doubt that by the 1980s the British electorate was characterized by high volatility in the periods between elections.

The best recent evidence that we have for mid-term volatility comes from a series of surveys known as the British Election Panel Survey (BEPS), which involved interviewing the same respondents every year from 1992 to 1997 and asking them how they would vote in a general election. Although the panel suffered from 'attrition' (respondents dropping out over the years) this series provides much fascinating data, and Table 4.6 is an example.

Table 4.6 Mid-term volatility (percentage of 1992 voters still supporting party in subsequent years)

	1993	*1994*	*1995*	*1996*	*1997*
Conservative	63	54	49	56	59
Labour	87	88	92	89	83
Liberal Democrat	73	63	49	49	50

Source: Data from British Election Panel Survey, 1992–7.

This shows the percentage of 1992 voters for each of the three main parties who indicated at each subsequent interview that they would still support the same party. This was a time when the Conservative government was very unpopular and this is reflected in the figures. By 1995, just under half of 1992 Conservatives were intending to vote Conservative again. But there was also massive defection from the Liberal Democrats: in 1995 only around half of those who voted Liberal Democrat in 1992 said that they would do so again. Labour, on the other hand, largely held on to its 1992 supporters. However, even these data underestimate the extent of party switching in mid-term as they do not tell us about respondents who nominated different parties in the different interviews. Considering those who were interviewed on all six occasions we find that only 27 per cent of 1992 Liberal Democrats (N = 188) indicated each time that they would vote Liberal Democrat. Only 33 per cent (N = 468) of Conservatives were consistently loyal, as were 66 per cent (N = 329) of 1992 Labour voters. Clearly, in the mid-1990s, party support was extremely fluid between general elections.

Campaign swithering

This form of volatility takes two main forms: switching parties, or moving between indecision and a firm voting intention ('churning', as the pollsters describe it). Evidence of net campaign volatility between 1964 and 1992, based on the results of campaign polls, suggests that this too increased sharply after 1970 and, with the exception of 1987, remained at a higher level thereafter (see Farrell, McAllister and Broughton, 1995). Campaign panel surveys enabling us to measure this form of individual volatility during campaigns are relatively recent and still rare (because they are expensive). However, the polling company, MORI, conducted panel surveys for *The Sunday Times* at each election between 1979 and 1992. It is difficult to summarize these data but it is worth noting that during the 1992 campaign the amount of movement found among the electorate was greater than ever before (see Fallon and Worcester, 1992). Nonetheless, one such study, which involved four separate interviews during the 1987 election, led Miller *et al.* (1990, p. 234) to conclude that 'a huge 38 per cent of the electorate changed their party preferences one or more times in the short period between March 1987 and the election in June'. Worcester and Mortimore (2001, p. 14) estimated that in 1997 around 28 per cent of the electorate was involved in some sort of 'churning' during the campaign, while their estimate for 2001 was 34 per cent (larger than MORI had ever found). BES research on the 2005 election involved interviewing a panel of voters just before the official campaign began and again immediately after the election. In the pre-campaign survey, fully 46 per cent of respondents ($N = 2,298$) said that they had not decided how to vote. Of those who had decided and named their party preference ($N = 1,369$), 75 per cent eventually voted for the party (18 per cent didn't vote and 7 per cent voted for another party). Of those who were undecided but indicated which party they were leaning towards ($N = 985$), only 48 per cent eventually voted for it while 38 per cent opted for another party and 24 per cent didn't vote. These figures indicate that there was a high level of campaign swithering even in an election in which opinion polls indicated relatively little change in net levels of party support over the campaign period and the result was thought by many to be a foregone conclusion.

Although campaign panel surveys are relatively recent, the main BES surveys provide a valuable series of data going back to 1964 which measures what Heath *et al.* (1991) call 'hesitancy' during campaigns: the percentage of voters who decided which party to support during the election campaign itself, and the percentage who thought of voting for a party other than the one that they ended up voting for. The figures are shown in Table 4.7. There were clearly more late deciders from 1974 onwards, and the proportion reached a peak in the 2005 election when a third of those who responded ($N = 2,157$) claimed that they made up their minds about which party to

Table 4.7   'Late deciders' and 'waverers', 1964–2005 (%)

	Decided during campaign	Thought of voting for other party
1964	12	25
1966	11	23
1970	12	21
1974 (Feb.)	23	25
1974 (Oct.)	22	21
1979	28	31
1983	22	25
1987	21	28
1992	24	26
1997	27	31
2001	26	–
2005	33	–

Note: The question asking whether respondents thought of voting for another party was not asked in the 2001 and 2005 surveys.
Source: Data from BES surveys.

support during the campaign itself. Similarly, Worcester, Mortimore and Baines (2005, p. 55) report that at the start of the 2005 campaign 41 per cent of MORI respondents indicated that they had not definitely decided and might change their minds about which party to support; by some distance, this was the largest figure that MORI had found in elections going back to 1987. The trend in the proportion of waverers is less clear, but the figures from 1979 onwards are generally larger than those for the previous five elections.

To sum up on volatility, we can say that while survey evidence of increased inter-election volatility is less than clear-cut, in the sense that there is no steady increase matching the clear decline in strength of party identification, the data do suggest that its extent is greater than it used to be in the age of alignment. In addition, if volatility is defined more widely, there is plenty of evidence – from both surveys and election results – that the electorate is much more unstable than it was when strong party identification was widespread. Certainly the potential for short-term electoral change is greater. Although analysis of the various dimensions of volatility is handicapped by the absence of suitable data from the 1950s, there is little reason to doubt that, as would be predicted by the dealignment thesis, when we take account of mid-term movements and campaign swithering the modern British electorate is unpredictable and volatile.

A paradox: electoral stability, 1979–92 and 1997–2005

The picture that I have drawn of the modern electorate – hesitant, volatile and unpredictable – is persuasive (I hope) and certainly widely accepted. At first sight, therefore, it seems odd that in one major respect this volatile electorate produced stable electoral outcomes in general elections from 1979 to 1992 and then again between 1997 and 2005. The Conservatives won all four elections in the first period, and their share of the vote in each varied only slightly (see Table 1.2) while Labour won all three elections from 1997. It is true that in the periods between their electoral successes the Conservatives experienced lengthy periods of unpopularity and suffered spectacular losses in parliamentary by-elections and local elections; but when a general election came round voters appeared to forget their mid-term misgivings and regularly returned the Conservatives to power. How can this be explained in terms consistent with dealignment?

In fact, it is a mistake to regard the 40-odd per cent of the vote that the Conservatives consistently garnered from 1979 to 1992 as constituting a solid bloc of core supporters. Data on party identification from the relevant

BES surveys show that the true Conservative core – those who identified very strongly with the party – never amounted to more than 9 per cent of the electorate in this period. The interpretation which is consistent with the picture of a dealigned electorate is that, at successive elections, the Conservatives were able to put together a temporary coalition of voters, which then dissolved in the inter-election periods. These coalitions were based on electors' short-term judgements about the competing parties. In particular, these judgements related to the relative competence of the parties in running the economy, the party leaders and the general images of the parties. These considerations will be discussed in more detail in the next chapter, but here it is worth noting that for most of this period the Conservatives were thought to be best at running the economy, Labour leaders were much less popular than Margaret Thatcher and John Major, and the Labour Party was hopelessly divided. Short-term factors all tended to push the electorate into the arms of the Conservatives. The electorate remained potentially volatile, but the potential was not translated into actuality largely because of the unattractiveness of Labour (for a fuller discussion of this period see Denver, 1998a).

The run of Labour successes can be explained in a similar way. After the 1997 election little changed. Labour never lost its lead in opinion polls and the 2001 election result showed very little change from 1997. The reason was that Labour continued to hold all the short-term cards: by a large margin Tony Blair was thought to be the best Prime Minister, the economy was in good shape and the government was thought to be economically competent while the Conservatives were seen as being out of touch with the modern electorate. Between 2001 and 2005 Labour (and Tony Blair) did become markedly less popular and there was a return to the familiar pattern of bad results for the government in by-elections and local elections. As the election approached, however, it was clear that on economic competence and assessments of party leaders Labour still had a significant lead over the rival parties and the Conservatives had failed to revitalize their appeal. These short-term advantages were enough to see Labour home even if the margin in terms of vote share was relatively narrow. It will be intriguing to see whether Labour can retain these advantages into a third term especially given the impending departure of Tony Blair as Prime Minister and the emergence of a new leader on the Conservative side.

1992–7: dealignment vindicated

Any doubts that might have remained about whether British voters were now thoroughly dealigned were swept away by events after the 1992 election. The Conservatives rapidly lost their reputation for economic competence and came to be seen as 'sleazy' and divided; Labour acquired a new popular leader and a new image. For these and other reasons Conservative support plummeted. The party experienced its worst-ever local election defeats, received its lowest vote share of the century in a national election (27.9 per cent in the European Parliament election in June 1994), and lost all eight of the seats it defended in parliamentary by-elections. In opinion polls, the Conservative share of voting intentions plunged further and faster than ever before.

The 1997 general election itself can be seen as a classic 'dealignment' election. As we have seen, class voting and identification with the major parties reached historically low levels. The swing from Conservative to Labour (10.2 per cent) was almost double the previous post-war record (5.3 per cent in 1979), and the vote share of 'other' candidates was close to twice what it had been in 1992. The volatility score on the Pedersen Index was 12.4 – the second highest since 1945 – and a quarter of voters switched parties as compared with 1992 (Table 4.5). The evidence suggests that these extraordinary results had little to do with voters' traditional loyalties but were a product of their judgements about party policies, the record of the government in office and the capabilities of the party leaders. Around ten years on, strange as it may seem, the 1997 election can be interpreted as giving encouragement to the Conservatives (and, possibly, the Liberal Democrats). The fact that a volatile electorate could produce such a turnaround means that it could always happen again. After 2005, the Conservatives still need a large swing to regain power, but with a dealigned electorate such a swing is always possible. Far from being fixed and rigid, the distribution of party support among voters is fluid and unpredictable.

5

Issues, the Economy and Party Leaders: The Emergence of 'Valence Politics'

If a political commentator or politician of the 1920s or 1930s were able to read the previous two chapters then he or she would be amazed at the relative lack of attention given to party policies or to topical events and political issues. Before survey studies of voting behaviour began, elections and voting were conceived of largely in terms of choices between competing sets of policy proposals. The voter was pictured as weighing up the policies of the different parties, or the qualities and positions of candidates, and on that basis deciding whom to support. The party which won an election was thought to have a 'mandate' from the electorate for all of its policy proposals as detailed in its election manifesto. In the nineteenth century, the political philosopher, John Stuart Mill (1963 edition, pp. 302–4), said this about the voter:

> His vote is not a thing in which he has an option . . . he is bound to give it according to his best and his most conscientious opinion of the public good . . . the voter is under an absolute moral obligation to consider the interest of the public, not his private advantage, and give his vote to the best of his judgement exactly as he would be bound to do if he were the sole voter and the election depended upon him alone.

This idealized view of the voter informed much comment upon elections until well into the twentieth century.

In the preceding two chapters, in contrast, I have considered voting behaviour as almost entirely a function of the voter's social location (class, religion, and so on), socialisation experience or psychological attachments (party identification), hardly mentioning party policies or 'the interest of the public'. It would, of course, be going too far to claim that before 1970 not a single voter decided how to vote after carefully evaluating the parties' policies and considering the public interest or that policy considerations played no part at all in the decision processes of most voters. Similarly, the qualities of party leaders no doubt influenced some voters. Indeed, the Michigan model explicitly contains 'issue orientation' and 'candidate orientation' as short-term factors affecting party choice. Most studies of British voters also found that voters did have generalized images of the parties that were not without policy content. Thus the Labour Party was widely perceived as the party which was 'for the working class' or in favour of nationalization and higher welfare spending. Nonetheless, when researchers in the 1950s and 1960s tried to be more precise about the effects of electors' political opinions and judgements on their voting choices, their results did not suggest that there was a very strong connection between the two. In the post-alignment period, however, as the impact of class and party identification declined, the importance of voters' assessments and judgments increased. In terms of the theories outlined in Chapter 1, as social determinism and the Michigan/Butler–Stokes model became less relevant, so voting as a form of rational choice came to be seen as a more useful way of explaining voters' decisions.

Conceptualizing issue voting

There is no consensus about what voting on the basis of issue or policy opinions should be called. The terms used include 'issue voting', 'policy voting', 'consumer voting' and 'instrumental voting'. Two variants on the basic idea are 'investment voting' and 'retrospective voting'. All of these are inspired, in part at least, by rational choice theory and involve the voter making a more or less calculated decision about which party to support (or, as we have seen, about whether to vote at all) on the basis of his or her policy preferences and assessments of the parties' positions or performance.

   In their discussion of issue voting Butler and Stokes (1974, p. 292) make an important distinction between what they call 'position' issues and 'valence' issues. The former are issues on which people take positions: for or against fox hunting, privatized railways, student tuition fees, tax increases to fund social welfare spending or whatever (although, of course, on many issues there are more than two possible positions). On the other hand, there are many issues on which there is broad agreement among the electorate about the goals that government should pursue. What is at issue is the competence or performance of the parties in seeking to achieve these goals. Not many people, for example, are in favour of increased crime and poor economic growth; not many are against improving standards of health care, or opposed to peace and prosperity. These are valence issues and the disagreement is about which party would be best at achieving what people want. In a much later piece, Stokes (1992) elaborated the idea of valence and argued convincingly that valence concerns have become increasingly important in elections.

As far as position issues are concerned, Butler and Stokes (1974, pp. 276–95) suggested that four conditions must be met if an issue is to affect voting and a voter is to qualify as an 'issue voter':

1   The voter must be aware of the issue concerned. Clearly if someone failed to notice that in 2004 the government introduced 'top-up' tuition fees for university students, then that policy could not affect his or her vote in a subsequent election.
2   The voter must have some attitude towards, or opinion about, the issue. I might be well aware that many people have strong views about whether or not the UK should have been involved in the Iraq war but be completely indifferent myself, or else unable to make up my mind on the question. In these cases the issue could not affect my vote.
3   The voter must perceive different parties as having different policies on the issue. Again, if this is not the case, there is no logical way in which the voter's opinion on the issue can be related to the choice of a party in an election. In the 1960s, for example, many voters had strong opinions on the question of immigration but believed (correctly, as it happened) that there was no real difference between the parties on the issue. As a result, the immigration issue did not, on the whole, influence party choice (see Butler and Stokes, 1974, pp. 303–8).
4   Finally, and obviously, the voter must vote for the party whose position on the issue is, or is perceived to be, closest to his or her own position. That is the 'rational' response.

The 'issue voting model' implied by these conditions is sometimes referred to as a 'spatial' model. This is because the voter – and the parties – can be seen as occupying a space on a continuum running from, say, 'strongly against' to 'strongly in favour' with respect to a particular position. It is a spatial conception of political issues that underlies the frequently heard references to 'the centre ground' of British politics. More recently (Clarke *et al.*, 2004) the model has been more helpfully labelled the 'issue proximity' model.

Methodological problems in analysing issue voting

It is generally agreed among voting researchers that the dealignment of the electorate has been accompanied by an increase in issue voting, in one form or another. Nonetheless, debates relating to this changed situation have raised two important methodological difficulties as well as problems of measurement.

The first methodological difficulty concerns the problem of causation. If we find that there is a positive relationship between voters' policy opinions and their choice of party, then at least two interpretations of this are possible. The first, deriving from the 'partisan alignment' model, suggests that voters base their party choice on factors such as their class location or family tradition. Insofar as they have policy opinions, these are formed by following the lead of the party: thus a voter who is a lifelong Labour supporter would tell a survey interviewer that he or she supports Labour policy on taxation, whatever that policy may be. The issue voting model suggests, on the other hand, that long-term influences on voters are relatively weak and that they make their decisions by comparing their policy preferences with the stances taken by the parties. The problem is that a strong correlation between issue positions and party choice is consistent with both interpretations. It tells us that there is a relationship between opinions and vote, but nothing about the processes by which the two come to be related. There is no simple way of resolving the problem of causal direction empirically. We can demonstrate the extent to which voters fulfil the conditions for issue voting, but ultimately it cannot be proved that issue preferences cause or determine party choice.

The second methodological problem is sometimes referred to as the problem of 'decision-rules' or 'trade-offs'. A voter might be pro-Conservative on some issues (say, Europe), pro-Labour on others (say, welfare spending), and pro-Liberal Democrat on yet others (reforming the electoral system, perhaps). The difficulty is that we do not know how the issue voter decides which issues are the ones that will determine his or her vote. How does a voter 'trade off' a preference for changing the electoral system against a preference for withdrawing from the European Union? The problem can be illustrated from the 1992 BES survey. The view that the government should introduce stricter laws to regulate trade unions, which was a Conservative policy, was supported by 35 per cent of respondents. But almost one-third (29 per cent) of these respondents also inclined to the view that taxes should be increased 'a lot' to pay for increased spending on health and social services, a Labour position, and 44 per cent of them favoured the introduction of proportional representation (a Liberal Democrat policy). Sixteen per cent of those who preferred the Conservative position on trade unions preferred Labour on taxation *and* the Liberal Democrats on electoral reform. Similarly, in 2005 the economy was a strong suit for Labour with 62 per cent of BES respondents thinking that the government had managed the economy very or fairly well. Of these, however, 26 per cent thought that the government had handled the National Health Service badly and 34 per cent that it had handled crime badly. Only 23 per cent consistently said that the government had done either well or badly on all three issues.

Clearly, many people's policy preferences or evaluations of government performance do not all point in the same direction. In practice, the commonest way out of this problem is simply to tot up the balance of voters' preferences over a number of issue areas. This is not entirely satisfactory, however, since it involves imposing a decision rule under which all issues are weighted equally, when in reality a voter's opinion on one issue may outweigh his or her preferences on all others.

Issue voting in the era of alignment

When aligned voting was the norm in Britain, relatively few voters fulfilled the conditions for issue voting. As in the Grand National, large numbers fell at every fence. First, on the question of awareness of issues, studies consistently found that large numbers of electors managed to get through life with only the haziest notion about the nature of the issues exercising the interest of MPs, political journalists and lobby correspondents, and little understanding of the language in which political debate was conducted. Butler and Stokes (1974, p. 277) commented that:

> the simplest evidence about the extent of popular attention to the affairs of government must challenge any image of the elector as an informed spectator. Understanding of policy issues falls away very sharply indeed as we move outwards from those at the heart of political decision-making to the public at large.

In 1964, around 40 per cent of respondents to the British Election Study survey were unable to name two important questions facing the country (quoted in Franklin, 1985, p. 128), while Butler and Stokes (1974, p. 334) reported that fully 80 per cent had minimal or no recognition of the meaning of the terms 'left' and 'right' in a political context. Politics and political issues were simply peripheral to most people's concerns.

Even when electors had some awareness of issues and were prepared to nominate the position that they held, Butler and Stokes suggest that many failed to fulfil the second issue-voting condition because they did not really have genuine attitudes towards the issues concerned. This argument is supported by evidence relating to opinions on the question of the extent to which major industries should be nationalized (publicly owned). This issue had been at the centre of political controversy in Britain for a long time and in the 1960s the parties took clearly different stances on the question. Yet, over four separate interviews, less than half (43 per cent) of BES respondents were consistent in either supporting or opposing further nationalization. According to Butler and Stokes (1974, p. 281) this indicated 'the limited degree to which attitudes are formed towards even the best-known of policy issues'.

Perception of differences between the parties on issues (the third condition for issue voting) varied considerably depending upon the nature of the issue. On 'big' or broad issues, such as welfare spending or nationalization, voters were mostly able to see a difference between the Conservatives and Labour, but on a whole series of more precise or detailed policy questions (and on immigration, as noted earlier) this was not the case. In addition, 1960s voters were notably unable to assign policy stances to the Liberals.

Finally, even voters who successfully passed the first three issue-voting tests frequently fell at the last fence. Despite having an opinion which they knew was contrary to a party's policy, some would nevertheless go ahead and vote for that party. This was particularly true of Labour supporters, a majority of whom were regularly found to oppose the party's central policy of nationalization. A survey of Bristol voters in 1955, for example, found that 39 per cent of Labour voters were pro-Conservative in their policy preferences with a further 27 per cent being neutral (Milne and MacKenzie, 1958, p. 119). The authors of the report on this survey also noted that 'the proportion of electors claiming that an issue had finally decided their vote is minute' (p. 160).

In sum, then, voting in the era of alignment can fairly be described as virtually 'issueless'. Voters were as likely to change their policy preferences to fit their party as they were to change their party to fit their policy position. There was, of course, *some* issue content in voting decisions and some electors were, no doubt, fully-fledged issue voters. But using the criteria suggested by Butler and Stokes, issue voting was the exception rather than the rule. To that extent, voting studies were justified in emphasizing the social and psychological bases of voting behaviour.

Issue voting after 1970

In a series of reports on general elections from October 1974 to 1992, Ivor Crewe used Gallup opinion poll data to provide a simple and distinctive account of issue voting (Crewe, 1981b, 1985b, 1992b, 1992c). This involved, first, the *salience* of different issues – the extent to which they are in people's minds at the time of the election – which is indicated by the percentage of voters mentioning an issue as one that they thought important when they were deciding how to vote. Second, there is the *party preferred* on the issue (the party thought to have the best policy). The third factor is the *credibility* of party proposals, or the extent to which voters believe that parties will or will not be able to achieve their policy goals. Crewe contended that the outcomes of these elections can largely be explained by a combination of changes in the salience of issues and changes in the electorate's judgements about the party having the best policies on the issues, together with voters' assessments of the credibility of party policies.

Initially at least, this approach seemed to work rather well. In 1979, for example, price inflation was easily the most salient issue (mentioned by 42 per cent) followed by unemployment (27 per cent), taxation (21 per cent), strikes and trade unions (20 per cent) and law and order (11 per cent). Labour was the preferred party on prices with a score of +13 (the percentage choosing the leading party on the issue minus the percentage choosing the second-placed party) as it was on unemployment (+15). The Conservatives were preferred on taxation (+61), trade unions (+15) and law and order (+27), and these big leads effectively wiped out Labour's advantage on prices and unemployment. In these circumstances, the Conservative victory in the election was no surprise.

In later elections, however, this mode of analysis ran into some difficulties. In 1987 Labour led very clearly on three of the four most salient issues and in 1992 they also had clear leads on the top three issues: the NHS, unemployment and education. In both cases, if electors had voted purely on the basis of their policy preferences then Labour would have won the election, but they lost both decisively. In attempting to resolve this paradox as far as 1987 is concerned, Crewe (1992b) shifted his ground somewhat, arguing that in 1987 voters were mainly concerned with their own private prosperity and the Conservatives were seen as the party most likely to create or maintain prosperity. Issue voting is still implicit in this argument but the issue concerned, prosperity, is a valence issue. Prosperity is not a 'problem' but a goal, and the voters opted for the party they judged most likely to attain it. Similarly, in 1992 Labour's leads on specific issue areas were outweighed by more general perceptions that Labour could not be trusted to run the economy effectively, which brings in the question of a party's credibility.

Gallup no longer do regular political polling but in recent elections MORI has consistently asked respondents to name the issues that were important in helping them to decide which way to vote and which party had the best policy on these issues. Results for 1997–2005, covering the most salient issues, are shown in Table 5.1. The first thing to notice is that so-called 'Labour issues' – those such as health and education on which the electorate consistently appears to prefer Labour policies – came at the top of the issue agenda in each of these elections. Some traditionally 'Conservative issues', such as defence, simply do not appear at all while on another – law and order – Conservative leads were relatively small. Under Blair, Labour successfully changed its image (to being 'tough on crime, tough on the causes of crime') and has reaped an electoral benefit, at least in 1997 and 2001. Second, it is interesting to note the changes in the issue agenda in this period. Unemployment (another 'Labour issue) was highly salient in 1997 but, although Labour maintained large leads on the issue, it slipped down the list of voters' concerns (at least partly because the government was relatively successful in dealing with it). On the other hand, asylum seekers and immigration were hardly mentioned in 1997 but these matters were clearly exercising voters by 2005. Third, although the detailed figures changed, on only two issues was there a big turnaround in opinion leading to a change in the party preferred overall: the economy and pensions. Both of these are not difficult to understand. Chancellor Gordon Brown was widely credited with managing the economy very effectively; on the other hand he presided over (and, some argue, contributed to) a crisis in the pensions industry. Finally, looking over the figures it is not really surprising that Labour won each of

Table 5.1 Issue salience and parties' policies preferred in 1997, 2001 and 2005

	1997		*2001*		*2005*	
	Salience	*Party preferred*	*Salience*	*Party preferred*	*Salience*	*Party preferred*
Health	1	Lab. +48	1	Lab. +35	1	Lab. +14
Education	2	Lab. +28	2	Lab. +34	2	Lab. +15
Unemployment	3	Lab. +39	7	Lab. +53	11	Lab. +31
Law and order	4	Con. +1	3	Con. +2	3	Con. +12
Economy	5	Con. +15	6	Lab. +34	7	Lab. +30
Pensions	6	Lab. +35	5	Lab. +30	4	Con. +2
Taxation	7	Lab. +2	4	Con. +3	5	Con. +6
Asylum/immigration	–	–	8	Con. +22	6	Con. +41

Notes: The *salience* columns show the order of salience as indicated by the proportion of respondents mentioning the issue. The party preference score is the percentage of those mentioning the issue who preferred the policies of the leading party on the issue minus the percentage preferring the other major party.
Sources: Data from Worcester and Mortimore (1999, 2001); Worcester, Mortimore and Baines (2005).

these elections. In each case Labour had substantial leads on the most important issues and these outweighed Conservative leads on issues that were less central to voters. This was less true in 2005 than in 1997 or 2001 and that may help to explain why that election was a much closer contest that the previous two.

This method of measuring and analysing issue voting has been severely criticised, however (Heath, Jowell and Curtice, 1985, pp. 89–90). The survey question used to find out which party a respondent prefers on an issue is some variant of 'Which party do you think has the best policies on . . . (the issue concerned)?' In the first place, there is no mention of what the policies concerned are and, in the second, the question is heavily loaded with partisan cues. If someone is going to vote for a particular party, or generally supports it, they are likely to say that it is best on most issue areas, without necessarily knowing what the party's policies are or even caring about the issue in question. It could be said that the fact that at a single election there are considerable variations in responses to the party preference question across the different issues casts some doubt on this argument. Nonetheless, the contention that these sorts of question tend to tap generalized support for the parties rather than support for the specific policies in question is difficult to deny.

Fortunately, more detailed and satisfactory tests of the issue voting hypothesis have been pursued using BES data. These have involved using questions which ask survey respondents to indicate their own policy preferences and what they believe to be the positions of the parties on a series of policy issues. In their report on the 1979 BES, for example, Sarlvik and Crewe (1983) analysed opinions on eight 'position' issues by asking respondents to choose between policy alternatives in each case. They found that most respondents (an average of 88 per cent) fulfilled the first two condition for issue voting: being aware of the issue and taking a position on it. An average of 78 per cent fulfilled the third step in the model: perceiving the parties as having different positions. Sarlvik and Crewe then examined the influence of policy preferences and perceptions by calculating correlation coefficients measuring the extent to which respondents voted for the party that they thought was closest to their own position on each issue. In every case the coefficients were positive and significant, averaging 0.36 and ranging from 0.19 on how to improve race relations to 0.48 on whether there should be more or less nationalization. In addition, Sarlvik and Crewe attempted to tackle the problem of 'decision rules' discussed earlier by grouping respondents according to their rating of each issue as 'extremely important', 'fairly important' or 'not very important'. In each case the correlations between issue position and party choice were consistently strongest among respondents who considered the issue extremely important (averaging 0.49) and weakest among those who considered it not very important (0.30).

Another part of Sarlvik and Crewe's analysis concerns four valence issues: strikes, unemployment, prices, and law and order. These are valence issues since few people would actually favour more strikes, heavier unemployment, higher prices or crime, and what issue voters do in these cases is assess the relative competence of the parties in handling these problems. In this case, almost all respondents in 1979 (average 96 per cent) were willing to offer assessments of the ability of the Conservative and Labour parties to handle the problems, and again opinions correlated strongly with party preference (average coefficient of 0.49, rising to 0.53 among respondents considering the issue extremely important).

Summing up on issue voting in 1979, Sarlvik and Crewe report that the votes of 69 per cent of their respondents could be correctly predicted on the basis of their issue opinions and assessments. If only those predicted to vote for the two major parties are considered (it is notoriously difficult to predict third-party voting), 86 per cent of respondents actually voted for the party that was predicted on the basis of their issue opinions. Comparing the effect of policy opinions and assessments with the effect of social characteristics on party choice, they say (p. 113) that 'the voters' opinions on policies and on the parties' performances in office "explain" more than twice as much as all the social and economic characteristics taken together'.

Numerous other studies have corroborated Crewe and Sarlvik's conclusion that issue voting became more evident from the late 1970s onwards. Franklin (1985), for example, used complicated statistical techniques to examine the relative extent to which class and issue positions contributed to explaining party choice between 1964 and 1979. He found that whereas in 1964 class exerted a stronger influence, by 1979 it was issue opinions that had the greater impact. In a later piece, Franklin and Hughes (1999) confirmed that in elections from 1987 to 1997 issue opinions remained significantly more important than class, even though 'class' was widely defined to include factors such as education level, parents' class and trade union membership, as well as occupation.

Issues or ideology?

If 'aligned voting' was the orthodoxy of electoral analysis in the 1950s and 1960s, then 'issue voting' quickly became the orthodoxy of the 1970s and 1980s. As more attention was paid to voters' opinions, however, the model of issue voting and the ways in which it had been studied came to be criticized.

Some critics argued that voters continued to know little about specific issues or policy areas but that they did have broader political values and preferences which they could link to parties. Ideology – a set of interlinked values relating to politics – rather than issue opinions was what was important in determining party choice.

In *How Britain Votes,* the main BES report on the 1983 election, Heath, Jowell and Curtice (1985) described issue voting as a 'vogue' and dismissed the argument that people vote on the basis of their policy opinions. They criticized the practice of previous researchers in using voters' judgements about the performance or competence of parties to measure issue voting, on the grounds that these judgements are inextricably bound up with a pre-existing party preference. Those who vote Labour usually think that Labour is best at dealing with unemployment but that is because they are Labour supporters in the first place. The judgement is a consequence of party preference, not a cause of it. Heath, Jowell and Curtice concentrate, therefore, on position issues. But because they see no logic in imposing a 'decision rule' about the weight attached to different issues, they do not attempt to construct any kind of index which would summarize a person's issue preferences and then see how this relates to his or her party choice. Instead, they show that if people had voted in the 1983 general election for the party which they saw as closest to them on the issue they considered most important, then the election would have resulted in a dead-heat between Labour and the Conservatives. Since Labour was in fact trounced, Heath, Jowell and Curtice argue, the policy voting model can be rejected. It should be said that Heath and his colleagues deliberately adopt a very narrow conception of issue voting (which they call 'consumer' voting), describing it as relating to 'the detailed stands which competing parties take on issues of the day' (p. 89), 'detailed appraisals of party manifestos and policies' (p. 99) and 'the small print of the manifesto' (p. 107). A better model, they suggest, is what might be called 'ideological voting'. Voters do not choose a party on the basis of policy preferences, but on the basis of their 'general values and their overall perceptions of what the parties stand for' (p. 107).

In the 1960s there was little evidence that voters could be described as 'ideological'. Electors did have views about what the main parties stood for, but these were expressed mainly in terms of class and rarely in terms of ideology. In the 1980s, however, Heath, Jowell and Curtice (1985) used survey respondents' answers to questions about issues and policies to demonstrate the existence and role of more general enduring values. In 1983, the issues which were most important in differentiating between Conservative and Labour supporters were nationalization, trade union legislation, income redistribution, defence spending, private education and job creation (p. 109). Not all of these were campaign issues in the election, say Heath and his colleagues, but they were bound up with the overall images of the parties and 'constitute[d] the main ideological divisions between the parties' (p. 109). The Labour Party, for example, was recognized as the party favouring nationalization, the trade unions, equality and so on, irrespective of the particular issues of the day. So, while they utilized responses to issue questions, and showed that opinions on these issues were clearly associated with party choice, Heath, Jowell and Curtice saw the questions as 'not so much tapping discrete issues as a general ideological dimension' (p. 111). Further support for this contention was presented in the BES study of the 1987 election which showed (Heath *et al.*, 1991, p. 174) that opinions on a variety of issues were inter-correlated in ways that would be expected if voters did indeed subscribe to general political values.

A somewhat similar account of the role of issues and opinions in influencing party choice was put forward by Rose and McAllister (1986) after the 1983 election. They too reject the view that issues – defined as 'topical issues of the moment, which are transitory by definition' (p. 117) – are an important influence on voting behaviour. They say (p. 147) that 'how a person votes is a poor guide to what a person thinks about most issues today' (and, presumably, *vice versa*). What is important, however, are the 'political principles' which voters hold: 'underlying judgements and preferences about the activities of government [which] are general enough to be durable . . . [and] . . . concern persisting problems of public policy' (p. 117). Rose and McAllister (1990) returned to this topic after the 1987 election. Although they now talked about political 'values' rather than 'principles', their position was unchanged. They concluded that 'durable political values are more than ten times as important in explaining voting as is the government's handling of issues' (p. 141).

Despite using different methods of analysis and data sources, and despite some differences in detail, Heath, Jowell and Curtice and Rose and McAllister are agreed on a central point: in the dealignment era the attitudes and opinions of voters became more strongly associated with their choice of party while the influence of family background decreased. Heath *et al.* (1991, p. 33) reported, for example, that: 'In 1983 and 1987 voters' attitudes towards the issues were more closely associated with the way they voted than had been the case in previous election studies. Attitudes have become better predictors of how people will vote.' This seems good evidence in favour of the view that electors' opinions increasingly came to influence their choice of party as the electorate became dealigned. Perhaps surprisingly, however, Heath *et al.* concluded that voters in the 1980s were not more influenced by issues than previously.

The argument underlying this apparently perverse conclusion is a little complicated but worth setting out in some detail. As mentioned above, finding a correlation between opinions and vote is not enough to show that the issue voting model applies. It could also be consistent with the model of aligned voting. Heath *et al.* (1991) suggest that the stronger correlations found for elections in the 1980s simply reflect the fact that political circumstances had changed, not the extent of issue voting. They argue that the strength of the correlation between opinions and vote is related to the extent to which voters see a difference between the parties. If the major parties move further apart (or are perceived by the electorate as doing so) such that their policies are more distinctive, then a stronger statistical relationship between issue positions and party choice would be expected under the aligned voting model because those who support their party's policies for the reasons suggested by this model now appear to be more polarized in terms of attitudes. Although there is a stronger correlation between opinions and vote, it is not necessarily the case that voters are more likely to weigh up the issues than they used to be. This, claim Heath *et al.,* is precisely what happened in 1983 and 1987, and they present data showing that their respondents saw a much greater difference between the two main parties in these elections than was the case before. As far as the declining influence of parents is concerned, Heath *et al.* suggest that this is simply due to increased inter-generational social mobility. More people now defect from their parents' party because more are in a different social class from that of their parents, and their voting reflects this.

These are logically sound arguments; but it is worth remembering that stronger correlations between opinions and party choice would *also* be expected if there were increased issue voting as described by proponents of that model. In addition, the point about inter-generational mobility does not fully explain why parental influence should be replaced by the influence of opinions rather than something else.

Heath *et al.* (1991) attempt to overcome the problem of the direction of causation between opinions and party choice by looking at trends in perceived party differences. These are certainly suggestive but do not entirely support their interpretation that it is changes in the perceptions of the parties which explain the increasingly strong relationship between attitudes and vote. It is also worth noting that others have tried to show empirically that it is opinions which determine vote and not vice versa. Franklin (1985) uses causal modelling techniques to take account of a variety of factors and concludes that the importance of issues from 1970 onwards was substantially greater than it was before. Denver and Hands (1990) show that even among people who receive no partisan cues from their parents or friends the relationship between opinions and vote remains strong, and argue that it is difficult to explain this other than in terms of an issue voting model.

Apart from the important methodological point concerning causation highlighted by Heath *et al.* (1991), the debate about whether it is opinions on issues or more general ideological values which influence party choice is, in the end, really much ado about not very much. In the first place, a great deal depends on simply how 'issues' are defined, and most proponents of the view that issue voting has increased are not claiming that voters weigh up every fleeting issue that happens to surface in an election campaign or pore over the small print of election manifestos (as some critics imply). Second, in practice, most of those who have sought to discover the broad principles or values that voters hold have done so on the basis of responses to questions on specific issues. They may not have been issues that were prominent in particular campaigns but they are nonetheless specific (nationalization or privatization being a case in point). Totting up issue positions and deriving more general values look like very similar activities. Third, whatever the phenomenon is called, the evidence for the most part suggests that voters' opinions on matters of public policy have come to play a larger part in determining their choice of party as opposed to a reliance on family tradition and class location. For these reasons, it does not seem to matter very much whether we talk about 'ideological' or 'issue' voting.

The economy and electoral cycles

During the 1992 US presidential election the communications director of Bill Clinton's campaign hung a sign over his desk which said, 'It's the economy, stupid!' This was to remind him that, no matter what happened, the state of the economy was the issue that would win the election for Clinton (and he was proved right). The view that the economy is *the* issue that matters above all others is one that many other politicians and commentators have long shared. Harold Wilson, Prime Minister in the 1960s and early 1970s, believed that 'all political history shows that the standing of a Government and its ability to hold the confidence of the electorate at a General Election depend on the success of its economic policy' (quoted in Norpoth, 1992, p. 2).

The state of the economy is a classic 'valence' issue. In broad terms everyone wants prosperity, and few would be opposed to more specific economic goals such as full employment, stable prices and increasing real incomes. What is at issue is how well different parties have performed, or might in future perform, in delivering these shared goals. In analysing the impact of the state of the economy on voting two distinct approaches have emerged, one focusing on individual economic perceptions and the other on economic and political cycles, although the subject matter of both is called 'economic voting' (see *Electoral Studies,* 2000).

Individual economic perceptions

The first approach focuses on the state of the economy at the time of elections. It is almost a psephological law that governments get re-elected in good times but get punished when they have presided over bad times. In the past, governments have tried to manage the economy such that 'booms' were timed to coincide with an election, and this usually worked. As Norpoth (1992, p. 1) puts it, 'In the dictionary of political economy, prosperity spells r-e-e-l-e-c-t-i-o-n for governing parties at the polls, whereas recession spells d-e-f-e-a-t.' Considerable doubt was cast on this simple formulation in the 1992 and 1997 general elections, however. In the run-up to the former the economy was in a severe recession but the Conservative government was re-elected comfortably; for some time before the latter most economic indicators were steadily improving, and yet the government was thrashed (see Newton, 1993; Gavin and Sanders, 1997).

More elaborate analysis concentrates not on the 'real' economy but on voters' opinions about the economy. Newton (1993) finds, for example, that the voters were well aware that the economy was not performing well in 1992 but they did not blame the government, as the former Prime Minister, Mrs Thatcher (whom they did blame), had been replaced by John Major some 16 months before the election. The phrase 'opinions about the economy' is rather vague, and in the course of research two important distinctions relating to these opinions have emerged. On the one hand, opinions about the economy may involve *retrospective* or *prospective* judgements, and on the other they may be *sociotropic* or *egocentric*. 'Retrospective' judgements refer to the recent economic performance of the government and the economic well-being of individuals and their families, while 'prospective' judgements concern how well the parties might run the economy in future, if elected, and how individuals view their economic prospects. 'Sociotropic' (society-centred) is the term applied to assessments of national economic conditions, while assessments of how the individual concerned has fared, or might fare in future, are labelled 'egocentric' (self-centred).

There is an abundance of evidence that economic perceptions at election time are strongly associated with party choice (see Norpoth, 1992) and much research has been undertaken to assess the importance of the different types of perception. In general, it has been found that economic voting is asymmetrical, in that it focuses on the performance of the governing party rather than the opposition and is more likely to involve punishing a bad performance rather than rewarding a good one. There is no agreement, however, as to whether retrospective judgements or prospective evaluations are more important. Similarly, researchers differ on the relative importance of sociotropic and egocentric evaluations. Although Butler and Stokes (1974, p. 370) noted that 'changes in personal economic conditions are overwhelmingly salient to the mass of electors and evoke in them strong and definite attitudes', they also cautioned that 'many will be responsive to the more generalized information about economic conditions that reaches them through the mass media'. Heath *et al.* (1991) concluded from their analysis of 'pocket-book voting' in the 1987 election, however, that in the economic sphere 'individual experiences do not seem to carry as much weight as collective ones' (p. 142). On the other hand, other studies have found that both sociotropic and egocentric considerations have a role to play (see Miller *et al.*, 1990, pp. 248–55).

The BES survey results from the 2005 election (Table 5.2) show the expected relationships between economic perceptions and party choice. In every case a majority of those with positive perceptions voted heavily for the incumbent government (Labour), while there were large anti-government majorities among those with negative perceptions. Interestingly, economic perceptions appear to have made little difference to the level of support for the Liberal Democrats. The problem of causation is again an issue here, of course. People who are basically Labour supporters are unlikely to think that the government has made a mess of the economy or is about to do so; those who are anti-Labour are unlikely to think that they have been, or are about to be, highly effective in running the economy. It is also difficult on the basis of the evidence in the table to decide which particular perceptions are most important. In fact, they are all strongly correlated with one another: those with positive personal expectations tend also to think that the economy in general will do well, and that they themselves and the economy as a whole have done well in the recent past. For what it is worth, however, in a regression analysis with voting Labour versus voting for another party as the dependent and the four types of perception as independent variables, the first variables to enter the equation (and, therefore, the best predictors of vote) are sociotropic prospective evaluations followed by sociotropic retrospective evaluations. The same was found for the 2001 election. It would seem, then, in line with Heath *et al.*'s (1991) analysis of 1987 data, that in both 2001 and 2005 how voters viewed the general economic situation, and prospects for the country as a whole, were more important influences on their vote decision than concerns relating to their individual economic circumstances. It should be mentioned, however, that this is a very crude and simple analysis and too much weight should not be put on the results given the inter-correlations between the variables mentioned above.

The first step in a more satisfactory test of the impact of economic perceptions would be to incorporate other variables – social characteristics, opinions on other issues, perceptions of leaders, and so on – into the analysis. When this is done for the 2001 election (using logit models) the result is that sociotropic (but not egocentric) economic perceptions remain a significant influence on party choice but they are much less influential than opinions about leaders or party identification (Clarke *et al.*, 2004, ch. 4). A

Table 5.2 Economic perceptions and party choice in 2005 (%)

	Retrospective			
	Egocentric		Sociotropic	
	Positive	*Negative*	*Positive*	*Negative*
Conservative	19	47	13	49
Labour	50	23	60	20
Liberal Democrats	22	23	21	22
Others	8	7	5	9
(*N*)	(636)	(926)	(509)	(1,236)
	Prospective			
	Egocentric		Sociotropic	
	Positive	*Negative*	*Positive*	*Negative*
Conservative	18	50	15	51
Labour	54	19	62	17
Liberal Democrats	21	22	17	23
Others	7	9	6	10
(*N*)	(614)	(854)	(655)	(1,173)

Notes: The figures are based on answers to questions asking how the financial situation of the respondent's household (egocentric) and the general economic situation of the country (sociotropic) has changed over the past year (retrospective) and will change over the next (prospective). Those who believe that things have got/will get better have positive perceptions; those thinking that they have got/will get worse have negative perceptions. Respondents thinking that things have stayed/will stay the same are not included in the table.
Source: BES 2005 post-election cross-section survey.

broadly similar story emerges from a preliminary and less detailed analysis of voting in 2005. In 'composite' models including a number of variables, economic evaluations, combined and more broadly defined, are a significant predictor of Labour and Conservative voting (although again less powerful than other factors). On the other hand, they appear to have no impact on voting for the Liberal Democrats (Clarke *et al.*, 2006). We can conclude that while individual economic perceptions – especially relating to the economy as a whole – have some influence on party choice, this is far from the whole story. Positive perceptions certainly help the incumbent government but, since other factors intervene, are not a guaranteed ticket to electoral success.

Electoral cycles and the economy

A second and rather different way of studying economic voting focuses not on elections but on the period between elections. Using monthly opinion poll reports on voting intentions, trends in the popularity of the various parties can be charted, and early research quickly established that there was a regular cycle in government popularity between each pair of general elections. Just after an election, the winning party usually enjoys a 'honeymoon' with the voters and its support increases for a short while. Quite soon, however, the government begins to become more and more unpopular – it suffers from 'mid-term blues' – but, as the next election approaches, there is an upswing in support. This cycle is reflected in by-election results as well as in opinion polls (see Norris, 1990) and a typical example, for the years 1987 to 1992, is illustrated in Figure 5.1. The basic 'U' shape of the graph is clear enough, although another feature of cycles is also illustrated: they are subject to 'random shocks'. Government popularity suddenly shot up in late 1990; this was caused by John Major replacing Margaret Thatcher as Prime Minister. It is also clear, however, that the effect of this soon faded and the basic underlying pattern was reasserted. That is what normally happens when there is a random shock.

Recent cycles have not conformed to the familiar pattern, however. Between 1992 and 1997 support for the Conservative government fell as expected (although more rapidly and further than usual), but there was hardly any upswing as the election approached. With Labour in power between 1997 and 2001 the government remained very popular throughout most of the period. There was something of a decline and surge of support but the surge came very late in the day, in the last few months before the election. The cycle of support between 2001 and 2005 was again unusual (see Figure 5.2). There was a definite 'honeymoon' and then a steady decline

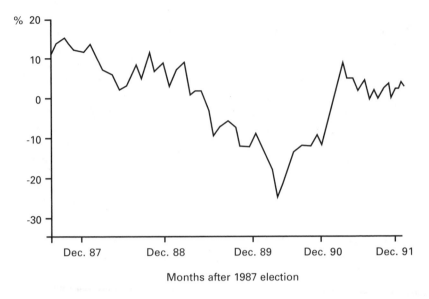

Note: Voting intention figures used are the monthly means for each party in the major regular polls.

Figure 5.1   The electoral cycle, 1987–92 (Conservative lead over Labour in monthly voting intentions)

in the government's popularity but no significant increase in support as the election approached; indeed, in the last few months of the Parliament the trend was again downwards.

In the context of economic voting, the first question to be asked about electoral cycles is whether and how they are related to the actual performance of the economy. The first statistically advanced attempt to tackle this question in relation to Britain was made by two econometricians (Goodhart and Bhansali, 1970). Analysing polls and economic data covering the period 1947–68, they found that a good prediction of the level of government popularity could be obtained using just two economic indicators: the level of unemployment and the rate of inflation. This came to be known as 'the misery index' but, as time passed, it became less useful. Indeed, if Goodhart and Bhansali's original equation is worked out using 1983 figures for inflation and unemployment, then it suggests that the Conservatives should have received *minus* 156 per cent of the vote in the 1983 election! (See Crewe, 1988, p. 28.) Other writers have taken up the topic, however, and produced increasingly complex models of the relationship between government popu-

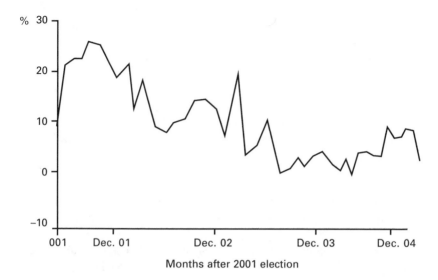

Note: Voting intention figures used are the monthly means for each party in the major regular polls.

Figure 5.2 The electoral cycle, 2001–5 (Labour lead over Conservatives in monthly voting intentions)

larity and the health of the economy, using a variety of economic indicators (see Denver and Hands, 1992, Part III). In one case, however, the authors argue that the relationship between government popularity and economic performance is largely spurious: that is, they claim that there is simply a cycle of government popularity no matter how the economy is performing, and that even if a government did not try to boost the economy as an election approached, there would still be a upswing of support in its favour (Miller and Mackie, 1973).

In recent years the best-known writer on the economy and electoral cycles in Britain has been David Sanders (see, for example, Sanders, Ward and Marsh, 1987; Sanders, 1993, 1995, 2005; Sanders *et al.*, 2001). The innovation originally made by Sanders was that he did not use objective economic indicators as the basis of his model, but opinion poll results about personal economic expectations (commonly known as 'the feel-good factor'). His model is, then, based on *egocentric, prospective* evaluations, although more sophisticated versions also take account of objective economic and other variables, as well as random 'shocks'. It should be stressed that in Sanders' analyses individual respondents' expectations are not matched to their individual voting intention. Rather, the net aggregate level of expectations in each month (the percentage of respondents who think that the financial situation of their household will get worse subtracted from the percentage who think that it will get better) is related to monthly aggregate voting intentions. Using aggregate figures reduces the possibility that the analysis is affected by individual respondents' economic perceptions being influenced by their attitude to the government of the day.

The statistics used by Sanders can become very complicated but the basic idea of the model is easy to grasp. A simple schematic representation is as follows:

State of   → Personal economic   → Level of government
economy   expectations   popularity

As a shorthand measure of the state of the economy Sanders initially used interest rates, which were set by the government and have a direct effect on how much people have to pay for their mortgages. The interest rate influences how optimistic or pessimistic voters feel about their economic prospects and this is turn affects their reactions to the government. On the basis of variations in interest rates and economic expectations Sanders (1993) was able to explain over 90 per cent of the variation in government popularity between 1987 and 1990. Further, he found that variations in expectations themselves could in turn be explained by changes in the levels of inflation and interest rates and (temporarily) by the introduction of the poll tax in 1990. Eighteen months before the 1992 election, when the Conservative government was very unpopular, Sanders (1991) suggested that if interest rates and inflation were steadily reduced, personal expectations would become more optimistic and government popularity would recover enough for the Conservatives to win the election. Moreover, he forecast what the Conservative share of the vote would be, given different levels of interest rates and inflation, and these forecasts turned out to be extremely accurate.

As with economic assessments at election time, there is no consensus on Sanders' argument that personal prospective economic judgements are the key ones. Clarke and Stewart (1995) tested all four possible economic models, defined by the egocentric–sociotropic and the retrospective–prospective categorizations, for the period from 1979 to 1992. They found, as has already been seen, that the four different economic assessment variables were strongly correlated with one another and that over this period there was little to choose between the four models in terms of how well they predicted government popularity. Clarke and Stewart argue, however, that in the immediate run-up to the 1992 election, and in predicting the election result, the national economic expectations variable performed better than personal expectations, which in turn was more successful than the two retrospective variables.

Recent electoral cycles have presented something of a challenge to Sanders' argument. As already indicated, the cycle of popularity between pairs of elections since 1992 were each rather unusual. The relevant graphs do not have a definite and clear 'U' shape. The rapid and very steep fall in support for the Conservative government after 1992 was almost entirely due to the collapse of a central element of the government's economic policy: UK membership of the European Exchange Rate Mechanism (ERM). In the autumn of 1992 Britain was forced to withdraw from the ERM in humiliating circumstances (see Denver, 1998b). For the rest of the Parliament the government, dogged also by accusations of 'sleaze', lagged badly behind Labour in voting intentions. In the last year before the election the economy was actually performing well and there was an improvement in personal economic expectations, but this produced only a very modest increase in government support (see Gavin and Sanders, 1997). Although the personal expectations model did not explain the pattern of government popularity very well, therefore, economic considerations were nonetheless important to the voters. Following the ERM disaster the Conservatives simply lost their long-standing reputation for being competent managers of the economy and they never recovered it.

During the 1997–2001 electoral cycle the (Labour) government never once lost its lead over the Conservatives in the monthly averages. In his analysis of this cycle, Sanders finds that the performance of the 'objective' economy – unemployment, interest rates, inflation and so on – had little effect on the trend in government popularity. On the other hand, personal economic expectations again played a significant role once other factors are taken into account. As with the Conservatives in 1997, there was a rising trend in expectations in the last months before the 2001 election. On this occasion, however, the 'feel-good factor' worked: it did have an impact upon party support and made a significant contribution to Labour's victory. Nonetheless, Sanders again shows that simple estimations of the relative competence of the major parties in running the economy tracked patterns of party support very closely (Sanders *et al.*, 2001).

Between 2001 and 2005 the simple relationship between the 'feel-good' factor and government popularity was weak (the relevant bivariate correlation coefficient is not statistically significant). Clearly the trend in government popularity was being driven by other factors and Sanders (2005) recognizes this by bringing more political factors – such as the popularity of the party leaders and the Iraq war – into his explanation of the pattern that occurred. Expectations are significant once other factors are taken into account but not nearly as important as they once were. On the other hand, ratings of the parties' ability to manage the economy were very closely related to trends in popularity; so closely, indeed, that one begins to wonder whether voting intentions and these perceptions are actually two sides of the same coin and not really distinguishable.

In a previous discussion of this topic (Denver, 1994, p. 105) I suggested that the ultimate failure of Goodhart and Bhansali's 'misery index' is a reminder that there is no 'last word' in this area: there is no guarantee that models which can explain past electoral cycles will continue to do so. With each new inter-election period models must be re-tested and it may be that personal economic expectations will at some point go the way of the 'misery index'. It is possible that we have now reached this point. The 'feel-good factor' failed to save the Conservatives in 1997 and did not make much difference to Labour in 2005. In both cases, 'politics' rather than 'economics' can better explain the inter-election trends in government popularity.

Our understanding of how 'the economy' affects voters and hence the outcomes of elections has changed over the years. Initially what seemed to matter was the performance of the 'objective' economy. The rate of unemployment was once thought to be the touchstone of economic performance, then it was inflation, then the balance of payments, then personal disposable income and then interest rates. Since 1997, the government has ceded control over interest rates to the Bank of England, however, and recent work has focused on tax levels. It would be foolish to say that the objective economy no longer matters. If there were to be a slump, for example, then the electoral effects would soon manifest themselves. In periods of relative and stable prosperity, however, economic considerations seem to fade in voters' minds. Governments get punished for bad times to a greater extent than they are rewarded for good times. In addition, it seems likely that the relative importance to the voters of different aspects of the economy will change depending on economic circumstances.

Later work has directed attention to the 'subjective' economy: how voters perceive their own and the country's economic situation and how they evaluate the economic competence of the parties. Others have focused on how people perceive the economic situation in their locality (Johnston and Pattie, 2001). The influence of these perceptions and judgements may also be somewhat dampened in 'good times' when other political issues and questions are more to the fore. Nonetheless, although few electoral analysts would want to argue that the economy is still *the* issue that determines the outcome of elections, few would dissent from the view that, in one form or another, economic considerations significantly influence party choice. Governments which ignored Harold Wilson's interpretation of 'political history', quoted above, would soon find themselves in trouble with the voters.

The impact of the party leaders

Just as we would anticipate that class and partisan dealignment would lead to an increase in issue voting, so also we would anticipate that the qualities and characteristics of party leaders would come to play a greater role in voters' calculations. In the period of alignment, the expectation would be that the personalities of leaders would have had relatively little electoral effect. The original Michigan model did allow for 'candidate orientation' as a short-term influence on party choice but that model was, of course, developed with presidential rather than parliamentary elections in mind. In Britain, the long-term forces of social class and family socialization would be presumed to have overridden the purely temporary consideration of who happened to be the leader of each party. Indeed, we would expect voters' assessments of the party leaders to have been themselves products of basic party loyalty. On the whole, each party's supporters would have approved of its own leader and disapproved of the others. With the erosion of the importance of long-term factors, however, we might expect an increase in the electoral impact of party leaders. The competence, personality and image of individual leaders might be regarded as akin to issues which could swing votes in the short term.

There are, as might be expected, problems in assessing the precise impact of party leaders. It is difficult to disentangle electors' views about the leader of a party or prime minister from views about the party or the government as a whole. Judgements of individual politicians will almost certainly be coloured by the political stance of the voter. It seems safe to assume, however, that in the days before extensive television coverage of politics the influence of party leaders on voting was minimal. For the great mass of voters, their only knowledge of political leaders was through photographs, newspaper reports of speeches and the occasional radio broadcast. It is instructive to note that the first survey study of voting in Britain (Benney, Gray and Pear, 1956) mentions each party leader only once (and then only to report the number of radio broadcasts they made during the election campaign).

By the 1960s, however, political television was well established and the faces, voices and personalities of party leaders became very familiar to voters. Butler and Stokes (1974, ch. 17) found that the Prime Minister and the Leader of the Opposition were highly visible figures about whom most voters had opinions. To assess the electoral impact of leaders, Butler and Stokes compared voters' attitudes to the parties and to the party leaders. They were then able to analyse the voting behaviour of those who were, on balance, favourable to one party but more favourable to the other party's leader. Only relatively small proportions of Butler and Stokes' sample fell into this category: 14 per cent in 1964, and 12 per cent in both 1966 and 1970. (The majority of respondents, 55 per cent, 64 per cent and 60 per cent respectively, had favourable attitudes to both a party and its leader; the remainder were neutral towards either parties or leaders.)

Among those who favoured one party but another party's leader, it was attitudes to parties that were decisive. Those who were pro-Conservative in terms of attitude to the parties, but pro-Labour in their assessment of leaders, voted Conservative by three to one; those who were pro-Labour in party terms, but pro-Conservative in terms of leaders, voted Labour by two to one. The conclusion reached by Butler and Stokes is judicious. They say that if there is a marked imbalance in the public's estimation of party leaders, if one is clearly preferred or more disliked than another, then that will have some impact on voting choice. If there is no great imbalance then the impact of leaders is likely to be small. In 1964 and 1966, the Labour leader Harold Wilson was clearly preferred to Sir Alec Douglas-Home and then to Edward Heath, his opposite numbers in the Conservative Party. This was an advantage to Labour but even in these cases Butler and Stokes counsel caution. They say that 'the pull of the leaders remains but one among the factors that determine transient shifts of party strength; it is easily outweighed by other issues and events of concern to the public' (p. 368). As if to prove the point, in 1970 Wilson was still clearly preferred to Heath but the Conservatives won the general election.

Table 5.3 presents some evidence about the relative popularity of the party leaders in elections from 1979. In 1979, when the leaders were James Callaghan (Labour), Margaret Thatcher (Conservative) and David Steel (Liberal), the electorate preferred Callaghan as Prime Minister but the Conservatives won the election. Crewe (1981b, pp. 274–5) explains this apparent paradox in a clear statement of the standard argument about the role of party leaders in British elections:

> The purpose of general elections is not primarily to choose a party leader to become prime minister but to choose a party to form a government. More importantly, the British electorate tends to vote according to what a party represents rather than who represents the party . . . British voters, if forced to choose between leader and party, tend to abandon the leader.

Table 5.3   Best person for Prime Minister, 1979–2005 (%)

1979		1983		1987		1992	
Callaghan	44	Thatcher	46	Thatcher	46	Major	47
Thatcher	33	Steel	35	Kinnock	22	Ashdown	22
Steel	24	Foot	13	Owen	12	Kinnock	21
		Jenkins	6	Steel	11		

1997		2001		2005	
Blair	38	Blair	52	Blair	37
Major	28	Hague	20	Howard	25
Ashdown	15	Kennedy	15	Kennedy	19

Note: The percentages do not total 100 as figures for 'don't know' are not shown.
Sources: Data from Gallup, *Political Index, Political and Economic Index*, Nos 226, 274, 322, 380, 441 and 489; YouGov final pre-election poll 2005.

Although Mr Callaghan was popular in 1979, Mrs Thatcher was not very unpopular. When not forced to choose between the two, voters gave Mrs Thatcher good ratings. It seems clear, however, that in this election the impact of the leaders was small.

In all other cases the party of the person thought likely to be the best Prime Minister won the election in question. In 1983 Michael Foot was Labour leader and he was a significant electoral handicap, coming a poor third in the prime ministerial stakes. Only 13 per cent of voters thought that he would make the best Prime Minister (and 63 per cent thought he would be the worst). Crewe comments (1985b, p. 181): 'Not since the war had a major party leader been regarded as so implausible a prime minister as Michael Foot.' Although Mrs Thatcher was much more popular, she was not an unqualified bonus for the Conservatives. Fewer than half of the voters believed that she would make the best Prime Minister, and her lead over David Steel in this respect was not large. In 1987, however, the Conservative leader maintained a handsome lead over the Labour leader (Neil Kinnock). Although Kinnock was more popular than Michael Foot had been, he was not highly rated as a potential Prime Minister by the electorate, and the same was true in 1992 when John Major was still enjoying something of a honeymoon with the voters.

By 1997 the situation had changed dramatically. On becoming Labour leader in 1994, Tony Blair immediately became the electorate's choice for

Prime Minister by a wide margin and he maintained his lead over John Major into the election. More detailed Gallup data show that larger proportions of the electorate believed that Blair was caring (82 per cent) and effective (64 per cent) than was the case for Major (62 per cent and 37 per cent respectively). Between 1997 and 2001 Blair's popularity was undiminished and (now facing the hapless William Hague, who was unable to hit it off with the voters) he had a huge margin as the best leader to be Prime Minister in 2001. By 2005, however, a lot of the shine had come off Tony Blair. Nonetheless, he was still clearly the electorate's choice as the leader who would make the best Prime Minister. Michael Howard, the Conservative leader, improved on William Hague's ratings but was still firmly in second place while Charles Kennedy – despite being well-liked as a person – again trailed in terms of potential as Prime Minister.

All of this is fascinating but it does not constitute very direct evidence about the extent to which evaluations of the leaders influenced party choice. Nonetheless, opinion poll data do provide support for the view that perceptions of leaders have become stronger influences on party preference. First, an analysis of the changing impact of party leaders (relative to party policies and performance) in elections from 1964 to 1992, using Gallup data, concluded that evaluations of leaders began to increase in importance during the mid-1970s and their effects became significantly more pronounced in 1987 and 1992 (Mughan, 1993). Second, in recent years the electorate's views as to which party leader would make the best Prime Minister have tracked voting intentions very closely (Sanders, 2005).

Even more impressive evidence of the increased importance of party leaders comes from recent BES surveys. In both 2001 and 2005 respondents were asked to indicate how much they liked or disliked each party leader on an 11-point scale. We can reduce these to three categories in each case ('like', 'dislike' and 'neutral') and then examine the votes of respondents with different combinations of feelings towards the different leaders. Even with just three categories that makes for 27 combinations of likes and dislikes for the three party leaders. In 2001 the most common pattern was liking Blair, disliking Hague and being neutral about Kennedy (14 per cent) followed by being neutral about all three (10 per cent). In 2005 feeling neutral about all three leaders was the most common pattern (12 per cent), followed by disliking Blair and being neutral about the other two (8 per cent).

Table 5.4 relates party choice in 2005 to feelings about the leaders. To simplify things, figures are given for those who liked each leader while also disliking or being neutral towards both of the others and then for those who disliked each leader while liking or being neutral about the other two.

Table 5.4   Feelings about party leaders and party choice, 2005 (row percentages)

	Conservative	Labour	Liberal Democrat	(N)
Like Blair/neutral or dislike others	4	86	7	(480)
Like Howard/neutral or dislike others	93	2	2	(334)
Like Kennedy/neutral or dislike others	15	18	59	(502)
Dislike Blair/neutral or like others	69	2	19	(622)
Dislike Howard/neutral or like others	2	65	26	(602)
Dislike Kennedy/neutral or like others	73	16	4	(51)

Note: Rows do not total 100 because votes for others are not shown.
Source: Data from BES 2005 cross-section survey.

The associations between feelings towards the party leaders and vote are very strong indeed. Those liking Tony Blair and Michael Howard while disliking or being indifferent to the other leaders overwhelmingly voted Labour (86 per cent) or Conservative (93 per cent) respectively. Charles Kennedy was more widely liked and some of those who liked him, while not being keen on the other two leaders, nonetheless voted for the other parties. Even so, among these respondents a clear majority (59 per cent) voted for the Liberal Democrats. The apparent impact of the party leaders is even stronger in the second part of the table. Hardly anyone voted for a party when they disliked its leader and felt even slightly more positive towards the other parties' leaders. The same sort of patterns occurred in 2001. This seems strong evidence that the party leaders now exert a considerable 'pull' (or, when they are disliked, 'push') on voters. Moreover, the conclusion is re-affirmed when relevant BES data are subject to more advanced and detailed analysis which takes numerous other variables into account (Evans and Andersen, 2005).

Not all electoral analysts agree that the personal appeal of the party leaders has become more important in swaying votes and there has been a limited rearguard action in defence of the traditional view (see Crewe and King, 1994; Bartle, 2002; Bartle and Crewe, 2002). The defence offered has not been very convincing, however, and the weight of evidence now clearly supports the argument that evaluations of leaders have come to play an important role in electors' calculations. Moreover, this is not difficult to understand given the extent to which the media reports and portrays politics in highly personalized terms. In addition, it strains credibility to suggest that the huge leads in personal popularity that Tony Blair enjoyed over his main opponents had little or nothing to do with Labour's triumphs in 1997 and 2001 or that the decline in his popularity was unconnected to his party's less impressive showing in 2005.

Even so, there remain caveats to be entered in conclusion to this discussion of leadership effects. First, in recent elections one leader (Blair) has had a clear lead over the other leaders in the electorate's estimation of who would make the best or most capable prime minister. One would guess that in circumstances in which the leaders were more evenly matched (perhaps Gordon Brown and David Cameron in the 2009/10 general election) the effect of leader evaluations on the election outcome would be less obvious. Second, the limits to the impact of leader evaluations are clearly demonstrated by the fact that, while the relative popularity of Liberal and Liberal Democrat leaders – at least in terms of being likeable – may have been a bonus for their party, it has never been nearly enough to make the party a serious contender for power. Third, the ever-present problem of causal direction remains. It is possible (if in this case rather implausible) that voters' feelings towards party leaders are consequences of their party choice rather than causes. Labour supporters would be expected to like Blair and dislike Howard in 2005, for example.

Conclusion: valence politics

The decline of the alignment between social–structural characteristics and party choice, together with the decrease in strong party identification, has not left a vacuum in which voters make almost random choices among competing parties. As we have seen, voting is now structured by opinions: about issues, perhaps especially economic issues, about values and principles and about party leaders. In trying to make sense of these changes the 2001 BES team developed an explanation of party choice based on what they called 'valence politics' Clarke *et al.*, 2004).

As noted above, Butler and Stokes (1974) introduced a distinction between valence issues and position issues and Sarlvik and Crewe (1983) paid significant attention to valence issues in their analysis of voting in the 1970s. In his later discussion of the subject, Stokes (1992) emphasizes the difference between position (or spatial) and valence issues, reminding us that the latter are those 'on which parties or leaders are differentiated not by what they advocate but by the degree to which they are linked in the public's mind with conditions or goals or symbols of which almost everyone approves or disapproves' (p. 143). The term 'valence' itself is borrowed from chemistry and refers to the link or bond (positive or negative) between the voters and the leader or party. Stokes suggests that election campaigning is dominated by valence concerns. Parties seek to avoid taking clear positions and instead try to associate themselves with generally approved goals (economic prosperity, being tough on crime) while associating their opponents with characteristics, performance or conditions of which there is wide disapproval (weak leadership, cutting public services, allowing large-scale immigration).

In their accounts of voting behaviour in contemporary Britain, the current BES team have used these ideas to develop, in *Political Choice in Britain*, a fully-fledged model of valence politics (Clarke *et al.*, 2004, 2006). The model has three main components. The first is people's judgements of the overall competence of the rival political parties. Making such judgements is difficult, however, and so voters use a convenient short-cut: their evaluations of party leaders. Evaluating leaders is a much simpler task since we can all react to people without necessarily knowing much about what parties have been doing or might do in future. The second is the priorities of the voters: which valence issues are they most concerned about? If they are mainly concerned with those on which one party has a strong reputation (Labour and the NHS, for example) then they will incline towards that party. Finally, Clarke *et al.* pay particular attention to economic competence: how voters rate the ability of the parties to bring economic prosperity. On the basis of some really forbidding statistical analysis Clarke *et al.* argue that focusing on these aspects of valence not only provides the best explanation of how electors decide to vote at the beginning of the twenty-first century but, contrary to what most analysts have thought, has always (at least since 1964) done so. They conclude that: 'The model always has been as, or more, compelling statistically as either models in the sociological framework or the issue proximity model' (p. 63). The view that valence is what matters is broadly confirmed in the team's preliminary report on the 2005 election, although the model is slightly expanded and the effect is clearer in determining votes for or against the government than support for the Conservatives and Liberal Democrats (Clarke *et al.*, 2006).

All of this is very powerfully argued. It should be said, however, that Clarke *et al.* are on firmer ground when dealing with more recent elections as opposed to those more distant in time. For earlier elections appropriate data are not always available. A more serious problem for the model, on the face of it, concerns party identification. Notwithstanding the clear decline in the strength of partisanship in Britain, in the analyses offered by Clarke *et al.* party identification stubbornly remains a statistically important influence on party choice. In their 'composite model' explaining voting in 2001, for example, which incorporates variables from a number of individual models,

Clarke *et al.* find that party identification remains highly significant (pp. 109–10) and the same is true in their preliminary account of the 2005 election. As traditionally conceived, party identification has little to do with judgements or evaluations but reflects a sort of 'tribal' loyalty to a party (an enduring attachment produced by the individual's socialisation experiences, particularly in the family). In order to encapsulate party identification within their valence framework, Clarke *et al.* reconceptualize the notion. Following Fiorina (1981), they suggest that identification is 'a storehouse of accumulated party and party leader performance evaluations' (p. 211). 'Valenced partisanship' is continually updated as voters acquire new information, react to events and make judgements about the competence of parties, governments and leaders. So it is less of an inherited tribal loyalty and more of a general inclination towards (or against) a party based on how the different parties and leaders seem to be doing. As such, it is another convenient shortcut in evaluating the performance of governments and parties. Although Clarke *et al.* provide statistical back-up, this treatment of party identification remains essentially a matter of interpretation. The alternative, traditional interpretation remains consistent with election results. Commentators regularly refer to Conservative and Labour 'heartlands' – areas where these parties have been consistently strong over many years – and it is difficult to explain the impressive continuities in levels of party support in different parts of the country in terms of continuously updated partisanship. It may be a little too early, therefore, to write the obituary of traditional party identification theory.

Nonetheless, *Political Choice in Britain* is undoubtedly a landmark in British electoral studies. Just like Butler and Stokes's *Political Change in Britain* (and the similarity of the titles is no accident), it will provide a starting point for much future research. For some time people professionally involved in politics and, in particular, in election campaigning have tended to think in valence terms; for the foreseeable future, academics will also use the valence framework in explaining individual party choice and election outcomes.

6

Campaigning and the Mass Media

For as long as there have been contested elections there has been election campaigning: that is, those standing for election and their supporters have endeavoured, by a variety of means, to persuade the relevant electorate to vote for them. Until well into the nineteenth century the main means of persuasion were 'treating' (providing electors with alcohol and other forms of largesse) and bribery. The earliest reference to treating was in 1467, while the first authenticated case of outright electoral bribery occurred in the reign of Elizabeth I (O'Leary, 1962, pp. 6–7). Campaigning remained overwhelmingly a local-level activity until the start of the twentieth century when the introduction of the first of the mass media – cheap, mass circulation, national newspapers – along with steady increases in the sizes of constituency electorates led to the development of national campaigning. Local campaigning continued, of course and, as we shall see, has recently been taken much more seriously by the parties. For much of the latter half of the twentieth century, however, the parties' efforts and the attention of the media were mainly focused on the national campaign.

National campaigning

In Britain, the period of the election campaign is legally defined. It must cover at least three weeks before polling day, but usually lasts four weeks. It is only during the legally defined campaign period that the various rules regulating candidates' spending, broadcasting and other campaign activities apply. During this period there is a massive increase in political activity. Media coverage reaches saturation point with the progress of the campaign being charted day by day. Over the past 50 years, however, the nature of the national campaign – what the campaigners do – has changed very dramatically (see Kavanagh, 1995; Scammell, 1995; Rosenbaum, 1997; Bartle and Griffiths, 2001).

During the 1950 general election campaign the then Prime Minister, Clement Attlee, undertook a 1,000-mile tour around Britain. He travelled in his pre-war family saloon car and was accompanied by his wife (who did the driving) and a single detective. If they were ahead of schedule they stopped by the roadside and Mrs Attlee would catch up with her knitting while the Prime Minister did a crossword puzzle and smoked his pipe (see Nicholas, 1951, pp. 93–4). The idea of a Prime Minister or major party leader travelling around in this way would be inconceivable today. During modern election campaigns party leaders are whisked hither and thither by jet, helicopter, battle-bus or car with an entourage of personal staff, security personnel, newspaper reporters, television crews and assorted other hangers-on. This partly reflects the fact that campaigns are now focused more on the party leaders. Campaign managers have to ensure that the leaders project a good image. Their itineraries are planned in detail, the meetings they address carefully controlled, they are coached on how to perform well on television, advised on how to dress, how to have their hair cut, what to say in public speeches and television interviews and so on. Mrs Thatcher even deliberately lowered the pitch of her voice in order to create a more favourable impression upon the voters (Atkinson, 1984, p. 113).

Modern national campaigns have five main characteristics. First, as has just been seen and as noted in the previous chapter, they are highly focused on the party leaders. The media follow the leaders everywhere, lengthy set-piece television interviews with the leaders are key events in the campaign and there are also programmes in which the leaders answer questions from members of the public. The possibility of having formal televised debates between leaders – as happens in American Presidential elections – is regularly discussed but has not yet been brought to fruition, although in 2005 there was a special edition of *Question Time* in which members of the audience asked questions of Charles Kennedy, Michael Howard and Tony Blair one after the other. Second, campaigning is not restricted to the formal campaign period. Pippa Norris (1997b) goes as far as to say that campaigning is now 'permanent' and plans are certainly made well in advance. For at least a year before an election is due (the precise date being determined by the Prime Minister), the parties clearly engage in campaign activity. Indeed, party officials routinely assert that on the day after an election they start preparing for the next one. Third, the parties use modern methods to find out what the voters are thinking and feeling about issues, events and personalities. Between the wars the Prime Minister, Stanley Baldwin, famously consulted his local station master if he wanted to find out what the people were thinking, and as late as 1979 a senior Labour figure preferred to consult his local constituency activists (Kavanagh, 1995, pp. 110, 132). Nowadays, however, the major parties engage polling firms and other professionals to monitor public opinion through conventional polling and 'focus group' research, which involves getting small groups of voters together to talk at length about their political opinions and reactions. Fourth, the parties employ a variety of professionals, specialists and consultants for campaigning purposes. The campaign is conceived of as an exercise in marketing (see Scammell, 1995) and advertising agencies are employed to design posters, suggest slogans, advise on election broadcasts and so on. 'Spin doctors' make every effort to ensure that the party and its personalities get the best possible media coverage. This professionalization of campaigning, much influenced by campaign activity in the United States, is one of the most important recent developments in British elections (Denver, Hands, Fisher and MacAllister, 2003). Finally, many campaign events are stage-managed for the benefit of television. It used to be – as late as the 1960s and 1970s – that party leaders would address large public meetings at which they would be interrupted by hecklers. Nowadays there are no such meetings. They have been replaced to a limited extent by 'rallies' of the party faithful to which admission is by ticket only, but generally large meetings are avoided. The daily press conferences, the leaders' tours and activities, the timing and locations of speeches, and the issues to be talked about are all carefully planned in advance. During the 2001 campaign two unscripted events received massive publicity: John Prescott punched a demonstrator who had hit him with an egg and Tony Blair was harangued in public by a woman complaining about the National Health Service. But it was the fact that this sort of thing now happens so rarely that made these incidents so newsworthy. In 2005 such embarrassments were entirely avoided.

These developments have made modern campaigns expensive. Before 2001 there was no legal limit on the amount of money that the parties could spend on national campaigning. The parties do not have to pay the broadcasting organizations for election broadcasts on television and radio (a major expenditure item in other political systems) but, nonetheless, in the 1992 election the Conservatives spent about £10 million, Labour about £7 million and the Liberal Democrats about £2 million (Butler and Kavanagh, 1992, p. 260). Campaign expenditure in the twelve months preceding the 1997 election reached around £28 million for the Conservatives, £26 million for Labour and £3.5 million for the Liberal Democrats (Fisher, 2001). Under the Political Parties, Elections and Referendums Act passed in 2000, however, a stop was put to the spiralling costs of campaigning. For the first time national campaign expenditure was 'capped' and for 2001 parties were not allowed to spend more than £16.3 million on campaigning between the Act coming into force in February and the election in June. This, of course, made little difference to the Liberal Democrats, who are permanently plagued by poverty and spent only around £1.4 million during the 2001 campaign. The Conservatives, on the other hand spent £12.8 million and Labour £11.1 million (Electoral Commission, 2001a). By 2005 the permitted expenditure had risen to £18.4 million. Both the Conservatives and Labour approached the maximum, each spending £17.9 million, while the Liberal Democrats spent £4.2 million (Electoral Commission, 2005). Clearly, national campaigns don't come cheap.

Is it worth it? Do campaigns have any effects or are they four weeks 'full of sound and fury, signifying nothing', as Pippa Norris (1987) asked in the title of an article on the 1987 campaign? She goes on to suggest (p. 458) that, at least as far as that election was concerned, it is arguable that 'for Labour and the Alliance, no matter how professional the presentation, how effective the grassroots organisation, how persuasive the party political broadcasts, how convincing the leader's speeches, how enthusiastic the rallies, they could not win against the Conservatives'. Similarly, Worcester and Mortimore (1999, p. 98) argue that in 1997, 'by the time the strategic phase was played out, the election about to be called and the short-term tactics of the campaign itself begun, the election was already effectively lost' (by the Conservatives).

As before, however, the shift from aligned to dealigned voting provides a context within which the effects of campaigns can be considered and, a priori, this would lead us to have different expectations. With aligned voting, the election campaign is merely one other short-term factor which might marginally affect the voters. When the great majority of voters had enduring party loyalties they were unlikely to be deflected from them by any incidents occurring in a short campaign. Compared to the deep-seated influences of class and party identification, campaigns paled into insignificance. As these enduring ties have loosened, however, it seems likely that voters have become more open to influence during campaigns. Fewer will have their minds already firmly made up when the campaign begins.

Some support for this interpretation has already been seen in Chapter 4 in the discussion showing that there has been increased 'campaign swithering' since 1964, and the figures quoted there are certainly consistent with the view that there are now plenty of voters 'up for grabs' during campaigns. In 2005, according to MORI, the proportion of voters who had yet to decide how to vote at the start of the campaign was larger than ever before. Even on the day before the poll, 27 per cent were still uncertain how to vote (Worcester, Mortimore and Baines, 2005, 54–7).

Given the fact that throughout general election campaigns there are now almost daily opinion poll reports of voting intentions, it is relatively easy to trace changes in the levels of support for the parties as campaigns progress. Figure 6.1 shows the trends in the 2001 election. Four pre-election polls at

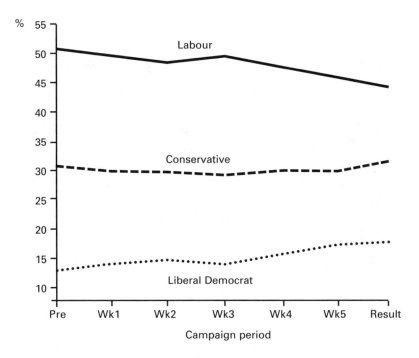

Note: The calculations – the simple mean in each case – are based on the 'headline' figures reported by the polls, whether these were adjusted or unadjusted. Each poll is assigned to the week in which the majority of the fieldwork was carried out.
Source: Results of published national polls.

Figure 6.1   Voting intentions in campaign polls, 2001

the start of May constitute the starting point and the chart then shows the average share of voting intentions in each week of the campaign and the parties' actual shares of the vote in Great Britain in the election itself.

Media reporting of the 2001 election generated a widespread impression that the campaign made no difference to the outcome. It is certainly true that Labour won easily, as expected, and the Conservatives 'flatlined', but Figure 6.1 suggests that there was some slippage in Labour's fortunes: having had more than 50 per cent of voting intentions in early May, support fell to around 45 per cent in the last week of the campaign. In addition, there was a clear upward trend in support for the Liberal Democrats. A similar increase in Liberal Democrat support occurred in 1997 (although not in 1992), and in part this simply reflects the fact that general election campaigns give the party (and its leader) more exposure than they can get in

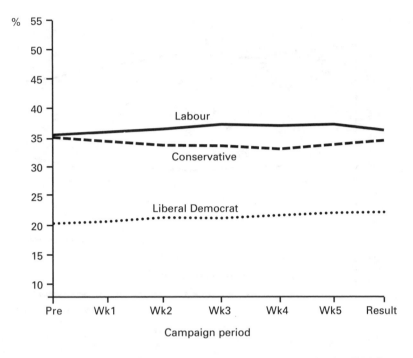

Note: The calculations – the simple mean in each case – are based on the 'headline' figures reported by the polls, whether these were adjusted or unadjusted. Each poll is assigned to the week in which the majority of the fieldwork was carried out.
Source: Results of published national polls.

Figure 6.2   Voting intentions in campaign polls, 2005

the periods between elections. In part also, however, the 2001 figures reflect the fact that the public increasingly warmed to the Liberal Democrat leader, Charles Kennedy. During the campaign, Gallup conducted a rolling series of polls on behalf of the British Election Study in which respondents were asked to indicate how much they liked each of the party leaders by giving them a score on a scale running from 0 (strongly dislike) to 10 (strongly like). When the series began on 14 May, Hague's mean score was 3.9, Blair's 5.6 and Kennedy's 4.9. By the end of the campaign Hague was still on 3.9 and Blair had increased to 5.9, but Kennedy made the biggest advance, scoring 5.4. Whatever interpretation is put on the figures, however, it seems clear that it is wrong to suggest that nothing changed over the weeks leading up to polling day in 2001.

Figure 6.2 shows a similar chart for the 2005 election. In this case, four pre-election polls at the start of April constitute the starting point. Campaign changes are not nearly as clear as they were in 2001. In the initial stages Labour support increased a little while the Conservatives fell back somewhat; towards the end support for the Conservatives steadied while Labour popularity eased downwards. As in 2001 the Liberal Democrats improved their position during the campaign, although not as markedly as in 2001 (in part, no doubt, because their starting point was higher). The likeability of Charles Kennedy may again have been a factor. On the same scale described above, he went from a score of 5.2 at the start to 5.5 at the end. Meanwhile, Tony Blair went from 4.0 to 4.1 and Michael Howard from 3.7 to 3.4.

The data in these two figures understate the case that campaigns make a difference, however. Party campaigns have three main aims: to *reinforce* voters who are inclined to support them but who may be wavering or not strongly committed, to *recruit* people who are genuinely undecided at the start of the campaign and to *convert* those who start off with a preference for another party. Reinforcement does not show up in opinion poll figures, but campaign panel polls suggest that there is some conversion and a good deal of recruitment from indecision. However, voters move to and from all of the parties and, if no one party does much better than the others at converting and recruiting, then the effects of all the campaign movements will be to leave the net levels of party support relatively unchanged. In other words, the aggregate figures can and do conceal much individual change during campaigns.

The mass media

During an election campaign only a tiny percentage of voters will actually see a party leader in the flesh or attend a rally to hear him or her speak. Even when party leaders visit particular constituencies, security concerns are such that they flash in and out without most local people even being aware that they've visited until they read about it in a local paper. Overwhelmingly, voters' awareness of the national campaign and their experience of it is obtained from the media, and in particular the national press and television. Modern campaigns are, therefore, media campaigns; they are a form of spectator sport. Most people do not participate in campaigns but watch them on television or read about them in the newspapers. Just after the 2005 election MORI found that 70 per cent of their respondents said that they had seen some party election broadcasts on television while 46 per cent saw the party leaders' 'debate' (Worcester, Mortimore and Baines, 2005, 196). Almost everyone must have seen campaign reports on television news. More generally, in a study for the Electoral Commission in 2001, MORI found that 88 per cent of respondents said that they used television as a source of information and news about politics while 74 per cent used daily newspapers for the same purpose (Electoral Commission, 2001b, pp. 58–61).

There are clear differences, however, between the national press and television in respect of their reporting of politics, and these are summarised below:

National Press	*Television*
Partisan	Balanced
Not trusted	Trusted
Segmented audience	Mass audience
Active audience	Passive audience
Printed messages	Audio/visual messages
Secondary source of information	Most important source of information

First of all, most national newspapers are partisan; they usually have a preference for one party or another and state it clearly. Television, on the other hand, is required by law to be impartial in its coverage of politics. In practice this is interpreted as meaning that coverage must be balanced between the parties in terms of time, and current practice is that the details are agreed by an informal committee on party political broadcasting, involving party and broadcasting representatives. The Electoral Commission (2003) has proposed, however, that somewhat more formal arrangements should be put in place. Second, partly because they are overtly partisan, newspapers are not greatly trusted to tell the truth whereas television news (especially the BBC) is trusted to do so. In 1997, for example, MORI found that 74 per cent of survey respondents generally trusted television news readers to tell the truth while only 15 per cent generally trusted print journalists, and there is little reason to think that things have changed significantly since then (see Worcester and Mortimore, 1999, p. 80).

Third, the audience for newspapers is 'segmented': different sorts of people read different papers. Readers of broadsheets (such as the *Daily Telegraph* or the *Guardian*) are generally better educated and better off than readers of tabloids such as the *Sun* and *Daily Mirror*. By contrast there is a mass audience for television. In this context 'mass' does not refer to the size of the audience (although it is, of course, enormous) but to the fact that it is relatively undifferentiated: all sorts of people watch television news, for example. Fourth, it is easy to ignore political coverage in the press; readers can simply turn to the sports pages or gossip columns or whatever it is that they are interested in. Only those who are actively interested in politics will look at the political coverage. The same is no doubt true of 'heavier' political coverage on television programmes such as *Newsnight*, but people watching the main news programmes will find themselves exposed to political news whether they are interested or not. It is this ability of television to reach a largely politically passive audience that makes it such an attractive medium to politicians. Fifth, television is also a much richer medium of communication than the press. The latter provides printed reports and some photographs. On television we can see and hear politicians: how they speak, move, interact with others and respond to questions; what gestures they use, whether they sweat under pressure, whether or not they seem sincere. Finally, and unsurprisingly, most people now regard television as their most important source of information about politics. At the start of the 2005 election campaign, for example, MORI found that 78 per cent of voters said that they regularly watched BBC 1 as a source of information about news and current affairs. Newspapers remain an important secondary source but, in election campaigns or at other times, when voters want political information it is to television that they mostly turn.

These differences have important consequences for the roles played by the press and television in election campaigns and for their potential impact upon voters. Before considering this in more detail, however, it is helpful to make a brief digression to discuss media effects on attitudes and behaviour more generally. Since the national campaign and media coverage of the national campaign are all but indistinguishable, examining the impact of the campaign on voters effectively means examining the degree to which they are influenced by what they read, hear and see in the mass media.

Media effects

The question of the extent to which people's attitudes, opinions and behaviour are influenced by the mass media, especially television, is one that has provoked an enormous amount of research in a variety of fields. People worry, for example, about the effects of presenting violent or obscene material, about the way women are frequently portrayed in advertisements or about the effect of showing people smoking cigarettes. Early media theorists, impressed by the apparent power of the media to influence ideas, posited what is called a *direct effects* or *hypodermic needle* model. This is illustrated in Figure 6.3. The source or sender (S) communicates information by a particular 'channel' (print, film, television or whatever) to a receiver (R). The receiver receives the message directly, accepts it and is influenced by it. In a sense, the whole advertising industry is based on this assumption, although modern marketing would recognize that it is very crude.

Empirical research on political attitudes quickly concluded that this model was far too simplistic (see Trenaman and McQuail, 1961; Blumler and McQuail, 1967). Voters did not come to mass media with empty minds available to be filled with media-provided information; instead, they already had opinions, values, experiences and predispositions which affected their perceptions and interpretations of media messages. The direct effects model was, therefore, replaced by the *filter* model, which is illustrated in Figure 6.4.

An important psychological theory underlies this model, known as the theory of *cognitive dissonance* (Festinger, 1962). Cognitive dissonance is a psychological state of unease or tension which occurs when an individual encounters facts or arguments that are at variance with his or her beliefs or attitudes. Thus a strong Labour supporter would feel uneasy if presented with evidence that ministers in a Labour government were not doing a good job. Subconsciously everyone wants to avoid this sort of unease, and does so by 'screening out' some information while being receptive to other information. Generally, people seek reinforcement of their own position from the media, and seek to avoid communications which contradict their views. This is done in three ways.

1   *Selective exposure*. We can't read all the newspapers or watch all television programmes. According to the model, we tend to read and watch material that supports our political viewpoint. Indeed, many people avoid 'political' material altogether and concentrate on sport, entertainment, soap operas and so on.

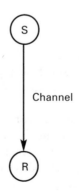

Note: 'S' refers to the source or sender and 'R' to the receiver.

Figure 6.3   Direct effects model of media influence

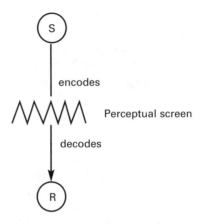

Note: 'S' refers to the source or sender and 'R' to the receiver.

Figure 6.4   Filter model of media influence

2   *Selective perception.* Even when we come across hostile media material, we reinterpret it to fit in with our preconceptions or don't even perceive its hostility. Thus Tony Blair might be seen by his supporters as very sincere, while opponents might perceive this as false sincerity; just as Margaret Thatcher was thought by opponents to be pig-headed, but was seen by supporters as resolute.
3   *Selective retention.* We remember selectively. We remember things that fit in with our views and quickly forget things that don't.

People employ these mechanisms subconsciously in 'decoding' the communications that have been 'encoded' by the sender. In doing so they erect a 'communications barrier' or 'perceptual screen' between themselves and the mass media. Despite all the propaganda efforts of the newspapers and of the parties in campaign broadcasts, the main effect of the media, as interpreted by this model, is to reinforce the voters' pre-existing predisposi- tions. An interesting example of these processes at work occurred in December 2001, although it had nothing to do with elections. The United States government released a video in which Osama bin Laden appeared to demonstrate at least prior knowledge of the previous September's terrorist atrocities in New York and Washington. The reaction of some of those opposed to subsequent American action in Afghanistan was to claim that the video was somehow faked. A letter-writer to the *Guardian* asked: 'May I be the first to nominate for an Oscar the actor who played bin Laden?' (see

Harris, 2001). The evidence of the video was thus interpreted to accord with, rather than challenge, existing views.

The filter model of media effects has been very influential and it has been supported by plenty of evidence. Nonetheless, as we shall see, in the context of electoral behaviour it has increasingly been called into question in recent years.

Television

Since the 1960s, television has utterly dominated national campaigns. The activities of the party leaders are 'media events' especially staged to be reported; 'photo-opportunities' are carefully arranged; schedules are timed to fit in with television news coverage. When leading politicians address meetings or rallies they do not really speak to their live audiences – who are occasionally glimpsed glassy-eyed with incomprehension – but to the television audience who will see clips from the speech ('sound-bites') later in the evening. Indeed, speeches are deliberately constructed so that they contain plenty of sound bites for television producers to use. Similarly, when leaders visit different localities campaign managers try to ensure that they are always surrounded by enthusiastic supporters so that a good impression is created for the television cameras. If the advent of mass-circulation newspapers provided the original impetus for national campaigning, then the highly professional modern campaign described above can be seen as a slightly delayed reaction to the advent of television. The question is whether watching the news, party election broadcasts, interviews with party leaders and campaign reports affects the attitudes and behaviour of voters.

The two pioneering studies of the effects of television on British voting behaviour (Trenaman and McQuail, 1961; Blumler and McQuail, 1967) supported the filter model described above. They found that among a variety of sources of political information only television was able to overcome the 'communications barrier' between people and the media, but it did so only to the extent of increasing the voters' level of political information; it did not change political attitudes and opinions. Thus, Trenaman and McQuail (p. 233) concluded that, 'in the field of attitudes a highly significant screening effect separates exposure to the campaign from changes in strength or direction of attitude'. They said (p. 192) that there was 'a definite and consistent barrier between source of communication and movement of attitudes in the political field at the General Election'.

Many people find the conclusion that television has little effect on political opinions difficult to accept. It seems to fly in the face of common sense to suggest that such a pervasive and powerful medium has little impact upon political attitudes and behaviour. I myself have already pointed to increased coverage of politics on television as a source of dealignment (Chapter 4). Moreover, if the medium has such little impact upon voters, why do the professionals in the political parties make such strenuous efforts to tailor their campaigns to the needs of television? Why are leading politicians extensively coached on how to come over well on the box?

The first point to make is that both studies mentioned above focus on party election broadcasts (paying little attention to other political reporting) and tend to assume that these broadcasts only have an impact if they result in changes in voting intentions and attitudes (rather than, for example, reinforcement or recruitment). More importantly, however, it is simply the case that times have changed. Both of these studies were undertaken a very long time ago. Trenaman and McQuail's book is concerned with the 1959 general election, while Blumler and McQuail's deals with the 1964 election. At that time political television was in its infancy. The quantity of political coverage on television today is vastly greater than it was then and the quality has vastly improved. Television commentators, interviewers and presenters concerned with political coverage are much more professional and less deferential to politicians; coverage of elections (and of the House of Commons) is much more detailed and sophisticated. Finally, the emergence of a dealigned electorate has serious implications for the filter model. It was the existence of party identification which to a large extent created the 'communications barrier' in respect of party preferences. It was because most voters had strong pre-existing party loyalties that they employed selective processes in response to political messages in the media. If people were strongly Conservative they would screen out pro-Labour information and remember pro-Conservative coverage. Since there has been a notable decline in the strength of party identification it would seem reasonable to infer that the 'communications barrier' has become rather more permeable since the 1960s.

There has been no full-scale survey study of the effects of television on political attitudes and behaviour in the dealignment era. Miller's (1991) painstaking study, *Media and Voters,* pays hardly any attention to television's effect on attitudes, while the data reported by Norris *et al.* (1999) are based on experiments rather than surveys. In part, this absence of major survey studies on television effects is a product of the fact that researchers have come to realize that demonstrating such effects is hugely difficult. There are three major problems.

First, a major criticism with the early studies mentioned above is that their focus is very much on short-term change. They concentrate on the election campaign period and it seems unrealistic to expect to find marked changes in political opinions in such a short space of time, especially in a situation where voting was highly structured by class and party identification. Effects could be long term, slow and subtle, but nonetheless significant. Party election broadcasts during campaigns might not convert people but that does not mean that attitudes might not be shaped over a long period by broader reporting of politics. The problem is that it would be difficult (and expensive) to construct a research programme to study the long-term effects of television.

Second, apart from party election broadcasts – which are clearly designed to persuade voters – television coverage of politics, as we have seen, is required to be balanced. Moreover, it is very diffuse, ranging from specialized regular features such as *Newsnight* and *Question Time* to documentaries, comedy and news broadcasts several times a day. Given this, it is difficult even to imagine how researchers could keep track of what information about politics viewers receive in order to try to measure its impact on their attitudes.

Third, as well as receiving information from television, voters are constantly exposed to a multiplicity of other influences, including family, friends, colleagues, newspapers, propaganda literature and so on. The mind simply boggles at the complexity of trying to separate out the effects of television from all of these other influences. This is related to the final difficulty: the perennial problem of demonstrating causal connections. It is well established that people who watch – or remember watching – a particular party's election broadcasts tend to vote for that party, but it is arguable that this is not because they are influenced by the broadcast; rather, they are supporters of the party in the first place and are using television to reinforce their views.

There is no doubt that television has profoundly affected the conduct of politics in general and of election campaigns in particular. Simple observation suggests that it has led to a greater concentration on personalities rather than policies or issues and, in particular, on the party leaders. Leaders who come across well on television appear to be at an advantage. Parties devote far more resources to presentation and to media management than they used to. Party conferences are now little more than media events staged for the television audience (such as it is). National campaigns revolve around television.

Finally, what remains unresolved and difficult to demonstrate, however, is the extent to which television affects voters' attitudes and hence their choice of party. Certainly the conditions for increased influence exist. Party identification, which previously filtered voters' perceptions of political communications, has declined in importance while voting on the basis of evaluations has become more prevalent. A pre-condition of making evaluations is possession of the requisite information, and television is by far the main supplier of political information (even if this amounts to little more than the impression created by a party leader when interviewed on *Richard and Judy*). More generally, the image that leaders project is largely communicated to the voters via television. It is also frequently suggested that television has an important role in setting the agenda for political discussion, by choosing to highlight certain issues and not others. Television producers and commentators, it is said, rather than politicians or voters, determine the campaign agenda – what people will think about – by choosing the issues to be discussed and which events will be reported. In fact, however, both Miller (1991, pp. 164–5) and Norris *et al*. (1999, pp. 182–3) suggest that the agenda-setting role of television is modest, at best. No matter what topics are being discussed on television, the electorate generally continues to believe that 'bread and butter' issues, such as prices, employment, the NHS and so on, are the most important.

Suggestive evidence that how politics is reported on television news does affect attitudes is provided by Norris and colleagues (Norris *et al.,* 1999, ch. 9). During the 1997 election they conducted an innovative experiment in London in which they asked people to view a specially compiled 30-minute video of news items. One of the videos was neutral so far as the parties were concerned but others included material favourable to, or not favourable to, one of the parties. It was found that, after viewing the videos, those who had been exposed to pro-Conservative messages were more likely to intend to vote Conservative, and those who had seen pro-Labour messages were more likely to intend to vote Labour.

This evidence can only be 'suggestive', however, as it was not based on a scientifically selected sample and the respondents' views were ascertained immediately before and after viewing the videos. It is not clear whether the effect demonstrated by Norris *et al*. would still be evident after even only a few days. It would appear that, in general, the influence of television is so pervasive, long term and mixed up with other factors that it is simply beyond the current ability of social science methods to measure it empirically.

The national press

Unlike television, the national press in Britain has traditionally been overwhelmingly and clearly partisan. On election day in 1992, for example, the whole of the front page of the *Daily Mirror* was taken up with Labour's red rose logo, a picture of Labour's leader, Neil Kinnock, and the slogan: 'The Time Is Now – Vote Labour'. It would be difficult to be more clearly partisan than that! Similarly, during the 2005 election a *Mirror* headline read 'Vote Labour – There's Too Much At Stake'. In 1997, the whole of the front pages of both the *Sun* and the *Mirror* consisted of a picture of Tony Blair and a banner headline: 'It Must Be Him' (*Sun*) and 'Your Country Needs Him' (*Mirror*). On the other side, a *Daily Mail* headline during the 2005 campaign read 'Blair Lied and Lied Again'.

Deacon, Golding and Billig (1998) suggest, however, that in recent elections simply categorizing papers as pro-Conservative or pro-Labour has become more problematical. Some papers tend to give out mixed or unclear opinions, and partisanship has been much less strident than previously. They argue, therefore, that it is now better to think of papers' stances as falling at different points on a continuum from 'strong Labour' through to 'strong Conservative' rather than categorizing them on an 'either/or' basis. Following this line, Deacon and Wring (2002) used campaign news reporting and comment, as well as editorials, to describe the overall partisan stance of the various papers in 2001 and their summary for national dailies (together with a similar classification for 2005 derived from the discussion in Bartle, 2005) is shown in Table 6.1.

Until 1992 there was a strong pro-Conservative bias in national daily newspapers. In 1992, for example, the circulation of pro-Conservative papers totalled 8.9 million, and all the rest only 4.8 million (Harrop and Scammell, 1992, pp. 181–2). This historic advantage for the Conservatives vanished in 1997 when papers calling for a Conservative victory had a combined circulation of around 4.5 million while the rest totalled 9.2 million

Table 6.1   Party 'supported' by national daily newspapers, 2001 and 2005

	2001	*2005*
Mirror	Strong Labour	Strong Labour
Guardian	Moderate Labour	Weak Labour
Star	Moderate Labour	None
Express	Moderate Labour	Moderate Conservative
Sun	Weak Labour	Weak Labour
The Times	Very weak Labour	Weak Labour
Financial Times	Very weak Labour	Weak Labour
Independent	None	Lib. Dem./Labour
Mail	None	Strong Conservative
Daily Telegraph	Strong Conservative	Strong Conservative

(Scammell and Harrop, 1997). By 2001, on Deacon and Wring's assessment, the Conservatives could count only on the support of the *Daily Telegraph*. In 2005, press support for the Conservatives increased somewhat but, even so, the preponderance of opinion among national dailies was still skewed in Labour's favour.

The fact that only two of the national daily papers gave strong support to a party in 2001 led Deacon and Wring to argue that there had been a 'partisan dealignment' among newspapers (see also Seymour-Ure, 2002). Just as voters' commitments to parties has weakened, so fewer newspapers now give strong, almost unquestioning, support to one of the parties. Readers can easily detect the partisan bias of papers that make their position very clear. In 2001 readers of the *Mirror*, *Guardian*, *Daily Telegraph* and *Mail* had little difficulty in describing the stances taken by these papers. In line with the dealignment argument, however, readers of other daily papers had rather less clear-cut opinions about where the papers stood on the merits of the respective parties (Worcester and Mortimore, 2001, p. 161). No comparable data are available for 2005 but it is worth noting that, in general, respondents found it more difficult to identify partisan bias in their newspapers in 2001 than they had done in 1997.

As with television, parties set great store by getting favourable coverage in the press – especially, perhaps, the mass circulation tabloids – and politicians certainly believe that the press can be highly influential in elections. After the 1992 election the former Conservative party treasurer, Lord McAlpine, wrote:

> The heroes of this campaign were Sir David English [editor of the *Express*] and Kelvin McKenzie [editor of the *Sun*] and the other editors of the grander Tory press. Never in the past nine elections have they come out so strongly in favour of the Conservatives. Never has the attack on the Labour party been so comprehensive . . . This is how the election was won. (*Sunday Telegraph*, 12 April, 1992)

The *Sun* itself was not slow to claim credit, asserting in a famous headline two days after the election, 'It's The *Sun* Wot Won It'. Whether this was actually true is debatable, to say the least (Curtice and Semetko, 1994), but after he became Labour leader Tony Blair made great efforts to court Rupert Murdoch (the paper's owner) and was rewarded with ringing endorsements in both 1997 and 2001 (and rather more qualified support in 2005).

As with campaigning in general, we have to ask whether this matters. Does what people read in the papers influence their opinions or voting behaviour? It is certainly the case that there is an association between the papers people read and the party they support. Table 6.2 shows the party preference of readers of the various papers in 2005. Although only quite

Table 6.2 Party choice by daily newspaper read, 2005 (row percentages)

	Conservative	Labour	Liberal Democrat
Mirror	11	67	17
Guardian	7	43	41
Independent	13	34	44
Sun	33	45	12
The Times	38	27	28
Financial Times	47	29	21
Star	21	54	15
Express	48	28	18
Mail	57	22	14
Daily Telegraph	65	13	17
None	27	37	27

Note: Rows do not total 100 as votes for 'others' are not shown.
Source: Data from Worcester, Mortimore and Baines (2005) p. 191.

small minorities of *The Times* and *Financial Times* readers followed their papers' advice and voted Labour, in broad terms voters tend to vote for the party supported by their paper (or, at least, not to vote for the party opposed by their paper). The relationship is far from perfect – there are, it seems, even some *Guardian*-reading Conservatives and non-Conservative *Daily Telegraph* readers – but it is fairly consistent and clear, and similar figures have been reported regularly at British elections.

What is not clear, however, is how these data are to be interpreted. They might indicate either that readers' political views are shaped by the paper that they read or that they choose to take a paper which is politically congenial to them. People may read the *Guardian* and vote Labour or Liberal Democrat, but that does not mean that they don't vote Conservative because they read the *Guardian*; rather, they may read the *Guardian* because they have anti-Conservative views in the first place. In other words, the data may reflect selective exposure. In fact, this has long been the standard interpretation of the relationship between newspaper readership and party choice. In the 1960s, Butler and Stokes (1974) noted that there was a strong relationship between newspaper reading habits and party choice but concluded (p. 118) that, in general, the relationship was spurious:

> The correlation is most likely to have been produced by the family's passing on a partisanship which the child has matched by his choice of paper, or by its passing on a more general social location to which both paper and party are appropriate . . . it is clear that newspapers often profit from, rather than shape, their reader's party ties.

There was evidence that the press helped to conserve or reinforce party loyalties and had a minor role in creating a party preference where readers were previously uncommitted, but little to support the hypothesis that people switched parties as a result of reading a paper with a particular partisan bias.

A similarly careful analysis of the political effects of reading different newspapers at the time of the 1983 election is provided by Martin Harrop (1986). He too finds some support for the view that papers can help to shape a party preference where readers previously had none, but he concludes that the main effect of the press is the reinforcement of existing party loyalties and finds no consistent evidence that newspapers convert their readers to the party supported by the paper.

When they were written, these interpretations represented the consensus among political scientists on the role of the press in influencing party choice and they are clearly in accordance with the filter model of communication. As with television, however, the weakening of party identification implies that voters could now be more open to persuasion by the press. Since they do not have a strong pre-existing preference for a party, they are less likely to filter information; lacking the 'anchor' of party identification they may be more likely to drift with the tides of opinion in the newspapers that they read. Proponents of the dealignment thesis would predict, therefore, that suitable research would find more positive evidence of press effects than hitherto, and in recent years some suggestive evidence has emerged.

As noted above, one of the problems that has bedevilled research on media influence is that it has tended to focus very much on the short term. Miller (1991), in the first major post-dealignment analysis of media effects, sought to overcome this problem by re-interviewing the same panel of respondents at widely different points in time. His results relating to readers of tabloid papers were impressive. Over the year between the summer of 1986 and the election of 1987, the change in the Conservatives' lead over Labour among Miller's panel as a whole was +10 per cent. Among readers of the *Express* and *Mail* it was +17 per cent, for *Sun* (then rabidly pro-Conservative) and *Star* readers it was +34 per cent, while among readers of the *Mirror* it was a mere +2 per cent. This suggests that the tabloids did influence their readers over this period. When Miller divided the readers of the different newspapers into those who were committed to a party (party identifiers) and those who were not, he found that the influence of the tabloids was particularly strong among the latter. When it is remembered that levels of political commitment in Britain have steadily declined, the message of Miller's analysis seems to be that there has been a corresponding increase in the scope for the national press to influence political attitudes and opinions and party choice.

Similar analyses using panel surveys from 1987 to 1992 and from 1992 to 1997 have been reported by Curtice and Semetko (1994) and Norris *et al.* (1999) respectively. Curtice and Semetko concluded that while newspapers had little influence on voters during the 1992 campaign, they had a small but significant effect over the longer term. Norris *et al.* remain more sceptical, however. They agree that newspapers 'can make a difference in mobilising their more faithful readers by playing them a familiar tune' but conclude that 'the partisanship of British newspapers is clearly part of the structure of British voting behaviour, but whether they can explain the flux is very much open to doubt' (pp. 168–9). On the other hand, Newton and Brynin (2001) suggest that newspaper effects are likely to be smaller in 'landslide' elections (such as 1997) than in closer contests, when voters may find it harder to make a decision. In addition, they find that when they take account of the 'selective exposure' argument by controlling for party identification and political attitudes (as well as a number of other relevant variables), newspaper readership has a statistically significant impact on party choice. Reading a paper that was consistent with respondents' party sympathies and attitudes significantly increased the likelihood of voting for the party in 1992 and 1997; reading a paper that was inconsistent with basic loyalties decreased the likelihood of voting for the party. In addition, in line with Miller's analysis referred to above, respondents with no party identification tended to follow their paper's politics even more closely than those who did identify with a party.

As with television, the conditions are ripe for increased press influence on voters' opinions with the development of a more free-floating and easily mobilized electorate. It is also true to say that both media cover much more than politics, especially outside election campaigns. Political scientists are highly interested in the political content of newspapers but the great majority of readers may give it scant attention, preferring to concentrate on sports coverage, celebrity news and so on. In that case, we should not be surprised that the influence of newspapers in shaping political opinions is easily exaggerated. It is worth saying again that it is extremely difficult to isolate the effects of one specific factor upon voting behaviour. As well as reading a newspaper, voters are exposed to a multiplicity of other influences upon their opinions: television, family, friends, colleagues at work and so on. It is impossible to control for all of these at once and so measure newspaper influence. Even so, some of the recent research discussed above suggests that the filter model no longer gives an adequate interpretation of the effect of press partisanship upon party choice.

Opinion polls

Public opinion polls are a familiar feature of general election campaigns. (Accounts of the history and methodology of political opinion polls can be found in Broughton, 1995; and Moon, 1999.) They are closely related to media campaign coverage, since it is newspapers and television programmes which commission many of the polls, and the voters read and hear about polls in the press and on television. Different types of poll are published during campaigns (polls in specific regions, in marginal seats, of specific groups of voters and so on). In addition, the major parties regularly commission private polls, the results of which are not published. Most attention focuses, however, on the regular nationwide polls tracking voting intentions: Table 6.3 shows the number of such polls published during the campaign period in elections since 1959. To some extent the numbers are affected by the length of the campaign concerned, but there was clearly a slow increase in the number of campaign polls from 1959 to 1979. The number then increased sharply in 1983, increased further in 1987 and peaked in 1992. In the 1997 and 2001 elections, however, there was a falling-off in the number of polls undertaken. This was probably a product of the fact that in advance of these elections the outcomes were not thought to be in doubt. In addition, some people's faith in the polls had been shaken by their relatively poor performance in predicting the result of the 1992 election. In 2005, however, there was a resurgence in polling activity, at least partly because a rather closer contest was expected.

Although a number of smaller companies are involved from time to time, political polling in Britain is dominated by three major firms: ICM, MORI and YouGov (which conducts polls via the Internet). A smaller and more

Table 6.3 Number of nationwide polls published during the campaign period, 1959–2005

Election	N *(polls)*	Election	N *(polls)*
1959	20	1979	26
1964	23	1983	46
1966	26	1987	54
1970	25	1992	57
1974 (Feb.)	25	1997	44
1974 (Oct.)	27	2001	36
		2005	52

Source: Data from Crewe (2005).

recent arrival, Populus, also conducts regular political polls. Although political polling is a high-profile activity, it is a very small part of the business of these companies and they don't do it on their own behalf or in the public interest. Rather, they are commissioned (and paid) by clients – mainly in the media – to conduct political polls. In the 2005 election, YouGov worked for the *Daily Telegraph, Sunday Times* and Sky Television, while ICM polled for the *Guardian,* MORI mainly for the *Financial Times* (with occasional polls for other papers) and Populus for *The Times*. National Opinion Polls (NOP), having virtually withdrawn from political polling, returned to conduct campaign polls for the *Independent*. In addition, on polling day an exit poll (see below) was undertaken jointly by MORI and NOP on behalf of the BBC and ITN.

Campaign poll results are sometimes portrayed as predictions of the outcome of the election in question; this is not the case. As we have seen, opinion fluctuates over the course of campaigns and what campaign polls actually provide is a snapshot of the electorate's voting intentions at a particular point in time, not a prediction of how they will vote at a later date. Nonetheless, the polling firms themselves treat their final polls as election forecasts and it is legitimate to assess the accuracy of polls by comparing the result of the final poll produced by each company with the actual election result. Here again we need to be careful. First, what the final polls estimate is the share of votes that each party will obtain in the election and each of these estimates is subject to a margin of error (usually plus or minus about two percentage points). Thus if, from a sample of around 2,000 respondents, the Conservative vote is estimated at 30 per cent then there is a very strong chance that it will actually be between 28 per cent and 32 per cent. Clearly, if we move from estimates of individual party shares to estimating the gap between them then there is a much larger margin of error (plus or minus four points). Second, poll figures are sometimes used to predict the number of seats that the parties will win. While this is an interesting and important exercise it has little to do with polling, since it involves making judgements about how the electoral system will translate votes into seats.

The fairest way to assess the accuracy of final polls is to compare their estimates of each party's share of the vote with the actual shares obtained, and Table 6.4 shows how the polls have performed in these terms in elections since 1964. Overall, the record up to 1992 was very creditable. Although in some elections some individual polling forms were less accurate, the mean errors were well within the margins expected in any poll. This was not enough to prevent embarrassment for the pollsters in 1970, however. In a close election, four of the five polling firms involved at the time predicted that Labour would win, but when the results came in it was

Table 6.4 Average error in final campaign polls' prediction of party vote shares, 1964–2005

Election	Mean error	N (polls)	Election	Mean error	N (polls)
1964	1.0	4	1983	1.5	7
1966	1.3	3	1987	1.3	7
1970	2.0	5	1992	3.0	4
1974 (Feb.)	1.0	6	1997	2.0	6
1974 (Oct.)	1.5	5	2001	1.8	5
1979	0.3	5	2005	0.8	6

Source: Data from Crewe (2005), p. 39.

the Conservatives who came out on top. Post-mortems generally agreed that polling had finished too early – some days before the election – and that there had been a swing to the Conservatives in the last few days of the campaign.

In 1992, however, the polls came seriously unstuck. Only one of the four polls published on election day put the Conservatives ahead of Labour, and then only very slightly, and yet the Conservatives had a comfortable victory. This resulted in a series of post-mortems in which various explanations for the failure of the polls were suggested and investigated (see, for example, Butler and Kavanagh, 1992, ch. 7; Crewe, 1992a). There may have been a *very* late swing to the Conservatives; the methods used by the pollsters may have been faulty; the electoral register may have been more inaccurate than usual; Conservative supporters may have refused to answer questions ('shy Tories') or else deliberately lied to interviewers because they were ashamed to admit that they intended to vote Conservative; people may have realized that there is a qualitative difference between stating a preference in a poll and actually putting a cross on the ballot paper. As David Sanders (1992) pointed out, however, it is extremely difficult to determine what really went wrong without using survey-based data, and there is no guarantee that these do not suffer from the very same problems that led to misleading poll predictions. In any event, it seems likely that the widespread criticism of the performance of the polls in 1992 was part of the reason for the decline in the number of campaign polls commissioned in the two subsequent elections.

In 1997 and 2001, predicting the election winners was not difficult and all polls correctly did so. Even so, the polls came in for criticism, in particular because they mostly overestimated Labour's vote and underestimated that of the Conservatives, especially in 2001 (Crewe, 1997, 2001). Although

Labour's vote share was again overestimated by most pollsters in 2005, the average error in predicting the parties' shares of votes was very small (0.8 percentage points). This is a remarkable performance especially given that in modern elections the pollsters have had to cope with more 'late deciders' and 'waverers', as well as a more fragmented party system. In addition, very low turnouts make prediction more risky as it is difficult to know which poll respondents will actually turn out to vote. All polling companies now have techniques for dealing with this (by counting only people who say that they are certain to vote, for example). A more general problem for pollsters is that there is always a possibility that polls may be self-falsifying: the publication of their results may alter the very behaviour that they are trying to forecast.

'Exit' polls – polls conducted on the day of the election, usually on behalf of the television channels, by interviewing voters as they leave polling stations – are of relatively recent vintage, being first used by ITN in October 1974 but not fully adopted by the BBC until 1992. These are not campaign polls and their main purpose *is* to predict the election outcome, although they also sometimes provide data on the characteristics and opinions of voters for the various parties. Given that the problems caused by late swings and differential turnout are eliminated, exit polls ought to be more accurate than 'final' polls and, indeed, they are. In 2001, for example, the mean error of the two exit polls was –1.2 per cent on the Conservatives' vote share, +2.0 per cent on Labour's and –0.8 per cent on that obtained by the Liberal Democrats. In 2005, the joint MORI/NOP exit poll slightly overestimated Labour's share (+1.0 per cent) but otherwise was pretty well spot on.

Public opinion polls play a major part in election campaigns. Prime Ministers use them to help decide on an election date; the political parties closely monitor public polls and employ firms to do private polls on their behalf; campaign strategies are built around and adjusted in the light of what public and private polls are reporting. Party professionals, candidates and election workers can be encouraged or discouraged by poll results. Throughout campaigns, poll findings are regularly reported and the results analysed in depth.

It is more difficult to know whether the publication of poll results during campaigns influences voting behaviour. Certainly many voters say that they remember seeing the results of opinion polls: the figure was 89 per cent in 1992 and 63 per cent in 1997 (Worcester and Mortimore, 1999, pp. 179–80). In 2005, around 39 per cent described themselves as very or fairly interested in what the polls were saying (Worcester, Mortimore and Baines, 2005, p. 212). On the other hand, very few voters (4 per cent in 2001 and 3 per cent in 2005) say that opinion polls influence the way that they intend to vote (Worcester, Mortimore and Baines, 2005, p. 207).

There have been two main hypotheses about the possible impact of polls on voters: one suggests that there is a 'bandwagon' effect, the other that there is a 'boomerang' or 'underdog' effect. The first suggests that when one party is seen to be in the lead some voters will 'jump on the bandwagon' and its support will increase, while supporters of the losing party will lose heart and may not vote. The 'underdog' hypothesis says exactly the opposite: supporters of the leading party become complacent, the resolve of supporters of the losing party is stiffened and there is a growth in sympathy for the underdog. The effect is to produce an upsurge of support for the trailing party. Clearly both hypotheses cannot be true and early investigations of the question concluded that there was no consistent pattern supporting either hypothesis (Teer and Spence, 1973, ch. 6). In the last four general elections, however – 1992, 1997, 2001 and 2005 – the polls consistently overestimated the level of support for the party that was reported to be leading during the campaign. In each case the underdog has done better than expected. Also in each case, however, it was the Conservatives that were the trailing party. It remains an open question, therefore, whether the pattern of the polls in recent elections indicates an underdog effect or reflects problems with the pollsters' methods which cause them to include too many Labour supporters in their samples.

It is sometimes suggested that the publication of opinion poll results should be banned during election campaigns in Britain, as it is in some other countries. The Speaker's Conference on Electoral Reform recommended this in 1967 but the proposal was not accepted by the government; nonetheless, the issue continues to be raised from time to time. Those who favour banning them believe that polls do affect voting behaviour, and also argue that they 'trivialize' elections by reducing them to 'horse races', deflecting the attention of the voters from the serious issues at stake (see Whiteley, 1986).

If the publication of polls were banned, however, they would merely be replaced by leaks from private polls, rumour and deliberate dis-information campaigns. Local parties and candidates are not above referring to 'polls' of doubtful validity, or even inventing 'poll' results in their campaign literature. We are all familiar with the campaign organizer who claims that canvass returns show that his party is doing 'very well' and support is 'holding up', when the election result turns out to be a disaster. It seems better, on the whole, to have polls conducted by firms with no political axe to grind. More positively, reliable information about the relative support for parties is something that voters may wish to take into account before deciding how to vote, and why should they be denied it? Opinion polls by reputable companies should be counted as a benefit to the electoral process, not a problem.

The electorate seems to agree with these arguments as a declining minority (down to 15 per cent in 2005) think that the publication of polls should be banned during campaigns (Worcester, Mortimore and Baines, 2005, p. 210).

Constituency campaigning

For most people, the national campaign is *the* election campaign. It impinges most persistently and directly on their consciousness as it is played out before their eyes on television and, although the vast majority of the electorate are mere spectators, it generates a considerable degree of interest and excitement, even in supposedly lacklustre elections. Another kind of campaigning goes on at general elections, however, and that is local campaigns in the constituencies. These are inevitably much more humdrum affairs, largely concerned with canvassing the electorate for support, delivering leaflets and get-out-the-vote efforts on polling day. It is at constituency level, however, that voters have direct contact with the election campaign. In the 2005 election, 21 per cent of BES respondents remembered being canvassed on the doorstep by a party, 7 per cent being canvassed by telephone and 6 per cent being 'knocked up' by party workers on polling day, while 89 per cent of MORI's respondents remembered getting leaflets through the door (Worcester, Mortimore and Baines, 2005, p. 196). Most people are probably aware that there is a local campaign going on, but locally these campaigns rarely arouse much interest, let alone excitement. Nonetheless, in recent years constituency campaigns have played an increasingly significant part in elections.

Up to at least the 1980s, whether they knew it or not, the local campaigning strategies and techniques adopted by the political parties were based on the model of aligned and stable voting developed by Butler and Stokes. The main purpose of the campaign was to identify known or likely supporters and ensure that they voted. Each party knew where its supporters were to be found – in council estates and other working-class areas for Labour, in private housing estates and middle-class suburbs for the Tories – and concentrated their attention there. Party workers were actively discouraged from 'wasting time' by trying to persuade opponents or 'doubtful' voters of the merits of their candidate. The underlying assumption was that party loyalties were more or less fixed and the aim of the campaign was to maximize the turnout of supporters on election day. Constituency campaigns were not primarily intended to alter the party choice of electors but to mobilize known supporters. Even in this limited respect, however, the general view of electoral analysts was that, apart from rare special cases, constituency campaigns made no significant difference to election results. The consensus was that in general elections local campaigning was little more than a sideshow. It was frequently described as an anachronistic ritual and received scant attention from psephologists.

During the 1990s, however, constituency campaigning was transformed (Denver, Hands, Fisher and MacAllister, 2003). There were four main developments as outlined below:

1 Central party headquarters began to play a greater role in planning, co-ordinating and managing local campaigns. In part this was because the approach of headquarters staff to all aspects of campaigning became more professional. Partly also, however, it was due to a realization that the voters had changed and that effective campaigning could bring electoral rewards.

2 Resources and effort were increasingly concentrated on 'key' or 'target' seats. Parties had always known that some seats (those that might change hands) were more important than others (those that were safe or hopeless); they drew up lists of targets but this had little practical effect. From the 1990s, however, targeting was ruthless and highly effective, and extended to targeting specific types of voters as well as constituencies.

3 Technology began to be exploited to improve campaigning. In particular, the development of computers and the use of telephone 'banks' to canvass the electorate greatly increased the sophistication of local campaigns, allowing the parties, for example, to build a profile of individual voters and send them appropriate communications. Another innovation was the distribution of campaign videos and (in 2005) DVDs.

4 Campaigning began far in advance of the election. Whereas local activity used to be crammed into three weeks before polling day, many activities – including telephone canvassing and leafleting – now began a year or more before.

The Labour Party was in the forefront of these developments. In elections from 1997, indeed, it is not going too far to say that Labour's whole campaign strategy was built around the constituency campaigns (especially those in target seats). Other parties quickly learned the the appropriate lessons and by 2005, nationally directed local campaigns targeted on key seats, telephone 'voter identification', communications targeted at individual voters, nationally produced local literature, nationally appointed constituency organizers and conscious attempts to 'localise the national message' were commonplace (Fisher *et al.*, 2006).

The traditional view that local campaigning made little difference to election results was largely based on a single piece of evidence: the fact that swing tended to be uniform. In the 1950s and 1960s, it appeared that even if some local parties made great efforts and others did little, the outcome was just about the same. We have seen, however, that swing has become less uniform (Chapter 1) and this raises the possibility that differential local campaigning may explain the differences between constituencies. To investigate this possibility, however, researchers needed to devise some way of measuring campaign intensity across parties and constituencies. In the 1990s, three groups of researchers came up with different ways of doing this. Whiteley and Seyd (1994) used surveys of party members to estimate the activism of local parties; Pattie and colleagues (Pattie, Johnston and Fieldhouse, 1995) used campaign expenditure as a surrogate indicator of the level of campaign activity; Denver and Hands (1997a) undertook surveys of election agents and, based on these, derived direct measures of campaign intensity. When these different measures are compared with election results – which involves some rather advanced statistical techniques – then in most cases it is found that variations across constituencies in the intensity of campaigns mounted by the parties have been associated with variations in their electoral performance. The better the local campaign, the better the result. In addition, the more intense the campaign in a constituency the better is the turnout (Denver, Hands and MacAllister, 2004).

It should be emphasized that these studies find effects that are *statistically* significant. The authors would not claim that local campaigning is a *major* influence on election results; it is more a matter of stemming or accentuating a national tide. Denver, Hands and MacAllister (2004) estimate, for example, that in 2001 the gap in turnout between constituencies with the weakest and strongest campaigning was just over 4 percentage points. In the same election the best Conservative campaigns produced a share of the electorate that was 0.8 percentage points greater than their worst campaigns (after taking account of a large number of other variables), while the figures for Labour and the Liberal Democrats were 2.0 and 3.2 points respectively. These are not huge figures but are not to be sniffed at. The fact that Labour had very strong campaigns in their key seats in both 1997 and 2001 gave the party a clear advantage over the Conservatives, and the gains made by the Liberal Democrats in these two elections were clearly the products of highly targeted and effective local campaigning. Preliminary analysis of the 2005 campaigns (undertaken by the author) suggests that strong campaigning was again associated with higher turnouts, but that Labour campaigns were less effective than those of the Conservatives and Liberal Democrats in delivering an electoral payoff.

Conclusion

With a dealigned electorate more open to change in the short term, election campaigns and the mass media are, potentially, more likely to influence voters and election outcomes. Identifying, measuring and demonstrating the extent of such influence, of course, is fraught with difficulties. There is solid evidence that local campaigning makes a difference to election outcomes – which is in tune with the kinds of developments anticipated by dealignment theorists – but as far as the impact of the national campaign as transmitted by the mass media is concerned, things are less clear-cut. It seems likely that if all parties run careful, professional national campaigns then short-term instability among the voters is unlikely to be markedly to the benefit or disadvantage of any one of them. On the other hand, the campaign is decision time for increasing numbers of voters and, as the example of Charles Kennedy and the Liberal Democrats in 2001 showed, a vigorous and fairly distinctive campaign can have an impact. Even when there is little change in aggregate voting intentions during a campaign, however, this can be deceptive. Beneath the surface appearance of stability, voters are switching, hesitating and moving between decision and indecision. For that reason the parties' campaigns remain very important and worth spending money on, as any party which did not campaign seriously and well would soon find out.

7

Electoral Geography and Electoral Systems

Electoral geography focuses on spatial variations in electoral behaviour: that is, variations across regions, constituencies, wards or neighbourhoods (see Johnston *et al.,* 1998). There is nothing new about this approach. Indeed, comparing election results from one place to another is probably the oldest form of electoral analysis and is something which all psephologists do, not just those with specialist expertise in geography. Comparing turnouts in different constituencies, for example, involves examining spatial variations. In this chapter the focus is on variations in party choice and, in this respect, where people live is an important part of the context within which voters make their decisions; it is a contextual variable.

Regional variations

In analysing regional voting patterns, students of elections generally use the regions (currently known as 'Government Office regions') defined by the Registrar General's Office for census and other purposes. The boundaries of these census regions change from time to time and in the most recent definition (revised in the 1990s) England is divided into nine regions – North East, North West and Merseyside, Yorkshire and the Humber, East Midlands, West Midlands, Eastern, London, South East and South West – while Scotland, Wales and Northern Ireland are also defined as separate regions. Dividing up the country in this way is inevitably rather arbitrary and it is unlikely that everyone living in these regions feels a distinctive regional identity (excepting, of course, Scotland, Wales and Northern Ireland, where people would probably resent the use of the term 'region'). People living in Newcastle upon Tyne, for example, would consider themselves 'Geordies' rather than inhabitants of the North-East region, and it is unlikely that many people would describe themselves as an 'East Midlander'.

Despite the artificiality of official regional boundaries, however, very clear regional voting patterns have been reproduced in election after election

Table 7.1   Conservative share of the votes in regions, 1955 and 2005

1955		2005	
South East	58.2	South East	45.0
North West	52.2	Eastern	43.3
East Anglia	51.8	South West	38.6
South West	51.5	East Midlands	37.1
Scotland	50.1	West Midlands	35.0
Greater London	49.5	London	31.9
West Midlands	49.4	Yorkshire and the Humber	29.1
East Midlands	46.8	North West	28.7
Yorkshire/Humberside	44.3	Wales	21.4
North	43.0	North East	19.5
Wales	29.9	Scotland	15.8
Great Britain	49.3		32.7

Source: Data from Rallings and Thrasher (2000, 2005).

throughout the post-war period. This is illustrated, first, in Table 7.1 which shows the Conservative shares of the vote in the various regions (as they were then defined) in 1955 and in 2005. Already in 1955 there was something of a 'North–South divide' in patterns of party support. The Conservatives' vote share was larger than the national average in the South East, East Anglia and the South West and smaller in Wales, the North, and Yorkshire and Humberside. Scotland and the North West stand out as distinctive, however, in that the Conservative share there was greater than the national average. By 2005, the North–South divide was much sharper. Conservative support was markedly lower in Scotland, Wales and the three regions in northern England, and clearly higher in the South outside London (South East, Eastern, South West) than in the country as a whole.

A summary picture of what happened between these two elections, in terms of regional voting patterns, is given in Figure 7.1. This shows, for each election, how the Conservative 'lead' (in some cases negative) over Labour deviated from the national (Great Britain) figure in Scotland, Wales, the three southern regions outside London and the three northern regions. From 1959 to 1987, slowly at first but then more rapidly in the 1980s, Scotland and the North deviated more and more away from the Conservatives while the South swung more and more to the Conservatives. After 1987 the gap closed a little (although widening again in 2005) so that by the end of the series it remained much wider than it had been at the start of the period even although Wales, which was strongly anti-Conservative in 1955, has slowly but surely become less clearly out on a limb.

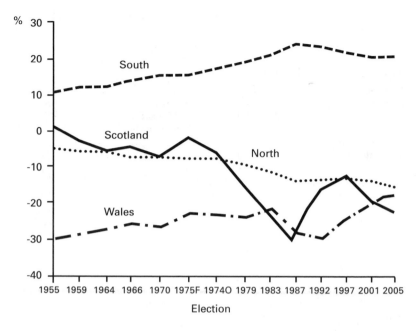

Figure 7.1   Regional deviations from national Conservative lead over Labour, 1955–2005

Figure 7.1 focuses on relative support for the Conservatives and Labour and so gives no information about two other distinctively regional features of elections during this period. The first was the distribution of support for the Liberals and their successors, which was markedly higher than average in the South West of England, in the Highlands and Borders of Scotland and in some parts of rural Wales. This continued their reputation as the party of the 'Celtic fringe'. Second, in the late 1960s there was an upsurge of political nationalism in Scotland and Wales and the SNP and Plaid Cymru emerged from the fringes of electoral politics in their respective countries. Thereafter, the two parties gained significant support in elections, further heightening the electoral distinctiveness of Scotland and Wales.

To an extent, regional differences in voting behaviour reflect differences in the social composition of the electorate. People living in the South are generally more affluent, more middle class and more likely to be home owners than those in Scotland, Wales and the North so that the Conservatives would be expected to do better there in any event. Survey data show, however, that even when social characteristics are taken into account regional differences persist. In the mid-1960s Butler and Stokes (1974,

p. 129) showed that among both working-class and middle-class voters greater proportions voted Conservative and smaller proportions Labour in the South than in Scotland, Wales and the North. Table 7.2 compares voting patterns in the South (outside London) and the North, Wales and Scotland in the 2005 election controlling for occupation, age and housing tenure. Within each category voters in the South were more likely to vote Conservative and Liberal Democrat and less likely to support Labour than their counterparts in the North, Wales and Scotland. It seems clear, then, that there is some regional factor at work – over and above simple social composition – which needs to be explained. It should be said, however, that there is an alternative (and minority) view which argues that apparent regional differences in voting disappear when a variety of controls are introduced (McAllister and Studlar, 1992). A problem with this analysis is that political attitudes are controlled before regional differences are considered and these attitudes are, of course, strongly related to party choice. The point is, of course, that people in the different regions have different political attitudes.

Table 7.2 Party choice in the 'North' and 'South' in 2005 (row percentages)

	Conservative	Labour	Liberal Democrat	(N)
Non-manual occupation				
North, Wales and Scotland	33	37	20	(755)
South	40	31	26	(717)
Manual occupation				
North, Wales and Scotland	13	62	12	(319)
South	28	40	30	(224)
Aged 65 and over				
North, Wales and Scotland	35	44	13	(298)
South	46	32	21	(268)
Owns home				
North, Wales and Scotland	30	40	18	(932)
South	40	30	27	(837)
Rents home				
North, Wales and Scotland	12	61	20	(217)
South	21	48	28	(195)

Note: Rows do not total 100 because votes for 'others' are not shown.
Source: Data from BES 2005 cross-section survey.

Urban–rural variations

The widening gap between regions in elections since 1955 has been accompanied by a less frequently noticed development: an increasing divergence between more urban and more rural areas. This is illustrated in Figure 7.2, which is based on a conventional definition of constituencies as very urban, mainly urban, mixed and rural, according to the number of electors per hectare and derived from Curtice and Steed (1992, p. 346). As can be seen, over time very urban areas have moved sharply away from the Conservatives (although there was a slight reversal of the trend in 2005, mainly due to the large swing away from Labour in London). Mainly urban constituencies have also moved against the Conservatives while, relative to the national results, mixed areas have become somewhat more Conservative and rural areas decidedly more so. The effect of this on party representation has been dramatic. Whereas in 1955 the Conservatives won 33 seats out of 74 in the ten largest British cities outside London – Birmingham, Bristol, Edinburgh, Glasgow, Leeds, Liverpool, Manchester, Newcastle,

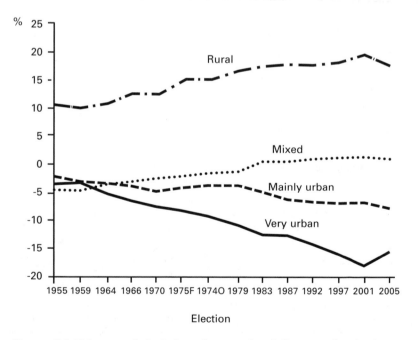

Figure 7.2 Urban–rural deviations from national Conservative lead over Labour, 1955–2005

Nottingham and Sheffield – they won none at all (out of 51) in the same cities in 2005.

When the urban–rural divergence is overlaid on the regional divergence then the extent of change in British electoral geography over the past 40 years or so is dramatic. Comparing 1966 and 2005 (both elections won by Labour), the Conservative lead over Labour in the rural south more than doubled – from 12.0 to 25.3 percentage points – while Labour's lead in the very urban parts of northern England rose from 21.5 to 37.4 points.

Explaining regional variations

The 'North–South' electoral divide, which opened up so spectacularly in the 1980s, has generated a large literature (see, for example, Johnston, Pattie and Allsop, 1988; McAllister and Studlar, 1992; Pattie, Johnston and Fieldhouse, 1993; Johnston *et al.*, 1998; Johnston, Pattie and Rossiter, 2005). Like most generalizations, the suggestion that there is an electoral dichotomy between the North and South of the country is an oversimplification – party support in London, for example, is very different from the pattern across the south as a whole – but it does highlight a major feature of the geography of party support in Britain. How can it be explained?

At the start of the 1980s, Curtice and Steed (1982) suggested that the long-term trend to increased regional polarization could be explained in three main ways. First, there had been slow changes in the distribution of socio-economic characteristics among the electorate. The proportion of broadly middle-class people tended to increase more quickly in the South (and in rural areas) and, relatively speaking, to decrease in the North and Scotland (and in urban areas). In part this could be due to migration, but research on the electoral effects of patterns of migration within Britain suggests that population movement has not in fact contributed significantly to the growth of the regional and urban–rural divides (see Denver and Halfacree, 1992a). Second, differential regional behaviour was a product of regional variations in economic well-being; put crudely, Scotland and the North have simply not been as prosperous as the South. Third, Curtice and Steed offered a purely political explanation. As the Liberals and their successors (and the nationalists in Scotland and Wales) increased in popularity from the 1970s onwards, this was generally at the expense of the locally weaker major party. Since the Conservatives were already weaker in the North and Scotland (and urban areas) they suffered more from the increase in support for 'minor' parties, and so performed more poorly relative to Labour. In the South and rural areas the picture was reversed, with Labour being the party to suffer.

Johnston and his colleagues have written extensively on this issue and they have argued that the growing regional electoral divide during the 1980s was closely related to uneven regional economic development. Areas which generally did less well under the Conservatives moved away from the party, while those which prospered deserted Labour. They suggest that government policy had a differential regional impact, making for differences in such matters as changes in levels of unemployment, in the occupational and industrial structure and in property values. Survey data showed that these changes resulted in regional variations in satisfaction with the country's economic performance and in optimism about the economic future. In turn, this was reflected in divergences in regional voting patterns. Subsequently, the slight narrowing of the divide after 1987 is again explicable in terms of reactions to regional economic circumstances.

Much of the literature on the North–South divide – especially explanations couched in terms of the rise of third parties or uneven economic development – is mainly directed towards explaining changes in regional patterns of party support since 1979 and certainly sheds a good deal of light on these changes (see Field, 1997, ch. 3, for a critical review of contemporary explanations). It is worth remembering, however, that regional differences were clear in 1955 and, indeed, long before that. Rose (1974, p. 490) demonstrates that the regional pattern of Conservative support in 1970 was very similar in every election stretching right back to 1918, while Field (1997, p. 37) shows that there was also a North–South divide in Conservative support in elections from 1885 to 1910. This suggests that a more general explanation is required than the regional effects of the policies of particular governments. Field himself suggests that such an explanation is provided by a version of 'core-periphery' theory (see also Steed, 1986). Put simply, this theory – which has been applied in a variety of disciplines – argues that Britain, like most other societies, is divided into a 'core' and a 'periphery'. The geographical core (London and the South East in this case) dominates the periphery culturally, economically and politically. Peripheral regions are poorer, suffer more in times of economic depression, have worse housing conditions, and so on. People living in these regions tend to resent the domination of the core. As a result, voters in the periphery tend to favour radical, non-establishment parties. This theory certainly does not fit the British case perfectly but it does offer some clues to understanding the long-term geographical pattern of voting in Britain. Nonetheless, in trying to explain regional electoral differentiation, analysts often invoke even vaguer ideas such as distinctive social, religious and political traditions or distinctive cultures. At root, as Curtice and Steed (1988, p. 333) imply, broad and long-lasting regional differences in party support are likely to be a product of 'cultural or historical differences and defy economic interpretations'.

Constituency variations

It hardly needs to be said that the pattern of party support varies across constituencies. Elections would be rather boring if it didn't! In general terms there is also nothing very surprising about how it varies. Given what we know about the parties and their supporters, it would raise few eyebrows to find that in the 2005 election the Conservatives performed worst in Blaenau Gwent (2.3 per cent) and best in Richmond, Yorkshire (59.1 per cent), while Labour's best show was in Bootle (75.5 per cent) and their worst in Newbury (5.9 per cent). Until the late 1960s, however, the analysis of aggregate election statistics was normally confined to the election results themselves (as in the statistical appendices to the Nuffield studies). There were very few examples of analysis that attempted to relate the distribution of party support in constituencies to their socio-economic characteristics in a systematic way. The ability of psephologists to undertake aggregate data analysis of this kind was greatly increased when census data for parliamentary constituencies were compiled and published following the 1966 sample census. Constituency data are now also available for subsequent censuses (1971, 1981, 1991, 2001).

In general terms, as suggested above, the results of these sorts of analysis are not exactly news to any observer of British electoral politics. Most people know that middle-class and rural areas usually return Conservative MPs and that working-class areas in cities tend to be Labour. With the availability of census data, however, analysts were able to bring a new precision to knowledge of this kind. Correlation coefficients enable us to tell exactly how strongly certain characteristics of constituencies are related to levels of party support; regression equations clarify the nature of such relationships and enable us to identify constituencies in which the pattern of party support deviates from what would be expected on the basis of their social composition. In short, the availability of appropriate social, demographic and economic data allows more subtle and sophisticated analysis of election results than had been possible before. Even though censuses usually take place only once every ten years, so that the data will become somewhat out of date if applied to an election that is distant in time from the census date, the fact is that in terms of their main characteristics most constituencies change only very slowly. Analysing the 2005 election on the basis of 2001 census data is, therefore, unlikely to produce seriously inaccurate results.

Table 7.3 shows correlation coefficients measuring the strength of the association between, on the one hand, the shares of the vote gained by the Conservatives, Labour and the Liberals/Liberal Democrats across constituencies in 1966 and 2005 and, on the other, variables relating to the social characteristics of the constituencies. (For an exhaustive analysis of the social correlates of constituency voting patterns in the 1966 general election see Miller, 1977.) The coefficient of 0.71 for the Conservative share in 1966 and percentage of professional and managerial workers, for example, means that the greater the proportion of the latter in a constituency, the bigger the Conservative share of the vote. On the other hand, the greater the proportion of households with no car, the smaller was the Conservative share of the vote (coefficient is negative).

In 1966, the pattern of support for the Conservatives and Labour across constituencies was clearly structured by the socio-economic characteristics of the constituencies. The class variables provide the strongest correlations but all of the others, except the percentage of residents belonging to an ethnic minority, are significant and in the expected direction. The absence of a significant association between major-party support and the proportion of a constituency's population belonging to ethnic minorities is a useful reminder of the pitfalls of inferring individual behaviour from aggregate statistics. We know from survey data that, as a matter of fact, ethnic minority voters disproportionately supported Labour. In most constituencies, however, they constituted such a small fraction of the electorate that variations in their numbers had no impact on the votes received by the parties, and

Table 7.3 Correlations between socio-economic characteristics of constituencies and party shares of vote, 1966 and 2005

	1966			2005		
	% Con.	% Lab.	% Lib.	% Con.	% Lab.	% L. Dem.
% professional and managerial	0.71	−0.82	0.24	0.57	−0.57	0.32
% manual workers	−0.68	0.71	−0.03*	−0.62	0.63	−0.33
% owner-occupiers	0.45	−0.49	0.18	0.61	−0.46	0.04*
% council tenants	−0.43	0.48	−0.13	−0.69	0.64	−0.23
% in agriculture	0.20	−0.46	0.55	0.31	−0.50	0.22
% households no car	−0.53	0.65	−0.30	−0.73	0.65	−0.16
% ethnic minority	0.01*	0.06*	−0.27	−0.22	0.24	−0.05*
Electors per hectare	−0.16	0.28	−0.34	−0.32	0.33	−0.03*
(No. of constituencies)	(617)	(617)	(310)	(625)	(625)	(625)

Notes: Asterisks indicate non-significant coefficients. The Speaker's seat is excluded in both cases and Staffordshire South (delayed election) and Wyre Forest (no Liberal Democrat) from the 2005 analysis. In 1966, '% ethnic minority' was measured as percentage born in the New Commonwealth and Pakistan.

hence the correlations are very weak. The correlations between Liberal support in 1966 and these social characteristics are only moderate. The coefficients suggest that in general the pattern of Liberal support was a sort of pale reflection of that of the Conservatives, but the level of Liberal support in a constituency was much less predictable on the basis of social characteristics than was support for the Conservatives or Labour.

Although the 2005 election was almost 40 years later, variations in party support across constituencies were patterned in much the same way as in 1966. The only major difference is that percentage ethnic minority was now significantly associated with variations in Conservative and Labour support (positively for Labour, negatively for the Conservatives). In 2005, variations in support for the Conservatives and Labour were less strongly related to the occupation variables, but most of the coefficients for the other variables are larger – indicating stronger associations – than they were in 1966. This reflects the divergences in the geography of party support discussed above. It is also the case that although the pattern of Liberal Democrat support across constituencies in 2005 was still similar to that for the Conservatives, it remained very weakly associated with variations in the socio-economic characteristics of constituencies.

The table shows that at the aggregate level there remain very strong associations between the class make-up of constituencies (measured by occupation and other class-related variables such as housing tenure) and the level of support for the Conservatives and Labour. This seems, at first sight, to contradict the argument advanced in previous chapters that, at the individual level, voting behaviour in Britain after 1970 was characterized by a loosening of the relationship between social class and party choice. In fact, however, the discrepancy between aggregate and individual data is more apparent than real. Although the strong positive correlation between the percentage of professional and managerial workers in a constituency and the percentage of Conservative voters means that the larger the proportion of these sorts of people in a constituency the greater is the Conservative share of the vote, this might reflect the fact that the more professionals and managers there are, the more *everyone,* irrespective of their class, votes Conservative. It tells us nothing about the extent of individual class voting.

In his work on this issue, Miller (1977, 1978, 1979) has shown that the relationship between the class character of constituencies and levels of support for the Conservative and Labour parties is stronger than would be expected on the basis of any given level of individual class voting. Where the Conservatives would be expected to do well on the basis of the class composition of the constituency, they do even better; where they would be expected to do badly, they do even worse. The same applies to Labour.

Constituencies, in short, are more polarized politically than people. The correlations at aggregate level are stronger than the correlation at individual level. Once again this is compatible with individual dealignment. Indeed, if more and more working-class people vote Conservative in predominantly middle-class areas, and more and more middle-class people vote Labour in predominantly working-class areas, the effect would be to produce both increased polarisation at the constituency level and decreased class voting at the level of the individual voter.

While the correlation coefficients shown in Table 7.3 are interesting and important, the various measures of social composition are themselves highly inter-correlated. Thus constituencies which have a large proportion of manual workers tend also to have large proportions of households with no car, council tenants and ethnic minority voters, as well as higher population density. As previously explained (Chapter 2), to sort out which variables are the most important influences on levels of party support and to assess the combined effects of different variables, we can undertake multivariate analysis by computing regression equations predicting party shares of the vote on the basis of the variables listed in Table 7.3. This form of analysis can select the combination of variables which gives the best prediction of the dependent variable. Remember that 'prediction' here has nothing to do with the future; what is 'predicted' is the share of the vote that the party concerned should have received in the actual election analysed, given its scores on the variables included in the equation. Equations for 2005 are shown in Table 7.4. Since the party system in Scotland and Wales is rather different from that found in England, due to the important role played by the SNP and Plaid Cymru, it would be helpful if that could be taken into account in the regression equations. The problem is that region (or in this case country) is a categorical variable. Different regions don't have different scores on 'regionality'. In order to overcome this problem, analysts frequently create what are called **'dummy' variables** by assigning scores of 0 to cases not in the category and 1 to cases which are. Here, for example, Scottish constituencies score 1 for the variable 'Scotland' and all other constituencies score zero. This is a somewhat artificial procedure and the created category has to be dichotomous (only two scores) but it does have the great advantage of allowing some categorical variables to be incorporated into ordinary regression analysis. In this case, two variables have been created: 'Scotland' and 'Wales'.

On the basis of each constituency's scores on the variables in the equations we can predict what each party's share of the vote should have been in 2005, given the constituency's characteristics. Thus, the Conservative percentage is predicted as:

Table 7.4   Multiple regression equations of party shares of vote in 2005

	% Conservative	*% Labour*	*% Liberal Democrat*
Constant	99.4	−111.1	65.4
% professional and managerial	−0.51	1.03	–
% manual	−0.82	1.35	−0.37
% owner-occupiers	–	0.57	−0.33
% council tenants	−0.16	0.45	−0.24
% agriculture	1.14	−2.34	1.29
% no car	−0.49	0.63	–
% ethnic minority electors per hectare	−0.07	0.10	−0.11
Scotland	−12.7	−4.96	–
Wales	−13.9	5.72	−3.9
r^2	0.755	0.715	0.201
(*N*)	(625)	(625)	(625)

Note: Only statistically significant coefficients are shown.

99.4 – 0.51 (% professional and managerial) – 0.82 (% manual workers) – 0.16 (% council tenants) – 0.49 (% no car) – 12.7 (Scotland) – 13.9 (Wales)

The variables for which coefficients are shown in the table are significant: they make a contribution to explaining constituency variations in support for the relevant party, even when the other significant variables are taken into account. Where no coefficient is given the variable in question is not significant. The r^2 statistics show that 75.5 per cent of the variation in the Conservative share of the vote across constituencies is explained by the equation; for Labour the figure is 71.5 per cent but for the Liberal Democrats only 20.1 per cent. The first two figures are respectable but even in these cases it is clear these regional and socio-economic factors are not the whole story (about a quarter of the variation remains unexplained) in accounting for spatial variations in Conservative and Labour support; for the Liberal Democrats they are a relatively small part of the story.

Having established the equation that best predicts a party's share of the vote across constituencies we can then calculate a predicted score for each constituency: what a party *should have* scored given the constituency's socio-economic characteristics. Comparing this with the *actual* share of vote obtained we have the **residual**, which is the difference in each constituency between the share of the vote predicted by the equations and the actual share in the election. Looking at the residual scores we can easily identify the

constituencies where each party performed exceptionally well or exception-
ally poorly. Thus, Labour underperformed most in Birmingham
Sparkbrook, Blaenau Gwent and Bethnal Green and Bow while the
Conservatives did so in City of Durham, Ceredigion and Hornsey and Wood
Green. The Liberal Democrats overperformed most in Ross, Cromarty and
Skye, Birmingham Yardley and Harrogate and Knaresborough. A look at
the 2005 election results in these constituencies should reveal why they
produced results which deviated sharply from the norm.

While examining residuals for individual constituencies is interesting,
they can also be used to explore reasons for cross-constituency variations
that are not captured by the variables in the original equations. In this case,
the residual scores suggest that the particular electoral context in constituencies – the parties which are in contention – clearly causes levels of party
support to deviate sharply from the levels predicted on the basis of social
characteristics. This can be seen in Table 7.5, which presents the mean residual scores for each party in differing electoral contexts. The Conservatives
did much worse than predicted in seats where Labour and the Liberal
Democrats were in contention, and Labour much worse where the contest
was between the Conservatives and Liberal Democrats. The Liberal
Democrats themselves performed much better than expected in these two
contexts but rather worse when the Conservatives and Labour were the top
two parties. If we add three dummy variables to the equations to take
account of these electoral contexts then the r^2 figures increase significantly
for the Conservative and Labour vote share (to 0.806 and 0.803 respectively)
while the figure for the Liberal Democrat share jumps to 0.600. In each case,
then, the ability to predict the party's share of the vote in constituencies is
markedly increased.

Table 7.5 Mean residuals for share of vote in 2005 in differing electoral
contexts

	First two parties in 2001		
	Conservative/ Labour	*Conservative/ Liberal Democrat*	*Labour/ Liberal Democrat*
Conservative	1.5	−1.3	−7.4
Labour	2.2	−8.6	−0.3
Liberal Democrats	−3.5	10.5	9.5
(*N*)	(413)	(101)	(60)

Tactical voting

The data in Table 7.5 suggest that constituency variations are partly explained by what has come to be called 'tactical voting'. This occurs when voters do not vote for the party that they prefer most, usually because it has no chance of winning the particular constituency, but vote for their second preference since that party is in a better position to defeat the party which the voter dislikes most. An alert Labour supporter in Westmorland in 2005, for example, would have been aware – or have had it drawn to his or her attention by the local Liberal Democrat campaign – that Labour had no chance of defeating the incumbent Conservative and that it might be more sensible, therefore, to vote for the Liberal Democrats who up to that point had regularly claimed second place. In Scotland and Wales, opportunities for tactical voting are even greater since the SNP and Plaid Cymru add an extra dimension to patterns of electoral competition.

Interest in tactical voting emerged in the 1980s and its extent is relevant to the main themes that I have discussed in previous chapters. We would expect voters to be more willing to vote tactically when they are dealigned rather than strongly aligned with one party or another (see Galbraith and Rae, 1989). In their report on the 1987 election, Heath *et al.* (1991, ch. 4) reported that in both 1983 and 1987 around 6 per cent of voters said that the main reason for their choice of party was tactical: that is, when asked in the BES surveys to indicate the main reason for their choice of party, they selected from the options offered: 'I really preferred another party but it had no chance of winning in this constituency.' (Other analysts, using more BES survey questions to classify voters as tactical or not, suggest that the proportion of tactical voters in 1987 was 17 per cent overall and was higher among those who were better educated, had weak party identification or lived in a constituency where tactical voting made sense: see Niemi, Whitten and Franklin, 1992.) Even on the somewhat narrow definition originally devised by Heath *et al.*, however, the proportion of tactical voters is creeping up: it was 9 per cent in both 1997 and 2001 and 12 per cent in 2005. Moreover, these voters would have been largely concentrated in seats where the structure of electoral competition lent itself to tactical voting so that in these the percentages would have been much larger.

Tactical voting is clearly reflected in election results. Although it can and does involve switching between all competing parties, Curtice and Steed's analysis of the 1997 results showed that 'voters exhibited a striking tendency to opt for whichever of the two opposition parties appeared best placed to defeat the Conservatives locally' (1997, p. 309). In the 2001 election, tactical switching by former Liberal Democrats helped to explain Labour's relatively good performances in their most marginal seats (Curtice and Steed, 2001, pp. 321–2). In 2005, however, there seemed to be an increased willingness on the part of Conservative supporters to switch to the Liberal Democrats in order to defeat incumbent Labour MPs (Curtice and Steed, 2005, pp. 243–5), so the precise form that tactical voting takes varies according to the political context.

Localities and neighbourhoods

In their pioneering study of British voting behaviour, Butler and Stokes (1974, pp. 130–7) provided survey evidence showing that the social composition of the locality in which people lived affected their party choice. Middle-class people living in mining communities were more likely to be Labour supporters, and those living in seaside resorts were more likely to be Conservatives, than the middle class as a whole; Labour support was stronger among working-class people in mining areas and weaker among the working class in seaside resorts than in the working class as a whole. Using NOP data, Butler and Stokes extended their analysis to cover a number of constituencies and showed that there was a tendency for local areas to become politically homogeneous. The more middle class a constituency, the larger the proportion of the middle class which voted Conservative; the more working class a constituency, the larger the proportion of the working class which voted Labour. Thus Butler and Stokes found evidence of a constituency effect at the individual level which was later demonstrated at aggregate level by Miller (see above).

Although Butler and Stokes described this as an effect of the local political environment, most constituencies are not natural communities; instead, they are simply slices of cities or other urban areas, combinations of towns and villages with little in common, or other contiguous areas which happen to include a convenient number of electors to form a constituency. The local political environment, it can be argued, is more local than the constituency and subsequent analyses have focused on neighbourhoods. Harrop, Heath and Openshaw (1992) used data relating to census enumeration districts (which typically contain about 190 households) to categorize the neighbourhoods lived in by 1987 BES respondents and found compelling evidence of a 'neighbourhood effect'. Whereas about 70 per cent of middle-class home owners living in 'select suburbs' voted Conservative, around 43 per cent of the same sort of people living in neighbourhoods characterized by working-class terraced housing did so. The effect of neighbourhood type persisted even when a variety of factors such as the voter's class, housing tenure, income and trade union membership were controlled. Indeed, Harrop, Heath and Openshaw's data showed (p. 105) that 'neighbourhood type proves to be just about the best single predictor [of vote] . . . knowing a person's address tells us at least as much about how he or she will vote as finding out about his or her class or [housing] tenure'.

A similar, although more complicated and fuller, analysis of neighbourhood and party choice in the 1997 election was undertaken by Johnston *et al.* (2000). Johnston and colleagues were able to place BES respondents in a variety of 'neighbourhoods' ranging from their immediate vicinity (nearest 500 persons) to the constituency as a whole. They found that there was a neighbourhood effect at every level (even after controlling for a variety of individual characteristics and the electoral context). The lower the status of the 'neighbourhood', the fewer people of all classes and types voted Conservative; the higher the 'neighbourhood' status, the more they voted Conservative. Johnston *et al.* suggest, however, that the strongest neighbourhood effect is found in 'neighbourhoods' comprising 2,500 to 5,000 residents. It is, therefore, very much a locality effect rather than a constituency-level effect.

Explaining the impact of the local political environment

In their original discussion of this subject, Butler and Stokes suggested that the tendency of localities to become politically homogeneous was caused by voters recognizing and conforming to local political values. The mechanisms by which this worked were informal: face-to-face contacts in pubs, clubs, shops, workplaces and so on. If almost everyone one meets appears to support the same party, then there is strong pressure on an individual to support that party too. A similar explanation relating to constituency effects was given by Miller (1977), who argues that the crucial feature of a voter's local environment is the concentration (or absence) of what he calls 'core' classes. These are 'controllers' (employers and managers) and 'anti-controllers' (manual workers who are trade union members). Concentrations of these classes set the tone, as it were, for an area and their influence is reinforced by personal contacts. As Miller (p. 65) puts it: 'Those who speak together vote together.' On the other hand, Dunleavy (1979, p. 413) poured scorn on the implication that 'political alignment brushes off on people by rubbing shoulders in the street' or that people picked up political signals in the bus queue or across the garden fence.

For some time the mechanisms by which people came to adopt locally dominant political norms remained a matter of speculation. In their 1992 article, however, Harrop, Heath and Openshaw went on to investigate various possibilities, including political discussion between neighbours, party activity in the locality, and parental partisanship. Their data do not offer much support for these suggestions but do suggest that there is evidence of neighbourhood self-selection. They say (p. 118) that 'consciously or not, the mobile minority migrate to politically congenial neighbourhoods'. In other words, when people move house they tend to move to areas which are predominantly of their own party colour. It is hard to believe that people weigh up the political complexion of an area to which they intend to move, however, and Harrop, Heath and Openshaw acknowledge that this pattern of behaviour is likely to be an unintended consequence of other considerations. They conclude (p. 118) that, while the evidence of a neighbourhood effect is clear, 'when we look for the mechanisms of neighbourhood influence we are less successful'.

More recently, however, Pattie and Johnston (1999, 2001) have examined in detail BES data on political conversation, considering who talks to whom and what the effects are. As it turns out, not many people talk to their neighbours about politics (only 3 per cent) but they do with their spouses (48 per cent), other family (38 per cent), friends (24 per cent) and workmates (16 per cent: see Pattie and Johnston, 1999, p. 887). In respect of vote switching between 1987 and 1992, Pattie and Johnston conclude (p. 889) that 'political conversation forms a distinct context within which people evaluate the parties and decide who to support. Conversations with supporters of a particular party encourage respondents to vote for it too.' In the context of the Labour landslide, the results for 1997 are less clear-cut but, even so, using panel data Pattie and Johnston (2001) show that conversations were associated with attitude changes and, to an extent, with vote changes. At last, it appears, we have evidence to support Miller's assertion that 'Those who speak together vote together.'

The neighbourhood effect underlies and helps to explain constituency effects, since constituencies are mostly collections of neighbourhoods. Arguably, constituency effects are then translated into regional and urban–rural divergences. This is, of course, not the whole story in terms of explaining the kind of regional variations and urban–rural differences discussed above; nonetheless it appears to be a significant piece in the puzzle of explaining long-standing spatial variations in party choice. In the next section, however, we turn from discussing the causes of spatial variation to a consideration of its consequences, particularly in relation to the operation of the electoral system.

Electoral systems in Britain

All voting takes place in the context of a particular electoral system. There has to be some agreed way of aggregating votes to produce a result. Votes indicate individuals' preferences and in public elections these have to be translated into seats (in Parliament, local councils or whatever) by some formula. There are many different electoral systems: in the 1990s, a cross-national study found 70 different systems in 27 democracies (Lijphart, 1994; for a useful introduction to the operation of different systems see Farrell, 2001). In evaluating electoral systems, or making an argument in favour of one system or another, it is important to consider what a particular (or an ideal) system is, or should be, for. What is it, or should it be, designed to achieve? There are at least three simple answers to this question:

(a)   to enable the representation of voters' opinions in rough proportion to their strength in the electorate;
(b)   to allow for the representation of geographically-defined areas;
(c)   to decisively confer power on a team of leaders or a party.

No system can do all of these at the same time, and ultimately a preference for one sort or another comes down to making a value judgement about which of these purposes should be given greatest priority.

In Britain, until recently almost all public elections were conducted under what is formally known as the Single Member, Simple Plurality system (SMSP). Each electoral district (constituency) has a single representative, and he or she wins by virtue of getting most votes (a simple plurality) in the area concerned. This is more commonly known – in an analogy with horse-racing – as the first-past-the-post system (FPTP). For a long time, interest in the possibility of changing the British electoral system was confined to a small band of enthusiasts (who might be labelled 'anoraks' by unfriendly critics) and few took the possibility seriously. That is not the case today. As part of its devolution programme, the Labour government elected in 1997 introduced new electoral systems for the Scottish Parliament and the Welsh and Northern Ireland Assemblies, and also brought in new electoral systems for the European Parliament and for electing mayors in England and the London Assembly. The various electoral systems now in operation in the UK are listed in Table 7.6.

FPTP is now confined to electing the House of Commons and local councils. From 2007, however, Scottish councils will be elected using the single transferable vote (STV), a much more proportional system. As far as the Commons is concerned, the incoming Labour government in 1997 initially

Table 7.6　UK electoral systems today

System	Body elected
Single Member, Simple Plurality	House of Commons
	Some English/Welsh local authorities
	All Scottish councils (until 2007)
Multi-Member, Simple Plurality	Some English/Welsh local authorities
Additional Member System	Scottish Parliament
	Welsh Assembly
	London Assembly
Single Transferable Vote	Northern Ireland Assembly
	All Scottish Councils (from 2007)
Regional Party (Closed) Lists	European Parliament
Supplementary Vote	Mayors in England

promised that there would be a referendum on whether to change the system. In preparation for this a commission (the Jenkins Commission) was set up to devise an alternative to FPTP that could be put to the people in a referendum. The commission reported in October 1998 (Jenkins, 1998), suggesting a mixed system whereby the majority of MPs would be elected by the Alternative Vote system in constituencies and additional members would also be elected in such a way as to produce greater proportionality (see Dunleavy and Margetts, 1999). Although the proposals were carefully crafted to have wide appeal, there has been no sign of the promised referendum.

Criticisms of first-past-the-post

Why has there been so much recent debate about, and activity in relation to, electoral systems in Britain? Why do so many people appear to have lost faith in the tried and trusted method of electing MPs? Two major reasons relate to how the system has operated in translating votes into seats, but other criticisms focus on the activities of the parties and effects on voters.

The first criticism is that FPTP is simply unfair. The shares of seats that parties receive do not reflect their shares of votes; in particular, the Liberal Democrats have been severely underrepresented. In the four elections from 1992 they won, respectively, 18.3, 17.2, 18.8 and 22.6 per cent of the votes but only 3.1, 7.2, 8.1 and 9.9 per cent of the seats. Put another way, in 2005 the number of votes cast for the Liberal Democrats per seat won was 96,539, while for the Conservatives it was 44,354 and for Labour 26,908. The next biggest party in terms of popular support (UKIP) won over 600,000 votes but no seats at all.

These sorts of discrepancies between votes and seats occur because the geographical distribution of a party's support is almost as important as its level: the system rewards parties with concentrations of support and penalizes those whose support is more evenly spread. Thus the system regularly produces disproportionality between votes and seats and, indeed, on two occasions (1951 and February 1974) the party winning most votes did not win most seats and thus 'lost' the election. In the past few elections, this disproportionality has strongly advantaged Labour to the extent that all commentators now agree that the system is biased in Labour's favour (see, for example, Blau, 2001; Curtice, 2001; Johnston *et al.,* 2001; Johnston, Rossiter and Pattie, 2006). In 2005, for example, the Conservatives polled more votes than Labour in England but won 92 fewer seats. If, at the election after 2005, the Conservatives achieved a uniform swing across the country of 1.5 per cent then that would bring them level with Labour in terms of votes, yet Labour would still have 111 more seats in the Commons. In fact, the Conservatives would have to be 6.4 points ahead of Labour before they would draw level in terms of seats (Curtice, Fisher and Steed, 2005, p. 251). The bias of the FPTP system in favour of Labour arises for three main reasons. First, seats won by Labour tend to have smaller electorates than those won by the Conservatives. Second, turnout is generally lower – fewer votes are cast – in seats that Labour wins. Third, the Labour vote happens to be more efficiently distributed across constituencies in that they win quite a lot of seats by fairly narrow margins rather than piling up huge majorities in a smaller number of bastions. Paradoxically, the Conservatives are strongly opposed to electoral reform (at present) even though they are severely penalized by the current system.

Supporters of FPTP see its unfairness or disproportionality as a virtue. In particular, it is claimed that in translating votes to seats the system exaggerates the lead of the winning party in a predictable way and thus ensures that the winner has a clear majority. Critics have suggested, however, that the changes in the geographical distribution of party support discussed above have led to a situation in which the system cannot be relied upon to do what it is supposed to do (see Curtice and Steed, 1982, 1986). In the 1950s and before, the share of seats that a party was going to obtain in the House of Commons, on the basis of a given share of the total national vote, could be predicted fairly well by using the 'cube rule' (sometimes also called the 'cube law'). If the share of votes between two parties were in the ratio A:B, then the share of seats would be in the ratio $A^3:B^3$. Thus, if the ratio of the two-party vote were 3:2, then the ratio of seats would be 27:8 (3 × 3 × 3:2 × 2 × 2). In other words, a party which obtained 60 per cent of the votes would get 77 per cent of the seats, while the other party with 40 per cent of the votes would get only 23 per cent of the seats. Clearly, then, the winning party's lead in terms of votes was greatly exaggerated by the electoral system when it was translated into seats, and it was widely assumed that the cube rule was an integral aspect of FPTP. In fact, the cube rule only worked if the votes of the major parties were geographically distributed across constituencies in a particular way, and regional and urban/rural divergence from 1955 to 1997 significantly changed the distributions. (For the cube rule to work, the distribution of the vote shares of each party across constituencies had to be close to a normal distribution with a standard deviation of 13.7.)

In general, the effect of regional divergence was to make Labour seats more safely Labour, and Conservative seats more safely Conservative. As a result, there were fewer and fewer marginal seats. In 1955, some 166 seats could be classed as marginal but by 1983 there were only 80 (Curtice and Steed, 1986, p. 214). There were thus fewer seats for a party to gain for each percentage point swing in its favour, and fewer to be lost by incumbents for each point of swing against their party. Much bigger swings in votes were now required for the party in opposition to gain enough seats to achieve a majority in the House of Commons. The exaggerative quality of the electoral system declined such that the ratio of seats to votes could no longer be predicted by a 'cube rule', or even a 'square rule'. Indeed, by the 1992 election the electoral system failed to produce any exaggerative effect at all. The ratio of Conservative to Labour votes was 55:45 and the ratio of Conservative to Labour seats won was also 55:45 (see Curtice, 1992). In the extraordinary circumstances of the 1997 Labour landslide, however, the ratio of Conservative to Labour seats was once again close to fulfilling the cube rule, while in both 2001 and 2005 there was an even greater disparity than the cube rule would imply. Clearly, the operation of the system is not predictable; in the last three elections it is not simply that there was a 'winner's bonus' but rather a clear bias in favour of Labour.

From the point of view of the voters, a major criticism of FPTP is that it results in many votes being wasted. In 2005, only around 48 per cent of voters voted for a winning candidate; the votes of the remaining 52 per cent could be said to have been wasted in that they did not help to elect anyone. If the definition of wasted votes is extended to include those which only serve to pile up large majorities for one party or another then the percentage of votes wasted would be even larger. It is undoubtedly the case that many voters have voted in general elections for all of their lives without ever voting for a winner. It could be argued that these voters are, therefore, unrepresented and that there is little incentive for people to vote in constituencies where the same party always wins. In addition, critics suggest that FPTP limits the choices that voters can make. They have to 'plump' for one candidate or another (the one selected by local party members), whereas under some other systems they can rank their preferences or indicate their support for a particular candidate of their party.

The electoral system also affects how parties campaign. Increasingly campaigns are focused on 'target' or 'key' seats, and the major parties almost ignore constituencies in which they have little chance of winning (see Denver *et al.*, 2002). This sort of skewed campaigning would be avoided if all votes counted equally no matter where they were cast.

Two final (more general) points of criticism are worth mentioning. First, because FPTP produces even greater disproportionality at regional level than over the country as a whole, Conservative and Labour representation in the House of Commons is heavily weighted to specific areas. After the 2005 election 57 per cent of Labour MPs represented constituencies in Scotland, Wales and the North of England compared with 12 per cent of Conservative MPs. On the other hand, 61 per cent of Conservative MPs were from constituencies in the South of England outside London compared with 13 per cent of Labour MPs. Second, it might be argued that although the system produces majority governments, which can then operate as almost an 'elected dictatorship', governments actually lack legitimacy since they have not been voted in by a majority. Indeed, in the elections of 1992, 1997, 2001 and 2005 the percentages of the eligible electorate in the UK as a whole (rather than of those who voted) that voted for the party which went on to form the government were, respectively, 32.6, 30.8, 24.2 and 21.6. That is not exactly a solid basis on which to govern.

In defence of first-past-the-post

Although these criticisms have persuaded many people that reform of the electoral system for Westminster is long overdue, FPTP still has its defenders among academics as well as practising politicians (Chandler, 1982; Hain, 1998). Five main points are frequently made in defence of the system.

First, it is easy for voters to operate and understand. Survey evidence relating to the use of the Additional Member System in the Scottish Parliament election of 1999 suggests that operating it was not much of a problem: only 10 per cent found filling in the ballot papers very or fairly difficult. On the other hand, the translation of votes into seats under other systems can be complicated, and 48 per cent of Scottish respondents found it very or fairly difficult to understand how the allocation of seats was worked out (Paterson *et al.*, 2001).

Second, the system maintains a clear link between MPs and their constituents. This link is particularly valued by MPs themselves and their attachment to it represents a major stumbling block to radical reform, since any change would have to be approved by MPs elected under the current system. It was for this reason that the Jenkins Commission's proposed alternative to FPTP still allowed the great majority of MPs to be elected directly from constituencies.

Third, FPTP tends to prevent 'fringe' or extremist parties gaining representation. Whereas a more proportional system might allow the BNP or UKIP to win a few seats, they are effectively excluded under FPTP, since the voters are encouraged to concentrate on the parties having a reasonable chance of winning their constituency. In addition, it is suggested that the major parties are forced by the system to be moderate since they are aware that dropping only a few points in vote share can result in the loss of many seats.

Fourth, alternatives to FPTP give too much power and influence to small parties. Since neither of the major parties would win a majority under a more proportional system a small party – for which not many people voted – could effectively decide who formed the government. Thus FPTP militates against coalitions. A single party can form the government and thus the lines of responsibility are clear. The electors know which party to blame if things go awry or to reward if it is seen to be successful.

Finally, an associated argument claims that a strength of FPTP is that it enables the voters to choose the government. In proportional systems, which do not create majorities in legislatures where none exists among the voters, there is often a gap between an election and the formation of a government during which the politicians negotiate. Deals are struck without reference to the voters, and governments emerge which sometimes comprise surprising coalition partners.

Arguments about the electoral system go backwards and forwards (proponents of change could produce counter-arguments to the five listed in defence of FPTP), and there is certainly more interest in the subject than there used to be. As indicated above, however, coming to a decision about which electoral system is 'best', or whether the current Westminster system should be reformed, is ultimately a question of values. Is it more important to have a governing party with a majority or to give fair representation to various shades of opinion? Is it acceptable to make it difficult for fringe parties to win seats? Is maintaining the link between MPs and constituents more valuable than having a system which allows more voters to have an influence on who is elected? People will have different views on these questions and these views will lead them to different conclusions about the advisability or otherwise of retaining FPTP for Westminster elections.

Voting under different electoral systems

There have now been two rounds of elections to the Scottish Parliament and the National Assembly for Wales (1999 and 2003) with the third to follow in 2007. In these elections a modified 'additional member' electoral system is used. Electors are asked to cast two votes. The first is to elect a constituency representative under the familiar FPTP rules. In addition, however, they vote for a party list within regions (eight in Scotland and five in Wales), and these votes are used to elect 'additional' or 'top-up' members after taking account of the number of constituency seats that each party has already won in the region concerned (see Curtice and Steed, 2000).

In both countries and in both elections, Labour easily won a majority of seats on the basis of the constituency results but, when the additional or list members were included, things became more complicated. In Scotland in both 1999 and 2003 no party had an overall majority and a Labour–Liberal Democrat coalition was formed to govern the country. In Wales, a similar coalition was eventually formed after the 1999 elections but in 2003 Labour won exactly half of the seats in the Assembly and on that basis was able to govern alone. The new electoral system, therefore, has importantly affected the outcomes of the elections and subsequent political developments in the two countries.

Surveys have found that electors in both countries rather like the new system and recognize its advantages, although in Scotland at least there was some decline in the popularity of the system between 1999 and 2003 (Curtice *et al.*, 2000; Curtice, 2004). Voting behaviour has also clearly been affected by the new system. In Scotland, about 20 per cent of voters 'split their tickets' in 1999 by voting for different parties in the constituency and list contests and the figure was around 29 per cent in 2003. Clear evidence of the effects of this is that in 2003 there were 7 Greens, 6 Scottish Socialists and one Senior Citizens' Party representative elected on list votes. In addition, opinion poll evidence suggests that Scottish voters bring different considerations to bear when deciding which party to support in Scottish elections and UK-wide general elections. Scottish opinion polls regularly report that larger proportions intend to vote SNP and smaller proportions to vote Labour in the former than in the latter. Analysis of survey data leads Paterson *et al.* (2001, ch. 3) to argue that, in the context of Scottish Parliament elections, more voters are concerned to support a party (the SNP) which they think is more likely to 'stand up for Scotland', to promote and to advance the country's interests within the UK, than is the case at general elections. The same is true of Wales. Here, about 25 per cent of voters 'split their tickets' in 1999 and once again there is evidence that many voters did so for understandable reasons (Curtice and Steed, 2000). The surprisingly good performance of Plaid Cymru in 1999 – although no doubt influenced by the immediate context of the election – seems also to indicate a willingness on the part of voters to desert their normal party in the context of Assembly elections. In summary, then, both the electoral system and devolution itself appear to have influenced the voting decisions of significant proportions of the Scottish and Welsh electorates.

Londoners have also had experience of using a novel electoral system in elections for a Mayor and Assembly in 2000 and 2004. In these cases three votes could be cast: one for the Mayor (in which voters could indicate a first and second preference among candidates), one for a constituency Assembly member and one for a party list for the Assembly. If turnout is a guide, then London voters have been less enamoured of the new way of voting than the Scots and Welsh: only 31 per cent voted in the Assembly election in 2000 and 36 per cent in 2004. It should be remembered, however, that these are essentially local elections. In addition, significant proportions of those who voted did not appear to understand what they were being asked to do since in these elections there was a much larger number of rejected or invalid ballots than would be normal in first-past-the-post elections. Nonetheless, the mayoral results show, overall, perfectly logical patterns of first and second preferences. As far as Assembly voting is concerned, about one-third of voters chose different parties at constituency and list level in 2000 and about 40 per cent in 2004 (Dunleavy, Margetts and Bastow, 2001; Margetts, van Heerde and Dunleavy 2005). The effect of using the system was to produce fairer results. The FPTP constituency elections in 2004 produced 9 Conservative and 5 Labour Assembly members but, as a result of the list votes, 2 Labour, 5 Liberal Democrat, 2 Green and 2 UKIP members were added. In concluding their detailed study of the 2001 London elections, Dunleavy, Margetts and Barstow argue that the FPTP system has severely constrained the choices that voters can make and conclude (p. 32) that 'London voters have complex preference structures which they were able to signal in sophisticated ways . . . using the opportunities provided by the [new] electoral systems.'

Conclusion

These are, then, exciting times for electoral reformers and debates about the future of the Westminster system will continue for the foreseeable future. What is certain is that the context provided by the electoral system affects electoral behaviour. It is worth remembering that the influential Michigan model focusing on party identification, and the Butler–Stokes model derived from it, were both developed in the context of FPTP elections. When the electoral system does not require voters to 'plump' for a single party then the usefulness of party identification in explaining party choice is likely to be reduced. With more choices to be made, more subtle explanations are required.

There is no doubt that the ways in which electoral systems – especially FPTP – translate votes into seats is strongly affected by the geographical or spatial distribution of party support. Changes in that distribution have also been one of the key features of British elections over the past 50 years. It is something of an exaggeration to say that 'Geography reigns – supreme!', which is how Johnston *et al.* conclude their (2001) study of the operation of the electoral system in Britain. Nonetheless, in electoral studies, geography does matter.

8
Elections and Party Choice in Contemporary Britain

One of the pleasures – and, occasionally, frustrations – of studying elections is that they keep happening. No sooner, it seems, have the data from one general election been collected, analysed and pored over than people are looking forward to the next. In addition, once every five years there are elections to the European Parliament, and these tend to fall conveniently (for analysts, if not governments) in the mid-term of the Westminster Parliament (1999, 2004, and so on). There are now also elections to the Scottish Parliament and Welsh Assembly and, if that were not enough, there are annual rounds of local elections. 'Elections galore!', one might say, and certainly more than enough to satisfy the keenest enthusiast and keep electoral analysts busy. The fact that there is always another election just around the corner means that there can be no 'last word' as far as explaining voting behaviour is concerned. Explanations of how individuals come to make their choices have to be refined; the outcomes of particular elections require explanation. The simple passage of time – with associated social changes and changes in the parties themselves – means that well-established theories have to be re-examined. In addition, the introduction of more proportional electoral systems has meant that voting decisions have become more complex; there is more to understand than there used to be.

In this concluding chapter, I review the theories of party choice introduced in Chapter 1 and suggest how election outcomes are best explained in modern circumstances. Before doing so, however, it is worth making a few comments about the role of theories in electoral analysis. These theories – frequently also called models – attempt to provide explanations as to why people vote the way that they do (and whether they vote at all). It is clear, however, that no theory can possibly account for the millions of individual decisions made in an election. Over the whole electorate there is an immense variety of motives for party choice; individual voters also frequently have a number of different considerations in mind when marking their ballot paper for one party or another. Models of party choice are bound, therefore, to be partial, to simplify and to generalize. Nonetheless, they provide a framework within which relevant data can be collected and interpreted. Thus the 'social determinism' model suggested that belonging to certain social groups importantly affects party choice. Consequently, voting surveys ask respondents for the relevant details and analysts can check whether or not the claims made by the theory are borne out by the data. Other models point to different questions that should be asked. Models offer, therefore, different perspectives on the same problem, but none is going to tell the whole story.

Explaining party choice

'Social determinism'

I labelled the first model described in Chapter 1 as 'social determinism'. The name might imply a simple deterministic link: people vote for a party because of their social location. In its original version at least, however, it is not as simple as that. The link exists because different groups have different interests and different parties seek to represent those interests. However, there is broad agreement among those who study elections that the link between the social characteristics of individual voters and their party choice has weakened over the past 40 years or so. In the BES study of the 2001 election, Clarke *et al.* (2004, ch. 3), having described the weakening of the alignment between class and party, show that there has been no corresponding increase in the explanatory power of other social and demographic characteristics and conclude that, overall, what they call the 'sociological approach' has declined in importance. 'Those wishing to understand electoral choice in present-day Britain', they say, 'must look elsewhere' (p. 123). Nonetheless, it remains the case that some different social groups tend to vote in significantly different ways.

Table 8.1 shows, firstly, that in 2005 those with manual occupations were still more likely to vote Labour and less likely to vote Conservative than routine non-manual workers and those with professional and managerial occupations. There is also a class dimension to support for the Liberal Democrats, who were weakest among manual workers. The figures relating to age groups are a little more complicated but there are clear patterns. Support for the Conservatives tends to increase and that for Labour to decline with age. The oldest voters – presumably being more set in their ways – were also least inclined to support the Liberal Democrats who outpolled the Conservatives among the two youngest age groups. The fact that Conservative support increased with age in 2005, just as it did in 1970 (although at a generally higher level in the latter case: see Table 3.3), suggests that this tendency is to be explained in terms of 'life cycles' rather than 'political generations' or 'electoral cohorts' since it has persisted over 35 years as different generations have moved through the electorate.

According to the BES data, there was a slight tendency for women to be more Conservative than men in 2005 but they were just as likely to vote Labour or Liberal Democrat. More detailed analysis shows that it is only

Table 8.1   Social characteristics and party choice in 2005 (row percentages)

	Conservative	Labour	Liberal Democrat	(N)
Occupational class				
Professional and managerial	35	34	26	(1,057)
Other non-manual	39	35	20	(908)
Manual	21	53	18	(715)
Age				
18–24	18	46	30	(223)
25–34	23	45	27	(398)
35–44	22	48	21	(585)
45–54	36	35	25	(505)
55–64	39	33	21	(503)
65+	41	36	18	(724)
Sex				
Male	29	40	23	(1,390)
Female	34	39	22	(1,547)
Housing tenure				
Owner-occupier	36	36	22	(2,336)
Renter	15	54	25	(577)
Religion				
None	23	42	26	(1,143)
Anglican	44	35	18	(1,065)
Scots Presbyterian	25	41	20	(109)
Roman Catholic	28	49	20	(271)
Nonconformist	33	39	20	(138)
Non-Christian	22	53	26	(101)

Note: Rows do not total 100 because votes for others are not shown. The BES survey overestimated the Labour share of the vote (by 3.5 points) and slightly underestimated the shares obtained by the Conservatives and 'others'. What is important here, however, is not the precise shares of votes indicated but the differences between the different groups.
Source: Data from BES 2005 cross-section survey.

among those aged 35–44 and the over-65s that there is a significant difference in party choice between men and women, with the latter being more inclined to the Conservatives. We have already seen that by 1966 the difference between men and women in respect of party choice was relatively small (Table 3.4). Over the subsequent 40 years the position of women has changed markedly – a much larger proportion go out to work, for example – but traces of the traditional tendency for women to be more Conservative than men still remain.

The great majority of voters own (or are buying) their homes, and so it is also not surprising that the voting of owner-occupiers in 2005 was similar to the overall outcome of the election. However, those who rent, either from the local council or privately (which includes many young people), are strongly anti-Conservative and pro-Labour. Finally, religion or denomination continues to be related to party choice. The most strongly pro-Labour group is non-Christians (mainly members of ethnic minorities) followed by Roman Catholics and those with no religious attachment. The most Conservative group are Anglicans, while Liberal Democrat support is greatest among those with no religion and non-Christians. In the latter case, this is probably due to some ethnic minority voters (especially Muslims) switching to the Liberal Democrats in 2005 as a consequence of the Party's stance on the Iraq war. Hitherto, all available evidence suggested that members of ethnic minorities heavily favoured Labour. In the 1997 BES survey, for example, a special 'booster sample' of ethnic minority respondents was included and on the basis of these data Saggar (1998, p. 35) reported that 81 per cent of Asians voted Labour, as did 89 per cent of black voters. There was no similar study in 2001 or 2005, however, and the numbers of ethnic minority voters in the BES samples is too small for detailed analysis.

As explained in previous chapters, we can use logistic regression analysis to examine the combined effects of these variables on party choice. In particular, the results of this procedure tell us whether a particular variable has a significant independent effect while the others in the analysis are held constant. Table 8.2 reports the results of three such analyses. The first compares voting Conservative with voting for any other party, the second makes the same comparison for Labour voters while the third compares Conservative and Labour voters only. Summarizing all three analyses, it is clear that occupational class still makes some difference. Taking all the other variables into account, there were no significant differences between professionals and managers (the reference category) and the 'other non-manual' group, but manual workers were about half as likely to vote Conservative and around twice as likely to vote Labour. The effect of age is also clear: the analysis confirms that those aged over 45 were significantly more likely to vote

Conservative and less likely to vote Labour in 2005, other things being equal. There are no significant differences between men and women, but renters were clearly more inclined to Labour than owner-occupiers. In the straight Labour–Conservative comparison, the former were three times more likely to vote Labour than the latter. The figures for religious attachment show that those with no attachment, Roman Catholics, Nonconformists and Scottish Protestants were less likely to vote Conservative than Anglicans and, especially in the straight two-party comparison, more inclined to Labour. The coefficients for non-Christians are as would be expected, but (due to the small numbers involved) are not statistically significant.

Table 8.2   Logistic regression analysis of Conservative and Labour voting in 2005 (social variables)

	Conservative versus others	Labour versus others	Labour versus Conservative
Class (Reference = professional and managerial)			
Other non-manual	1.07	1.05	1.05
Manual	**0.53**	**1.93**	**2.31**
Age (Reference = 18–34)			
Aged 35–44	0.75	1.28	**1.39**
Aged 45–54	**1.34**	**0.74**	**0.66**
Aged 55–64	**1.66**	**0.66**	**0.53**
Aged 65 +	**1.82**	**0.72**	**0.51**
Sex (Reference = male)			
Female	1.06	1.11	0.98
Tenure (Reference = owner-occupier)			
Renter	**0.38**	**1.86**	**3.00**
Religion (Reference = Anglican)			
None	**0.45**	**1.31**	**1.95**
Roman Catholic	**0.54**	**1.71**	**2.06**
Nonconformist	**0.49**	1.37	**1.86**
Scottish Presbyterian	**0.39**	1.24	**2.03**
Non-Christian	0.15	1.34	1.54
Nagelkerke r^2	0.141	0.086	0.180
% correctly classified (original)	67.4	60.6	54.7
% correctly classified (equation)	70.4	63.5	66.3
% correctly classified (change)	3.0	2.9	11.6
(*N* of cases)	(2,755)	(2,755)	(1,886)

Note: Significant odds ratios ($p < 0.05$) are shown in bold.

It is instructive to compare Table 8.2 with the equivalent analyses of the 1964 election (Table 3.6). In this case, the r^2 statistics (estimating the amount of variation in party choice explained by the equations) are much smaller, as are the changes in the proportion of respondents whose party choice is correctly classified on the basis of the equations. Whereas in 1964 knowing voters' social characteristics improved our ability to classify them as Conservative or 'other' by around 12 points, as Labour or 'other' by 19 points and as Labour or Conservative by 20 points, the relative improvements in 2005 were only 3 points in the first two cases and 12 points in the third. This confirms that party choice is now less influenced than it used to be by these social variables at least, and that the 'social determinism' model is correspondingly less useful. In many ways this is not at all surprising. One of the aims of the New Labour leadership in the 1990s was to broaden the party's appeal and make it into a 'catch all' party (see Heath, Jowell and Curtice, 2001). Nonetheless, as Table 8.2 indicates, Labour still retains an edge among its traditional sources of support.

Few electoral analysts would now subscribe to 'social determinism' in its original form (although social background variables are almost always included in analyses as controls when the effects of other sorts of variables are being investigated). An alternative version focuses not on the objective social characteristics of voters but on their *social identities* (see Norris, 1997a). It is not whether a person is a manual worker that matters, for example, but whether he or she feels 'working class' or not. This is a more useful approach: national identity is an important influence on voting in Scotland and Wales, for example, and there are regional and local identities within England that might be important. It is also the case that class identity is a better predictor of party choice than objective class. It is not clear, however, that age or housing tenure can be clearly linked to the idea of identities.

The 'Butler–Stokes' model

Although it contained many nuances and subtleties, the central element of the model used by Butler and Stokes to explain voting in Britain in the 1960s, itself a version of the 'Michigan model' developed in the United States, was the concept of what they called 'partisanship'. More commonly called 'party identification', this referred to the enduring attachments that voters had to one party or another. At the time, it was widely accepted that party identification (together with class voting) provided a good explanation of party choice in Britain. As time has passed, however, doubts have arisen. As we have seen (Chapter 4), one area of doubt concerns the survey question used to elicit party identification. When respondents are offered the opportunity to say that they do *not* 'generally think of themselves as' party supporters, fewer party identifiers are found. Another concerns the stability of identification over time. If identification really does relate to an 'enduring attachment' to a party then the identification of individuals should be very stable over time. Clarke *et al.* (2004, ch. 6) cite various panel survey studies which suggest that for a sizeable minority of voters this is not the case. For example, in the 1960s over four interviews (1963, 1964, 1966 and 1970), only 61 per cent of respondents identified with the same party. Similarly, over four more recent interviews (1998, 1999, 2000, 2001) the proportion was 64 per cent. In addition, monthly data collected by Gallup between January 1992 and December 2002 showed that identification with the Conservatives ranged from 21 per cent to 37 per cent, with Labour from 30 per cent to 54 per cent and with the Liberal Democrats from 7 per cent to 19 per cent. These figures suggest that either many people do *not* have an enduring attachment to a party, which they stick to through good times and bad, or the standard survey questions do not tap the attachments that exist.

In any event, even on the basis of the standard question asked at each election we have seen that the strength of party identification in Britain has sharply declined (Figure 4.2). There are, of course, still some strong party identifiers around for whom supporting their party at an election is more or less automatic, but they are thinner on the ground. It is also the case that, as before, in 2005 those who said that they identified with a party overwhelmingly voted for it. Thus 91 per cent of Conservative identifiers voted Conservative, with the relevant figure for Labour being 87 per cent and for the Liberal Democrats 83 per cent. Nonetheless, the proportion of electors whose voting can be explained as being a consequence of their being socialized by their parents and other personal contacts into a specific party identity, which then colours their whole approach to politics, has diminished and looks likely to diminish further.

Models based on rational choice

No one imagines that voting decisions are, or ever have been, made on the basis of 'pure' rational choice criteria. That would involve voters consciously weighing up the costs and benefits to themselves of voting for one party or another, on the basis of ample information, and then supporting the one which would maximize the benefits and minimize the costs. Nonetheless, rational choice theory has inspired a whole family of explanations for party support, each of which sees the voter as making a more or less conscious choice. The two key approaches are issue voting and valence voting.

The *issue voting* approach suggests that voters make up their minds on the basis of what they perceive to be the key issues in an election. They have opinions about these issues, know the stances of the parties and vote for the one which, overall, advocates policies of which they approve most. A variant of issue voting suggests that it is not so much their preferences on issues of the day which influence voting choices but the more general political values or principles that voters hold. Proponents of this approach pay more attention to voters' stances on broader political questions that have been around a long time (nationalization versus privatization of industry, for example, or the balance between taxation and welfare benefits) than to their opinions on contemporary issues.

As described in Chapter 5, *valence voting* is basically about the voters making judgements. These relate to three overlapping areas. First, voters react to the performance of the government and/or the opposition. In this view, elections constitute a judgement on a party's tenure of office, enabling the people to hold their governors accountable. Taking everything into account – including how well the alternative government (the opposition) might have performed – voters decide whether to confirm the government in office or vote to 'throw the rascals out'. Second, voters are influenced in particular by how well the government has managed the economy. They may consider their own situation or the situation of the country as a whole; they may focus on past performance or future prospects. For some analysts, however, economic considerations such as these are uppermost in the voters' minds when an election comes along. Finally – and unsurprisingly in a television-dominated age – judgements about party leaders now weigh heavily in the scales when voting decisions are being made. Indeed, making a judgement about the leaders can be seen as a short-cut which avoids making more complex judgements. It may not be so much the details of the leaders' performances that are important but the general image that they convey: whether they seem likeable, honest, decisive, caring and have a strong personality, for example.

These two approaches do not exhaust the kinds of explanation for party choice that have their roots in rational choice theory. It is clear, for example, that voters react in understandable ways to changes or variations in the contexts of elections. Parties themselves may change. Labour's sharp move to the left in the 1980s clearly put off more moderate voters, while the change from 'Old' to 'New' Labour in the 1990s probably disillusioned some traditional supporters but also won new support among the less committed. Similarly, the electoral context (the scope for tactical voting or the electoral system used) influences party choice in ways that could be described as 'rational'.

The impact of issue and valence voting in 2005 is illustrated in Table 8.3, which again reports the results of three logistic regression analyses. Three preliminary points should be made about the table. First, it is not intended to be a comprehensive analysis of party choice in the 2005 election but merely to illustrate the importance of electors' judgements. A whole variety of other variables could have been selected for inclusion but, for my purposes, there is no need to debate this at length or to explain in detail how the variables used were created from the original data. Second, it should be emphasized that the social background variables shown in Table 8.2 were also included in these analyses. Thus the table shows the effects of various judgements while still taking account of the impact of class and the other social variables, although coefficients for the latter are not shown. Third, it is worth saying again that the coefficients listed are odds ratios, indicating the odds that a respondent in the category concerned voted for the first-named party in the column heading as compared to a respondent in the reference category, while holding all other variables constant. Thus, all things considered, compared with those who thought that the economic situation would stay the same, those who expected that the country's economic situation would get worse were less than half as likely to vote Labour rather than Conservative (0.46), just over half as likely to vote Labour rather than for another party (0.59) and 1.38 times more likely to vote Conservative than for another party.

The general pattern of coefficients in the main part of the table is much as would be anticipated. As has just been pointed out, economic pessimists were more likely to support the Conservatives and less likely to support Labour as opposed to other parties although the party preferences of optimists, who thought things would get better, were not significantly different from those of the reference group. Those who thought that the issue that they nominated as the single most important in the general election would be best handled by one of the parties were much more likely to vote for that party and less likely to vote for another than the reference group.

Attitudes to the government's handling of the economy appear to have made relatively little difference to whether people voted Conservative or not, once the other factors are taken into account. On the other hand, both those who thought that the government had handled the economy well and those who thought it had done so badly were significantly more likely to vote Labour than those who had no opinion. This is a somewhat quirky result. It should be emphasized that simple cross-tabulations show the expected pattern: Labour voting stood at 45 per cent among those who thought that the

Table 8.3   Logistic regression analysis of Conservative and Labour voting in 2005 (social plus issue/valence variables)

	Conservative versus others	Labour versus others	Labour versus Conservative
General economic expectations (Reference = same/don't know)			
Get worse	**1.38**	**0.59**	**0.46**
Get better	0.68	0.95	1.38
Best party to handle most important issue (Reference = none/don't know)			
Conservative	**6.00**	**0.27**	**0.10**
Labour	**0.26**	**4.40**	**7.19**
Liberal Democrat	**0.09**	**0.42**	**4.48**
Other	0.58	0.94	1.00
Government handled economy (Reference = neither/don't know)			
Well	0.76	**1.95**	**2.13**
Badly	0.90	**2.11**	**2.32**
Feelings about party leaders (Reference = neutral/don't know)			
Dislikes Blair	**2.78**	**0.20**	**0.09**
Likes Blair	**0.33**	**5.06**	**6.62**
Dislikes Howard	**0.12**	**2.32**	**15.02**
Likes Howard	**7.17**	**0.47**	**0.14**
Dislikes Kennedy	**2.18**	**1.89**	0.89
Likes Kennedy	**0.41**	**0.58**	1.61
Nagelkerke r^2	0.725	0.650	0.851
% correctly classified (original)	67.0	60.9	54.3
% correctly classified (equation)	88.1	84.6	92.4
% correctly classified (change)	21.1	23.7	38.1
(Weighted *N*)	(2,664)	(2,664)	(1,820)

Note: Significant odds ratios ($p < 0.05$) are shown in bold. Respondents' class, sex, religion, housing tenure and age were included in the analysis but, for the sake of clarity, the figures are not shown here.
Source: Date from BES 2005 cross-section survey.

government had done well in this area and 12 per cent among those who thought it had done badly. However, only a small minority of respondents (12 per cent) was unimpressed with the government's economic performance, and once the other variables are taken into account this did not seem to make much difference to their vote.

The last set of odds ratios relate to whether or not respondents liked or disliked the party leaders (or were neutral towards them: the reference category), and they tell a clear story. Those who disliked Blair were almost three times more likely than those who were neutral about him to vote Conservative (2.78) rather than for another party, and less than one-tenth as likely (0.09) to vote Labour rather than Conservative. Even more strikingly, those who disliked Howard were 15 times more likely to vote Labour rather than Conservative compared with those who were neutral towards him, while respondents who liked him were much more inclined to vote Conservative. Voters' feelings about Kennedy made no significant difference to their preference between the Conservatives and Labour, but those who disliked him were more likely to vote Conservative or Labour rather than for another party. Given that the odds shown indicate the impact of leaders when all other variables in the analysis are held constant, these data suggest that feelings about leaders played a big part in determining party choice. Liking Blair and Howard attracted voters to their parties; disliking them clearly put them off. A separate analysis of voting for the Liberal Democrats as opposed to another party shows that liking or disliking Kennedy was significant and had the expected effects.

As noted above, the details of the analysis and interpretation of the results need not detain us here. The most important point to notice is the extent to which the addition of these five issue and valence variables to basic social characteristics dramatically improves our ability to predict party choice. This can be seen clearly from the 'pseudo' r^2 statistics. When the social variables alone were included (Table 8.2), the analyses accounted for 14.1 per cent of the variation in Conservative versus other voting, 8.6 per cent of the variation in Labour versus other voting and 18.0 per cent of Labour versus Conservative voting. Adding the 'judgement' variables increases these to 72.5 per cent, 65.0 per cent and 85.1 per cent respectively. Moreover, as we have seen, classifying voters by party on the basis of the equations relating to social characteristics (Table 8.2) made for only modest improvements on simply putting every respondent into the largest category (3.0, 2.9 and 11.6 points respectively). In Table 8.3, however, the improvements are much larger: 21.1, 23.7 and 38.1 points.

There remains, of course, the problem of causation. What are described by the data are associations and it is theoretically possible that voters decided which party to support on some other grounds and that their judgements were consequences of, or rationalizations for, that decision rather than causes of it. That is possible but, on the whole, implausible. The most plausible interpretation of the data is that the voters' judgements and reactions influenced their choice of party in the election.

To sum up, explanations of party choice based on social location or social identities still have some value but are less successful than they used to be. Explanations based on party identification appear to apply to a steadily decreasing part of the electorate. In analysing the modern electorate attention must focus on their opinions, perceptions and attitudes. There is no agreement as to which opinions in particular are critical, and it may be that this will change over time or vary among different groups of voters. What is clear, however, is that in explaining party choice in modern elections, voters' opinions are all-important.

Explaining election outcomes

There is clearly an intimate connection between explaining how voters come to make their decision in a particular election and explaining the distribution of support for the parties in the election. The latter, after all, is simply the aggregated effect of millions of individual decisions. In fact, when the electorate was largely aligned, and 'social determinist' and party identification explanations predominated, it was quite difficult to explain election outcomes on this basis. Such models emphasized long-term influences on party choice and these changed only very slowly. The Conservatives might have benefited from the slow decline in the size of the working class, for example, but this would have taken a very long time to affect election results significantly. As would be expected under these models, electoral change was slow and small. Between 1950 and 1970 the Conservatives' share of the vote ranged between 41.4 per cent and 49.3 per cent, while Labour's was never higher than 49.4 per cent or lower than 43.9 per cent (Table 1.2). Most voters regularly supported the same party and short-term electoral change was produced by a small proportion of 'floating' voters who switched parties or (more commonly) in and out of non-voting. Unfortunately, it was difficult to determine what motivated 'floating' of this kind. As discussed in Chapter 3, those who switched parties were found to be less concerned and less knowledgeable about politics, and less interested in the outcomes of elections, than were those whose voting pattern was stable. It was not those who were interested in and knowledgeable about politics and current affairs who determined which party won elections – such people were mainly loyal party supporters – but the less concerned, less interested and less knowledgeable. Butler and Stokes (1969, p. 437) suggested that switchers in some way acted 'as surrogates for those who, although they [did] not change, recognised in themselves the reactions which . . . moved the less committed'. In other words, when an election came along the political wind would be blowing in a particular direction. All felt it and were inclined to move with it, but only those with weak class or party attachments were actually propelled into switching to the party in whose direction the wind was blowing. The rather convoluted nature of this explanation illustrates the difficulty of explaining election results on the basis of the traditional models of party choice.

In the modern era, however, things are rather easier. To explain election outcomes we need to examine the pattern of judgements that the electorate has made or is making. This is illustrated for the 1997, 2001 and 2005 elections below. Focusing on the various approaches which emphasize electors' opinions discussed above, the judgements made by the electorate as a whole provide good explanations for the results of these elections.

The 1997 election

Change in the context   There is no doubt that the Labour Party changed dramatically between 1992 and 1997. Under Tony Blair, the party cast off much 'ideological baggage' – including the historic commitment to the public ownership of major industries – and moved towards the centre-ground of politics. This was noticed by the electorate. BES data show that, in 1992, some 29 per cent of respondents believed that Labour was 'extreme' but by 1997 this had fallen to 16 per cent. Sanders (1999) has shown that voters overall believed that Labour was ideologically closer to them in 1997 than it had been in 1992. This change could only benefit Labour.

Performance of the government   The Major government elected in 1992 became very unpopular shortly afterwards. In the first three months of 1997, according to Gallup data, an average of 64 per cent of the electorate disapproved of the government's record, with only 25 per cent approving.

The economy   In the run-up to the 1997 election, the performance of the British economy was improving steadily, according to the usual indicators (such as unemployment, inflation and interest rates). This did not benefit the Conservatives as much as it should have, however, because the electorate's long-standing confidence in the Conservatives to manage the economy competently had been shaken by events: in particular, the UK's forced withdrawal from the European Exchange Rate Mechanism in late 1992, the consequent effective devaluation of the pound and numerous tax increases. By the time of the 1997 election they had failed to restore that confidence;

when asked which was the best party to handle Britain's economic difficulties, almost half (49 per cent) of Gallup's respondents in March 1997 chose
Labour compared with 35 per cent choosing the Conservatives. This was a
historic turnaround.

Party images   We have already seen that between 1992 and 1997 Labour
successfully changed its image of being an extremist party. At the same
time, the Conservatives were acquiring a less than helpful (but nonetheless
deserved) image. In particular, they were seen as divided. Just after the
1992 election Gallup found that 65 per cent of the electorate thought that
the party was united and 26 per cent that it was divided; by January–March
1997 the position was dramatically reversed: a mere 16 per cent thought
that the party was united and a huge 80 per cent that it was divided. Labour,
meanwhile, had gone from being seen as divided by 72 per cent of the electorate to 35 per cent in 1997 (see Denver, 1998b). In addition the
Conservatives came to be seen as 'sleazy and disreputable'. In November
1995 fully 75 per cent of Gallup's respondents agreed with this description
of the party and only 19 per cent disagreed. The mud stuck, as it were, right
through to the election.

Party leaders   As has already been seen (Chapter 5) the accession of Tony
Blair to Labour's leadership helped to transform the party's prospects. He
easily outscored John Major as the most popular choice for Prime Minister
and thus reversed a disadvantage that Labour had suffered from in the previous three elections.

Key issues and policies   Again, we have already seen (Table 5.1) that on
each of what voters believed were the five most important issues facing the
country (the National Health Service, education, Europe, law and order, and
unemployment) Labour was the preferred party, in most cases by a very
wide margin. More generally, MORI data show that whereas in 1992 Labour
had a slight lead over the Conservatives (33 per cent to 31 per cent) in being
thought to have the best policies for the country as a whole, the gap had
increased substantially (36 per cent to 20 per cent) by 1997 (Worcester and
Mortimore, 2001, p. 78).

*   *   *

With all these evaluations stacked up against them it is not difficult to understand why the Conservatives lost the 1997 election and Labour won a handsome victory.

The 2001 election

Change in the context   Being in government can cause electoral problems for parties since some people are bound to be disappointed and some policy failures are inevitable. There are also advantages, however, since the Prime Minister can name the election date and an economic upswing can be engineered as the next election approaches. Between 1997 and 2001, the modernization of Labour continued and the moderation of the government was plain for all to see. Unsurprisingly, 72 per cent of 2001 BES respondents described Labour as 'moderate' and only 15 per cent as 'extreme'. Despite much internal organizational reform, heart-searching over their defeat and debate about the direction to be taken, the Conservatives in 2001 were seen as being broadly the same party that had lost disastrously in 1997 (Norton, 2002). One other potentially significant change in the electoral context concerned the Liberal Democrats. Having won more seats than ever before (46) in 1997, the party could anticipate benefiting from an 'incumbency effect' in those constituencies. Moreover, having been in government in Scotland and Wales, it could be argued that the Liberal Democrats could no longer be described as inexperienced or peripheral to the party battle (Denver, 2001).

Performance of the government   Although the Blair government disappointed some of its own traditional supporters and did not fill many with enthusiasm, the electorate was generally satisfied with its performance. Apart from a rocky period during 2000, Gallup's monthly polls consistently found that more people approved of the government's record to date than disapproved. In March and April 2001, approximately 55 per cent and 52 per cent of respondents respectively said that they approved of the government's record.

The economy   In stark contrast to previous Labour governments, the 1997–2001 government's handling of the economy was believed by many to be particularly effective. Unemployment fell steeply, interests rates were low and inflation was at lower levels than had been experienced for a generation. Pluralities of MORI respondents at the time thought that all five of the budgets introduced by Gordon Brown, the Chancellor of the Exchequer, were good for the country while his last pre-election budget was the best-received ever recorded by MORI (Worcester and Mortimore, 2001, p. 27). Unsurprisingly, 62 per cent of 2001 BES respondents thought that the government had 'handled the economy generally' well, while only 9 per cent thought that they had handled it badly.

Party images   The image of sleaze that had dogged the Conservatives in 1997 had been largely dispelled by 2001. In addition, fewer people saw the party as divided (71 per cent on Gallup's figures for May 2001) than had been the case in 1997, although this was still a historically high proportion and contrasted with 44 per cent seeing Labour as divided (Gallup, *Political Index,* Report 489). On the other hand, despite the efforts of William Hague to make the party seem more inclusive, youthful and even trendy – or perhaps because of them – Gallup data (Report 489) also show that the Conservatives were now seen as being 'out of touch with modern Britain' (69 per cent) and 'going on too much about Europe' (65 per cent).

Party leaders   Tony Blair's lead over William Hague as the preferred Prime Minister was huge and greater than any party leader's since 1979 at least (see Table 5.3). It was not just Hague personally who had a problem connecting with the electorate, however; the people around him in the leadership team also failed to impress. When MORI asked just before the election which party had the best team of leaders, only 9 per cent of respondents chose the Conservatives (47 per cent chose Labour, 5 per cent the Liberal Democrats and 33 per cent said none or didn't know: see Worcester and Mortimore, 2001, p. 78). At the same time, Gallup found an astonishing 81 per cent agreeing that the Conservatives did not have a strong team of leaders. In contrast, the new leader of the Liberal Democrats, Charles Kennedy, made a favourable impression on the electorate. Thirty per cent of BES respondents said that they liked him, 59 per cent were neutral and only 11 per cent disliked him. For comparison, 23 per cent disliked Tony Blair and 41 per cent disliked William Hague.

Key issues and policies   In 2001 Labour remained the preferred party on the key issues nominated by voters, although their lead was generally smaller than in 1997. On the other hand, their lead over the Conservatives as the party thought to have the best policies for the country as a whole (47 per cent to 17 per cent) once again increased substantially as compared with the previous election.

*   *   *

In the light of these evaluations it is again not difficult to understand why Labour won the 2001 election, if not as overwhelmingly as in 1997 (and also why the Liberal Democrats improved their position).

The 2005 election

Change in the context   The context of the 2005 election was dramatically different from those of 1997 and 2005. Labour was very much on the defensive and the main reason for that was the Iraq war, which began in March 2005, and subsequent related developments. Although there were large anti-war demonstrations at the time, initially a clear majority of the public supported Britain's involvement (66 per cent to 29 per cent in April 2003, according to YouGov). As events unfolded, however, support waned. Among other things, the failure to find weapons of mass destruction, the impression that in making the case for involvement the government had been less than straightforward and the apparently unending chaos in Iraq itself all took their toll. By the start of 2005 only 35 per cent of YouGov's respondents were in favour of the war with 56 per cent opposed (see Quinn, 2006). Labour's difficulties on Iraq did not advantage the Conservatives – who had supported the invasion – but probably helped the Liberal Democrats who had opposed the war outright and picked up votes as a consequence, especially among Muslims.

Performance of the government   Quite unlike the period between 1997 and 2001, the electorate were generally dissatisfied with the performance of the government between 2001 and 2005. In every month from January 2003 (when the series started) to March 2005, YouGov reported large majorities saying that they disapproved of the government's record. Over the 27 months, the average figure for those disapproving was 59 per cent compared with 29 per cent approving.

The economy   On the other hand, Labour could take some comfort from the fact that it came to be seen as the party most likely to do a good job as far as managing the economy was concerned. YouGov data show that although the two major parties were virtually neck-and-neck on this issue for some time after January 2003, Labour's lead on the issue began to stretch in the early months of 2005. During the campaign itself, over five separate surveys, the proportion opting for the Conservatives as the party more likely to run the economy well averaged 28 per cent, while those choosing Labour averaged 47 per cent. The economy may not be the only thing that matters in an election, but it does matter a lot and Labour's record in this respect put the party in a strong position.

Party images   Labour's image in 2005 was less positive than it had been in 2001. On one set of measures produced by MORI, indeed, positive attributes (such as 'has a good team of leaders') were outweighed by negative ones (such as 'out of touch with ordinary people'). However, the Conservatives, despite a slight improvement from 2001, had an even more negative image. On the other hand, the image of the Liberal Democrats was generally positive (see Worcester, Mortimore and Baines, 2005, pp. 36–40). When the images of the two major parties were compared by YouGov, however, Labour clearly still had the edge. By more than two to one, respondents described the Conservatives rather than Labour as appealing to only one section of society, being stuck in the past, being old and tired and wanting to divide people instead of bringing them together (King, 2006, p. 168).

Party leaders   Following the 2001 general election, William Hague was replaced as Conservative leader by Iain Duncan Smith. The latter failed to make much of an impact with the voters and was replaced by Michael Howard in November 2003. YouGov data show that Howard scored better than Duncan Smith in terms of which party leader was thought to be the best person for Prime Minister but, even so, he did not challenge Tony Blair's lead for long. From mid-2004 through to the election Blair was the clearly preferred Prime Minister. YouGov continued to monitor opinion on this matter during the election campaign but little changed. Over five surveys, the proportion preferring Blair varied between 34 per cent and 37 per cent, while Michael Howard's scores were always between 23 per cent and 25 per cent and Charles Kennedy's between 15 per cent and 18 per cent. Blair's leads were much smaller than those he had recorded over William Hague in the 2001 election – and that, no doubt, helps to explain Labour's decline in popularity – but they were clear and sustained. Whatever their misgivings about the Labour leader and the fact that he wasn't particularly liked, the electorate clearly believed that he would be a better Prime Minster than either of his rivals and that goes a long way in explaining why Labour won.

Key issues and policies   Despite its importance in providing the context of the election and contributing to concerns about the extent to which the Prime Minister could be trusted, according to MORI data the Iraq war was not of itself particularly salient to the voters in the election. As already seen (Table 5.1), MORI data suggest that the three issues that concerned voters most were health, education, and law and order. Labour had handy leads as the most preferred party on the first two of these. BES data tell a slightly different story. In answer to a question asking what was the most important issue facing the country, the three most commonly referred to by post-election survey respondents were (in order) the NHS, asylum seekers and immigration, and law and order. Labour had a big lead on the NHS and a smaller one on law and order, while the Conservatives were clearly ahead on asylum seekers and immigration. Overall, however, Labour was named as the best party on what they thought was the most important issue mentioned by 36 per cent of respondents, compared with 20 per cent choosing the Conservatives and 7 per cent the Liberal Democrats. This certainly represented a narrowing of the 'issue gap' from 2001 (when the respective figures were 46 per cent, 16 per cent and 8 per cent) but still left Labour comfortably ahead of its rivals.

* * *

The judgements of the electorate in 2005 in respect of government performance, the economy, the parties, leaders and issues were decidedly more mixed than in the two previous elections. The government and the Prime Minister were clearly not very popular but the Conservatives had problems of their own and, despite a slight improvement in their performance, were not able to benefit as much as they could have. The main beneficiaries, it could be argued, were the Liberal Democrats and minor parties, in particular UKIP and the BNP.

It should be emphasized that the sorts of judgement made by the electorate that I have used to explain the outcomes of the last three elections do not, of course, tell the whole story. (For extended treatments of the 2001 election see Norris, 2001; Butler and Kavanagh, 2002; Geddes and Tonge, 2002; King, 2002. For the 2005 election see Geddes and Tonge, 2005; Kavanagh and Butler, 2005; Norris and Wlezien, 2005; Bartle and King, 2006.) A fuller account would also include consideration of the role of the media, for example. In addition, while electors' judgements may give strong clues as to why votes are distributed as they are, to understand the election outcome in terms of seats won we also have to take account of the electoral system and the geographical distribution of support which is influenced by, among other things, local campaigning. Nonetheless, if we are to use the insights that studies of individual voting behaviour have provided in order to explain overall election results, it is clear that the best starting point is to focus on the judgements made by individual voters about government performance, the parties, issues, policies and leaders. And that is how it should be if elections are to fulfil the functions prescribed for them in democratic political systems.

Conclusion

I suggested at the beginning of this book that one reason for studying elections is that they are fun events. Turnouts in recent elections might suggest that fewer people are now finding them quite as much fun. Terms such as 'disengagement' and 'alienation' are now commonly used in discussions of the electorate's attitudes to the electoral process. Nonetheless, students of elections should find elections more interesting, and even exciting, than they used to be. They should do so because – notwithstanding the fact that Labour has recently won three times in a row – elections are now unpredictable. The electorate's judgements on relatively short-term matters have come to play a key role in determining party choice, and short-term judgements are subject to rapid change. As Mrs Thatcher found to her cost, the transition from being perceived as resolute to being perceived as pig-headed can be swift. When governments these days run into a bit of heavy weather, the absence of the anchor provided by widespread and strong party identification among voters means that they can rapidly become critical and withdraw their support. As it happened, short-term factors in both 1997 and 2001 clearly favoured Labour and were very negative for the Conservatives. The resultant land-slide victories for Labour are not difficult to explain. In 2005, judgements were much more mixed and the electoral outcome (especially in terms of votes) was much closer.

Within a year of the 2005 general election much had changed in British politics. Towards the end of the year, David Cameron was chosen to succeed Michael Howard as leader of the Conservative party while in March 2006 Menzies Campbell took over as leader of the Liberal Democrats from Charles Kennedy. Meanwhile, Tony Blair had announced that he would step down as Prime Minister before the next election (the expectation being that Gordon Brown would take over as Labour leader). Given the argument that the electorate's evaluations of party leaders now play a major part in determining party choice, these changes will clearly be electorally signifi-cant although it is difficult to predict how the new leaders will be perceived by the time of the next general election.

After the election Labour had a six-month honeymoon period during which the party's support in the polls was at higher levels than it had been in the election itself. The share of voting intentions obtained by the Liberal Democrats slowly declined while the Conservatives made little headway. As has been argued in this book, however, with a dealigned and volatile elec-torate governments contemplating clear blue electoral skies can quickly find themselves under dark clouds. This happened to Labour in the run-up to the local elections of May 2006. Against a background of apparently continual bickering over the leadership succession, allegations of peerages being granted in return for backing the party financially and revelations of incom-petence in dealing with non-native released prisoners, Labour slumped to just 33.5 per cent of voting intentions in the April polls. In the local elections themselves, the 'national equivalent' vote shares were 39 per cent for the Conservatives, 26 per cent for Labour and 25 per cent for the Liberal Democrats. In these terms, this was the best local election performance by the Conservatives since 1992 while Labour's vote equalled the party's worst showing in over 25 years. Although the Liberal Democrats did only slightly worse than in 2003 and 2004, they gained fewer seats and the results were widely interpreted as something of a setback for the party. The April polls also indicated a sharp increase in support for 'other' parties (to 12 per cent) and in a number of areas the British National Party made significant advances in the local elections – further proof, if any were needed, that the electorate's attachment to the major parties is far from secure.

Given that these developments occurred within a year of the 2005 general election, it would clearly be foolish for anyone to attempt to predict what will happen in the next general election, which may be some years distant. The electoral context and the personalities involved will be different and it is impossible to know whether economic storms will suddenly blow up or unforeseen issues arise. Combine these uncertainties with a fickle and judgemental electorate and it is easy to understand why British elections will continue to be exciting and the study of British elections and voters fascinating.

Glossary of Statistical and Technical Terms

These explanations of statistical terms used in the text are not instructions about 'how to do it' as no formulae are given. If that is what is required, readers should consult an appropriate statistics textbook (for example, Rose and Sullivan, 1996; Bryman and Cramer, 2001) but, these days, all the necessary calculations are done by appropriate computer packages such as SPSS. Neither are the following explanations given in technical language. Rather, the intention here is to provide non-specialist readers with a basic, working knowledge of various statistical techniques and terms commonly used in electoral analysis. An understanding of what the various techniques measure and what the results mean is all that is required to engage with the electoral studies literature and even to undertake basic research. In what follows, terms in the text in bold type have their own separate entries.

Aggregate data

Aggregate data describes information referring to aggregates or collectivities rather than to individuals. Constituency data – such as election results or social composition figures – is a common example in electoral analysis. It is an important feature of aggregate data that they cannot be used to infer anything about the individuals comprising the collectivity concerned.

Binary logistic regression

Normal linear **regression analysis** can only be used with **continuous data**. Binary logistic regression has recently started to be used in electoral analysis and it enables the application of regression analysis methods, with their associated advantages, in cases where the **dependent variable** and associated **independent variables** are **categoric**. These advantages include being able to analyse a large number of **independent variables** simultaneously and to measure the separate independent effect of each, as well as the combined effect of all of them.

The dependent variable has to be reduced to two categories, such as voted Conservative or not (hence 'binary'), and for each independent variable a 'reference' category has to be specified with which other categories will be compared. The output produced by each analysis is voluminous and the initial coefficients difficult to interpret. The most important elements for interpretation are: the **odds ratios** given for each category of an independent variable (which show the extent to which cases in the category differ from the reference category); the **statistical significance** of each odds ratio (which shows whether the difference between the category and the reference group could have arisen by chance); the r^2 statistics (which estimate how much of the variation in the dependent variable is explained by the independent variables in the analysis) and the classification tables (which show the extent to which allocating cases to the categories of the dependent variable on the basis of the regression equation improves upon allocating all to the largest category).

Bivariate analysis

Analysis involving two variables.

Categoric variables

Sometimes called 'nominal variables', these are **variables** for which the information is such that each case can only be assigned to one of a number of discrete categories. Examples are party voted for, religion, sex, occupation group and opinion on taxation policy.

Chi-squared test

A test of **statistical significance** normally applied to **cross-tabulations**. The test indicates the probability that any difference between the categories could have arisen by chance; the lower that probability the more significant the difference. Normally a probability of 0.05 or less (usually reported as '$p < 0.05$') is taken to indicate a statistically significant difference. When the probability is larger, the difference found is normally interpreted as not being statistically significant.

Continuous data

When a **variable** is such that each case can be assigned a precise score on a scale, the resulting data are described as continuous. Examples for individuals could include height (the scale could be metres), weight (pounds), age (years) or score on a political quiz (marks out of ten). For constituencies, the parties' percentage shares of the votes, the percentage of manual workers in the work-force and persons per hectare would be examples.

Correlation (coefficients)

As most commonly used, these are measures of the strength of association between two **interval-scale** or **continuous variables.** The coefficients are signified as '*r*' and can vary between −1 and + 1. A positive sign indicates that as the scores on one variable increase, so do the scores on the other. A negative sign means that as one increases the other decreases. The closer the coefficient is to zero, the weaker the association.

Cross-tabulation

This is the standard way of presenting and investigating the relationship between two or more **categoric variables.** Tables are created by defining categories for the column (**independent**) variable and the row (**dependent**) variable. Thus we could allocate survey respondents according to sex (two categories – independent variable) and party voted for (say, three categories – Conservative, Labour, Liberal Democrat – dependent variable). This defines a table of six cells and respondents are allocated to the appropriate one. The figures in each column are then usually converted to percentages. More variables can be incorporated, but two problems quickly arise: first, the number of cells multiplies rapidly so that tables become unwieldy, difficult to present clearly and hard to understand; second, the number of cases in each cell becomes very small so that the percentages become unreliable.

Dependent variable

A **variable** that is presumed to be affected by other factors: for example, in examining the relationship between age and vote it is clear that vote must be the dependent variable.

Dummy variables

Categoric variables can be converted into *quasi* **continuous variables** by being reduced to two categories and assigning scores (usually 0 and 1) to each. Because they are not truly continuous, the created variables are known as 'dummy' variables. Thus, region could be converted into a series of 'dummies' scored 0 = Not Scotland, 1 = Scotland; 0 = Not North East, 1 = North East; and so on. The advantage is that dummy variables can then be used in ordinary **regression analysis**.

Independent variable

A **variable** that is presumed to affect other (dependent) variables: for example, in examining the relationship between age and vote, it is clear that age must be the independent variable.

Individual-level data

These are data which refer to individuals. Such data are most commonly collected by means of sample surveys and the individuals concerned are usually anonymous.

Interval-scale data

See **continuous data**.

Mean

The most common measure of the central tendency of a set of scores on an **interval-scale variable**. In everyday speech it is commonly called the average (although there are other relevant measures) and it is calculated by summing the scores and dividing the total by the number of cases. The mean can give a misleading impression if the number of cases is small and there are some extreme values (very high or very low scores compared to most cases).

Multiple regression analysis

Regression analysis involving more than one **independent variable**.

Multivariate analysis

Analysis involving two or more **independent variables.**

Nagelkerke r^2

This statistic gives an estimate of the proportion of **variation** explained by an equation produced by a **binary logistic regression** analysis.

Odds ratios

Odds ratios allow us to compare cases, which have been allocated to a two-category **independent variable**, in respect of a two-category **dependent variable**. For example, if the **independent variable** is class (working versus middle) and the **dependent**

variable is party voted for (Conservative versus Labour), then we can define the odds of voting Conservative (as opposed to voting Labour) for both working- and middle-class respondents. The odds can be expressed as probabilities (thus 50:50 equals 1; 60:40 equals 1.5; 40:60 equals 0.67) and the ratio between the figures for the two groups summarizes the comparison. In **binary logistic regression** odds ratios are produced comparing each category of each independent variable with the reference category in each case.

Regression analysis

This a shorthand way of referring to ordinary least squares linear regression (OLS), a technique for analysing the relationships between **continuous variables**. Simple regression analysis involves estimating the line (the 'regression line') that best fits a distribution of points on a scatter diagram plotting the **dependent variable** (vertical axis) against an **independent** or 'predictor' **variable** (horizontal axis). In the most common analysis the line is assumed to be straight ('linear regression') and is the 'least squares line' (i.e., that line which minimizes the sum of the squares of the vertical distances from each point to the line). It can be described by an equation of the form $y = a + bx$, where y is the dependent variable score, a is a constant, b is a measure of the slope of the line and x is the independent variable score. By extension, **multiple regression** is used to predict a dependent variable on the basis of more than one independent variable. The goodness of fit of the regression line to the data is measured by r, the **correlation coefficient** (either simple or multiple) and the *r-squared* statistic estimates the proportion of variation in the dependent variable statistically explained by the equation.

Residuals

On the basis of an equation produced by **regression** analysis, 'expected' scores on the **dependent variable** can be predicted for each case (the scores that would be expected given scores on the **independent variable**). The difference between this expected score and the actual score is known as the residual.

r-squared (r^2)

The square of the **correlation coefficient** (r) is a measure of the proportion of the **variation** in the values of one variable which is statistically explained by variations in the values of another (or others).

Standard deviation

This is a measure of the dispersion or spread of a set of scores on a **continuous variable**. The smaller the standard deviation, the more closely the scores are clustered together; the larger it is, the more the scores are spread out.

Statistical significance

Significance tests measure the probability that a statistical relationship found in analysis might have occurred by chance. There is a variety of such tests appropriate for different types of analysis. In all cases, however, the key indicator is the probability statistic and normally a probability of 0.05 or less (usually reported as '$p < 0.05$') is taken to indicate a statistically significant result. When the probability is larger the relationship found is not significant. It is important to remember that the *statistical* significance of a relationship does not necessarily imply that it is *theoretically* or *substantively* significant.

Variable

A variable is any characteristic, quality or other measure that varies. It can vary over time, from place to place, from person to person or across any other set of cases.

Variation

Any set of values on a **continuous variable** has a given amount of variation. The square of the **standard deviation** (called the 'variance') is a measure of this variation, and in **correlation** and **regression analysis** estimates can be made as to how much of the variation in a **dependent variable** can be explained or accounted for by variations in **independent variables**.

References

Alford, R. (1964) *Party and Society* (London: John Murray).

Atkinson, M. (1984) *Our Masters' Voices* (London: Methuen).

Bartle, J. (2001) 'The Measurement of Party Identification in Britain: Where Do We Stand Now?', *British Elections and Parties Review*, 11, 9–22.

Bartle, J. (2002) 'Why Labour Won – Again', in A. King (ed.), *Britain at the Polls 2001* (New York: Chatham House), 164–206.

Bartle. J. (2005) 'The Press, Television and the Internet' in P. Norris and C. Wlezein (eds), *Britain Votes 2005* (Oxford: Oxford University Press), 43–55.

Bartle, J. and Crewe, I. (2002) 'The impact of party leaders in Britain: strong assumptions, weak evidence' in A. King (ed.) *Leaders' Personalities and the Outcomes of Democratic Elections* (Oxford: Oxford University Press), 70–95.

Bartle, J. and Griffiths, D. (eds) (2001) *Political Communications Transformed: From Morrison to Mandelson* (Basingstoke: Palgrave Macmillan).

Bartle, J. and King, A. (eds) (2006) *Britain at the Polls 2005* (Wahington, DC: CQ Press).

Bealey, F., Blondel, J. and McCann, W. (1965) *Constituency Politics* (London: Faber & Faber).

Beer, S. (1982) *Britain Against Itself* (London: Faber & Faber).

Benney, M., Gray, A. P. and Pear, R. H. (1956) *How People Vote* (London: Routledge & Kegan Paul).

Berelson, B., Lazarsfeld, P. and McPhee, W. (1954) *Voting* (Chicago, IL: University of Chicago Press).

Birch, A.H. (1959) *Small Town Politics* (Oxford: Oxford University Press).

Blau, A. (2001) 'Partisan Bias in British General Elections', in *British Elections and Parties Review*, 11, 46–65.

Blumler, J. G. and McQuail, D. (1967) *Television in Politics* (London: Faber & Faber).

Broughton, D. (1995) *Public Opinion Polling and Politics in Britain* (London: Prentice Hall).

Bryman, A. and Cramer, D. (2001) *Quantitative Data Analysis with SPSS Release 10 for Windows* (London: Routledge).

Butler, D. (1952) *The British General Election of 1951* (London: Macmillan).

Butler, D. (1955) *The British General Election of 1955* (London: Macmillan).

Butler, D. (1998) 'Reflections on British Elections and Their Study', *Annual Review of Political Science*, 1, 451–64.

Butler, D. and Kavanagh, D. (1974) *The British General Election of February 1974* (London: Macmillan).

Butler, D. and Kavanagh, D. (1975) *The British General Election of October 1974* (London: Macmillan).

Butler, D. and Kavanagh, D. (1980) *The British General Election of 1979* (London: Macmillan).

Butler, D. and Kavanagh, D. (1984) *The British General Election of 1983* (London: Macmillan).

Butler, D. and Kavanagh, D. (1988) *The British General Election of 1987* (London: Macmillan).

Butler, D. and Kavanagh, D. (1992) *The British General Election of 1992* (London: Macmillan).

Butler, D. and Kavanagh, D. (1997) *The British General Election of 1997* (London: Macmillan).

Butler, D. and Kavanagh, D. (2002) *The British General Election of 2001* (London: Macmillan).

Butler, D. and King, A. (1965) *The British General Election of 1964* (London: Macmillan).

Butler, D. and King, A. (1966) *The British General Election of 1966* (London: Macmillan).

Butler, D. and Pinto-Duschinsky, M. (1971) *The British General Election of 1970* (London: Macmillan).

Butler, D. and Rose, R. (1960) *The British General Election of 1959* (London: Macmillan).

Butler, D. and Stokes, D. (1969) *Political Change in Britain,* 1st edn (London: Macmillan).

Butler, D. and Stokes, D. (1974) *Political Change in Britain,* 2nd edn (London: Macmillan).

Campbell, A., Converse, P., Miller, W. and Stokes D. (1960) *The American Voter* (New York: John Wiley).

Chandler, J. (1982) 'The Plurality Vote: A Reappraisal', *Political Studies*, XXX, 87–94.

Clarke, H. and Stewart, M. (1995) 'Economic evaluations and election outcomes: an analysis of alternative forecasting models', in D. Broughton, D. Farrell, D. Denver and C. Rallings (eds), *British Elections and Parties Yearbook 1994* (London: Frank Cass).

Clarke, H., Stewart, M. and Whiteley, P. (2001) 'The Dynamics of Partisanship in Britain: Evidence and Implications for Critical Election Theory', *British Elections and Parties Review*, 11, 66–83.

Clarke, H., Sanders, D., Stewart, M. and Whiteley, P. (2004) *Political Choice in Britain* (Oxford: Oxford University Press).

Clarke, H., Sanders, D., Stewart, M. and Whiteley, P. (2006) 'Taking the bloom off New Labour's rose: party choice and voter turnout in Britain, 2005', *Journal of Elections, Public Opinion and Parties*, 16 (1), 3–36.

Crewe, I. (1981a) 'Electoral participation', in D. Butler, H. R. Penniman and A. Ranney (eds), *Democracy at the Polls* (Washington, DC: American Enterprise Institute), 216–63.

Crewe, I. (1981b) 'Why the Conservatives won', in H. Penniman (ed.), *Britain at the Polls 1979* (Washington, DC: American Enterprise Institute), 263–305.

Crewe, I. (1984) 'The electorate: partisan dealignment ten years on', in H. Berrington (ed.), *Change in British Politics* (London: Frank Cass), 183–215.

Crewe, I. (1985a) 'Great Britain' in I. Crewe and D. Denver (eds), *Electoral Change in Western Democracies* (London: Croom Helm), 100–50.

Crewe, I. (1985b) 'How to win a landslide without really trying', in A. Ranney (ed.), *Britain at the Polls 1983* (Washington, DC: American Enterprise Institute), 155–96.

Crewe, I. (1986) 'On the death and resurrection of class voting: some comments on *How Britain Votes*', *Political Studies*, XXXV, 620–38.

Crewe, I. (1988) 'Has the electorate become Thatcherite?', in R. Skidelsky (ed.), *Thatcherism* (Oxford: Basil Blackwell), 25–49.

Crewe, I. (1992a) 'A nation of liars? Opinion polls and the 1992 election', *Parliamentary Affairs,* 45, 475–95.

Crewe, I. (1992b) 'The 1987 general election', in D. Denver and G. Hands (eds), *Issues and Controversies in British Electoral Behaviour* (Hemel Hempstead: Harvester Wheatsheaf), 343–54.

Crewe, I. (1992c) 'Why did Labour lose (yet again)?', *Politics Review*, 2, 2–11.

Crewe, I. (1997) 'The Opinion Polls: Confidence Restored?', in P. Norris and N. Gavin (eds), *Britain Votes 1997* (Oxford: Oxford University Press), 61–77.

Crewe, I. (2001) 'The Opinion Polls: Still Biased to Labour', in P. Norris (ed.), *Britain Votes 2001* (Oxford: Oxford University Press), 86–101.

Crewe, I. (2002) 'A New Political Hegemony', in A. King (ed.), *Britain at the Polls 2001* (New York: Chatham House), 207–32.

Crewe, I. (2005) 'The Opinion Polls: The Election They Got (Almost) Right', in P. Norris and C. Wlezien (eds.), *Britain Votes 2005* (Oxford: Oxford University Press), 28–42.

Crewe, I. and King, A. (1994) 'Did Major win? Did Kinnock lose? Leadership effects in the 1992 election' in A. Heath, R. Jowell and J. Curtice with B. Taylor (eds), *Labour's Last Chance? The 1992 Election and Beyond* (Aldershot: Dartmouth), 125–47.

Crewe, I. and Payne, C. (1971) 'Analysing the census data', in D. Butler and M. Pinto-Duschinsky, *The British General Election of 1970* (London: Macmillan), 416–36.

Crewe, I. and Thomson, K. (1999) 'Party Loyalties: Dealignment or Realignment', in G. Evans and P. Norris (eds), *Critical Elections: British Parties and Voters in Long-Term Perspective* (London: Sage), 64–86.

Crewe, I., Fox, T. and Alt, J. (1977) 'Non-voting in British general elections 1966–October 1974', in C. Crouch (ed.), *British Political Sociology Yearbook*, Vol. 3 (London: Croom Helm), 38–109.

Crewe, I., Fox, A. and Day, N. (1995) *The British Electorate 1963–1992* (Cambridge: Cambridge University Press).

Crewe, I., Sarlvik, B. and Alt, J. (1977) 'Partisan dealignment in Britain 1964–1974', *British Journal of Political Science*, 7, 129–90.

Curtice, J. (1992) 'The hidden surprise: the British electoral system in 1992', *Parliamentary Affairs*, 45, 466–74.

Curtice, J. (2001) 'The Electoral System', in P. Norris (ed.), *Britain Votes 2001* (Oxford: Oxford University Press), 239–50.

Curtice, J. (2004) 'Proportional representation in Scotland: public reaction and voter behaviour', *Representation*, 40 (4), 329–41.

Curtice, J. and Semetko, H. (1994) 'Does it matter what the papers say?', in A. Heath, R. Jowell and J. Curtice (eds), *Labour's Last Chance: The 1992 Election and Beyond* (Aldershot: Dartmouth), 43–63.

Curtice, J. and Steed, M. (1982) 'Electoral choice and the production of governments: the changing operation of the electoral system in the UK since 1955', *British Journal of Political Science*, 12, 249–98.

Curtice, J. and Steed, M. (1986) 'Proportionality and exaggeration in the British electoral system', *Electoral Studies*, 5, 209–28.

Curtice, J. and Steed, M. (1988) 'Analysis', in D. Butler and D. Kavanagh, *The British General Election of 1987* (London: Macmillan), 316–62.

Curtice, J. and Steed, M. (1992) 'The results analysed', in D. Butler and D. Kavanagh, *The British General Election of 1992* (London: Macmillan), 322–62.

Curtice, J. and Steed, M. (1997) 'The results analysed', in D. Butler and D. Kavanagh, *The British General Election of 1997* (London: Macmillan), 293–325.

Curtice, J. and Steed, M. (2000) 'And Now for the Commons? Lessons from Britain's First Experience with Proportional Representation', *British Elections and Parties Review*, 10, 193–215.

Curtice, J. and Steed, M. (2001) 'An analysis of the results', in D. Butler and D. Kavanagh, *The British General Election of 2001* (Basingstoke: Palgrave Macmillan), 304–38.

Curtice, J., Fisher, S. and Steed, M. (2005) 'The results analysed', in D. Kavanagh and D. Butler, *The British General Election of 2005* (Basingstoke: Palgrave Macmillan), 235–59.

Curtice, J., Seyd, B., Park, A. and Thomson, K. (2000) *Wise After the Event? Attitudes to Voting Reform following the 1999 Scottish and Welsh Elections* (London: Constitution Unit).

Deacon, D. and Wring, D. (2002) 'Partisan Dealignment and the British Press', in J. Bartle, R. Mortimore and S. Atkinson (eds), *Political Communications: The General Election of 2001* (London: Frank Cass).

Deacon, D., Golding, P. and Billig, M. (1998) 'Between Fear and Loathing: National Press Coverage of the 1997 British General Election', *British Elections and Parties Review*, 8, 135–49.

Denver, D. (1994) *Elections and Voting Behaviour in Britain,* 2nd edn (Hemel Hempstead: Harvester Wheatsheaf).

Denver, D. (1998a) 'The British Electorate in the 1990s', in H. Berrington (ed.), *Britain in the Nineties: The Politics of Paradox* (London: Frank Cass), 197–217.

Denver, D. (1998b) 'The Government That Could Do No Right', in A. King (ed.), *New Labour Triumphs: Britain at the Polls* (New York: Chatham House), 15–48.

Denver, D. (2001) 'The Liberal Democrat Campaign', in P. Norris (ed.), *Britain Votes 2001* (Oxford: Oxford University Press), 86–101.

Denver, D. (2005) 'Valence Politics: How Britain Votes Now', *British Journal of Politics and International Relations*, 7, 292–9.

Denver, D. and Halfacree, K. (1992a) 'Inter-constituency migration and party support in Britain', *Political Studies*, XL, 571–80.

Denver, D. and Halfacree, K. (1992b) 'Inter-constituency migration and turnout at the British general election of 1983', *British Journal of Political Science*, 22, 248–54.

Denver, D. and Hands, G. (1974) 'Marginality and turnout in British general elections', *British Journal of Political Science*, 4, 17–35.

Denver, D. and Hands, G. (1985) 'Marginality and turnout in British general elections in the 1970s', *British Journal of Political Science*, 15, 381–8.

Denver, D. and Hands, G. (1990) 'Issues, principles or ideology? How young voters decide', *Electoral Studies*, 9, 19–36.

Denver, D. and Hands, G. (eds) (1992) *Issues and Controversies in British Electoral Behaviour* (Hemel Hempstead: Harvester Wheatsheaf).

Denver, D. and Hands, G. (1997a) *Modern Constituency Electioneering* (London: Frank Cass).

Denver, D. and Hands, G. (1997b) 'Turnout', in P. Norris and N. Gavin (eds), *Britain Votes 1997* (Oxford: Oxford University Press), 212–24.

Denver, D. and Hands, G. (2004) 'Exploring Variations in Turnout: Constituencies and Wards in the Scottish Parliament Elections of 1999 and 2003', *British Journal of Politics and International Relations*, 6 (4), 527–42.

Denver, D., Hands, G. and MacAllister, I. (2003) 'Constituency Marginality and Turnout in Britain Revisited', *British Elections and Parties Review*, 13, 174–94.

Denver, D., Hands, G. and MacAllister, I. (2004) 'The electoral impact of constituency campaigning in Britain, 1992–2001', *Political Studies*, 52 (4), 289–306.

Denver, D., Hands, G., Fisher, J. and MacAllister, I. (2002) 'Constituency Campaigning in 2001: The Effectiveness of Targeting', in J. Bartle, R. Mortimore and S. Atkinson (eds), *Political Communications: The General Election of 2001* (London: Frank Cass), 158–80.

Denver, D., Hands, G., Fisher, J. and MacAllister, I. (2003) 'Constituency Campaigning in Britain 1992–2001: Centralization and Modernization', *Party Politics*, 9 (5), 541–59.

Downs, A. (1957) *An Economic Theory of Democracy* (New York: Harper).

Dunleavy, P. (1979) 'The urban basis of political alignment: social class, domestic property ownership and state intervention in consumption processes', *British Journal of Political Science*, 9, 409–43.

Dunleavy, P. (1980) 'The political implications of sectoral cleavages and the growth of state employment', *Political Studies*, XXVIII, 364–83 and 527–49.

Dunleavy, P. (1987) 'Class dealignment in Britain revisited', *West European Politics*, 10, 400–19.

Dunleavy, P. and Husbands, C. (1985) *British Democracy at the Crossroads* (London: George Allen & Unwin).

Dunleavy, P. and Margetts, H. (1999) 'Reforming the Westminster Electoral System: Evaluating the Jenkins Commission Proposals', *British Elections and Parties Review,* 9, 46–71.

Dunleavy, P., Margetts, H. and Bastow, S. (2001) 'Freed from Constraint: Political Alignments in the 2000 London Elections', Paper presented at the PSA annual conference, Manchester.

Edgeworth, F. (1905) 'The Law of Error', *Transactions of the Cambridge Philosophical Society,* 20, 35–65 and 113–44.

Electoral Commission (2001a) *Campaign Expenditure for Great Britain Parties,* Electoral Commission Website.

Electoral Commission (2001b) *Election 2001, The Official Results* (London: Politico's).

Electoral Commission (2003) *Party Political Broadcasting: Report and Recommendations* (Electoral Commission, London).

Electoral Commission (2005) *Register of Campaign Expenditure*, Electoral Commission Website.

Electoral Studies (2000) Special Issue on 'Economics and Elections', 19 (2/3).

Evans, G. and Andersen, R. (2005) 'The Impact of Party Leaders: How Blair Lost Labour Votes', in P. Norris and C. Wlezien (eds), *Britain Votes 2005* (Oxford: Oxford University Press), 162–80.

Evans, G. and Norris, P. (eds) (1999) *Critical Elections* (London: Sage).

Evans, G., Heath, A. and Payne, C. (1999) 'Class: Labour as a Catch-All Party?', in G. Evans and P. Norris (eds), *Critical Elections: British Parties and Voters in Long-Term Perspective* (London: Sage), 87–101.

Fallon, I. and Worcester, R. (1992) 'The use of panel studies in British general elections', Paper presented at EPOP/Political Communications conference, University of Essex, September 1992.

Farrell, D. (2001) *Electoral Systems: A Comparative Introduction* (Basingstoke: Palgrave Macmillan).

Farrell, D., McAllister, I. and Broughton, D. (1995) 'The Changing British Voter Revisited: Patterns of Election Campaign Volatility since 1964', in D. Broughton, D. Farrell, D. Denver and C. Rallings (eds), *British Elections and Parties Yearbook 1994* (London: Frank Cass), 110–27.

Festinger, L. (1962) *A Theory of Cognitive Dissonance* (London: Tavistock).

Field, W. (1997) *Regional Dynamics: The Basis of Electoral Support in Britain* (London: Frank Cass).

Fiorina, M. (1981) *Retrospective Voting in American National Elections* (New Haven, CT: Yale University Press).

Fisher, J. (2001) 'Campaign Finance', in P. Norris (ed.), *Britain Votes 2001* (Oxford: Oxford University Press), 125–36.

Fisher, J., Denver, D., Fieldhouse, E., Cutts, D. and Russell, A. (2006 forthcoming) 'Constituency Campaigning in 2005: Ever More Centralization?', in D. Wring, J.

Green, R. Mortimore and S. Atkinson (eds), *Political Communications: The British General Election of 2005* (Basingstoke: Palgrave Macmillan).

Franklin, M. (1985) *The Decline of Class Voting in Britain* (Oxford: Oxford University Press).

Franklin, M. (1996) 'Electoral Participation', in L. LeDuc, R. Niemi and P Norris (eds), *Comparing Democracies: Elections and Voting in Global Perspective* (London: Sage), 216–35.

Franklin, M. (2002) 'The Dynamics of Electoral Participation', in L. LeDuc, R. Niemi and P. Norris (eds), *Comparing Democracies 2: new Challenges in the Study of Elections and Voting* (London: Sage), 148–68.

Franklin, M. and Hughes, C. (1999) 'Dynamic Representation in Britain', in G. Evans and P. Norris (eds), *Critical Elections: British Parties and Voters in Long-Term Perspective* (London: Sage), 240–58.

Galbraith, J. and Rae, N. (1989) 'A test of the importance of tactical voting: Great Britain 1987', *British Journal of Political Science,* 19, 126–36.

Gallup, *Political Index.*

Gallup, *Political and Economic Index.*

Gavin, N. and Sanders, D. (1997) 'The economy and voting', in P. Norris and N. Gavin (eds), *Britain Votes 1997* (Oxford: Oxford University Press), 123–32.

Geddes, A. and Tonge, J. (eds) (2002) *Labour's Second Landslide* (Manchester: Manchester University Press).

Geddes, A. and Tonge, J. (eds) (2005) *Britain Decides: The UK General Election 2005* (Basingstoke: Palgrave Macmillan).

Goldthorpe, J. H., Lockwood, D., Bechhofer, F. and Platt, J. (1968) *The Affluent Worker* (Cambridge: Cambridge University Press).

Goodhart, C. and Bhansali, R. (1970) 'Political economy', *Political Studies,* XVIII, 43–106.

Hain, P. (1998) *Proportional Misrepresentation* (Aldershot: Gower).

Harris, R. (2001) 'The Left blinds itself to the truth about bin Laden', *Daily Telegraph,* 18 December 2001.

Harrop, M. (1982) 'Labour-voting conservatives: policy differences between the Labour party and Labour voters', in R. Worcester and M. Harrop (eds), *Political Communication: The General Election Campaign of 1979* (London: Allen & Unwin), 152–63.

Harrop, M. (1986) 'Press coverage of post war British elections', in I. Crewe and M. Harrop (eds), *Political Communications: The General Election Campaign of 1983* (Cambridge: Cambridge University Press).

Harrop, M. and Scammell, M. (1992) 'A Tabloid War', in D. Butler and D. Kavanagh, *The British General Election of 1992* (London: Macmillan), 180–210.

Harrop, M., Heath, A. and Openshaw, S. (1992) 'Does neighbourhood influence voting behaviour – and why?', in I. Crewe, P. Norris, D. Denver and D. Broughton (eds), *British Elections and Parties Yearbook 1991* (Hemel Hempstead: Harvester Wheatsheaf), 103–20.

Hart, J. (1992) *Proportional Representation: Critics of the British Electoral System 1820–1945* (Oxford: Clarendon Press).

Heath, A. and Taylor, B. (1999) 'New Sources of Abstention?', in G. Evans and P. Norris (eds), *Critical Elections* (London: Sage), 164–80.

Heath, A., Jowell, R. and Curtice, J. (1985) *How Britain Votes* (Oxford: Pergamon Press).

Heath, A., Jowell, R. and Curtice, J. (2001) *The Rise of New Labour: Party Policies and Voter Choices* (Oxford: Oxford University Press).

Heath, A., Jowell, R., Curtice, J., Evans, G., Field, J. and Witherspoon, S. (1991) *Understanding Political Change* (Oxford: Pergamon Press).

Heath, A., Jowell, R., Curtice, J. with B. Taylor (eds) (1994) *Labour's Last Chance? The 1992 Election and Beyond* (Aldershot: Dartmouth).

Himmelweit, H., Jaeger, M. and Stockdale, T. (1978) 'Memory for Past Vote: Implications of Bias in Recall', *British Journal of Political Science*, 8, 365–84.

Jenkins, R. (1998) *Report of the Independent Commission on the Voting System* (London: The Stationery Office).

Johnston, R. and Pattie, C. (2001) 'It's the economy, stupid – but which economy? Geographical scales, retrospective economic evaluations and voting at the 1997 British general election', *Regional Studies*, 35, 309–20.

Johnston, R., Pattie, C. and Allsop, J. (1988) *A Nation Dividing* (London: Longman).

Johnston, R., Pattie, C. and Rossiter, D. (2005) 'The election results in the UK regions' in P. Norris and C. Wlezien (eds), *Britain Votes 2005* (Oxford: Oxford University Press), 130–45.

Johnston, R., Rossiter, D. and Pattie, R. (2006) 'Disproportionality and bias in the results of the 2005 general election: evaluating the electoral system's impact', *Journal of Elections, Public Opinion and Parties*, 16 (1), 37–54.

Johnston, R., Pattie, C., Dorling, D. and Rossiter, D. (2001) *From Votes to Seats: The Operation of the UK Electoral System since 1945* (Manchester: Manchester University Press).

Johnston, R., Pattie, C., Dorling, D., MacAllister, I., Tunstall, H. and Rossiter, D. (2000) 'The Neighbourhood Effect and Voting in England and Wales: Real or Imagined?', in *British Elections and Parties Review*, 10, 47–63.

Johnston, R., Pattie, C., Dorling, D., Rossiter, D., Tunstall, H. and MacAllister, I. (1998) 'New Labour Landslide – Same Old Electoral Geography?', *British Elections and Parties Review*, 8, 35–64.

Kavanagh, D. (1995) *Election Campaigning: The New Marketing of Politics* (Oxford: Basil Blackwell).

Kavanagh, D. and Butler, D. (2005) *The British General Election of 2005* (Basingstoke: Palgrave Macmillan).

King, A. (1975) 'Overload: problems of governing in the 1970s', *Political Studies*, XXIII, 284–96.

King, A. (ed.) (2002) *Britain at the Polls 2001* (New York: Chatham House).

King, A. (2006) 'Why Labour Won' in J. Bartle and A. King (eds) *Britain at the Polls 2005* (Wahington, DC: CQ Press), 151–84.

King, A. and Wybrow, R. (2001) *British Political Opinion 1937–2000* (London: Politico's).

Lazarsfeld, P., Berelson, B. and Gaudet, H. (1968) *The People's Choice*, 3rd edn; first published 1944 (New York: Columbia University Press).

Lijphart, A. (1994) *Electoral Systems and Party Systems* (Oxford: Oxford University Press).

Lipset, S. M. and Rokkan, S. (1967) *Party Systems and Voter Alignments* (New York: Free Press).

McAllister, I. and Studlar, D. (1992) 'Region and voting in Britain: territorial polarization or artifact', *American Journal of Political Science*, 36, 168–99.

McCallum, R. B. and Readman, A. (1947) *The British General Election of 1945* (Oxford: Oxford University Press).

McKenzie, R. and Silver, A. (1968) *Angels in Marble* (London: Heinemann).

McLean, I. (1982) *Dealing in Votes* (London: Martin Robertson).

Margetts, H., van Heerde, J. and Dunleavy, P. (2005) 'Explaining Voters' Choices in London Elections 2004', Paper presented at the PSA annual conference, Leeds.

Mill, J. S. (1963) *Considerations on Representative Government*, World Classics edn (Oxford: Oxford University Press).

Miller, W. (1977) *Electoral Dynamics in Britain since 1918* (London: Macmillan).

Miller, W. (1978) 'Social class and party choice in England: a new analysis', *British Journal of Political Science*, 8, 257–84.

Miller, W. (1979) 'Class, region and strata at the British general election of 1979', *Parliamentary Affairs*, 32, 376–82.

Miller, W. (1981) *The End of British Politics* (Oxford: Clarendon Press).

Miller, W. (1991) *Media and Voters* (Oxford: Clarendon Press).

Miller, W. and Mackie, M. (1973) 'The electoral cycle and the asymmetry of government and opposition popularity', *Political Studies*, XXI, 263–79.

Miller, W., Tagg, S. and Britto, K. (1986) 'Partisanship and party preference in government and opposition: the mid-term perspective', *Electoral Studies*, 5, 31–46.

Miller, W., Clarke, H., Harrop, M., Leduc, L. and Whiteley, P. (1990) *How Voters Change* (Oxford: Clarendon Press).

Milne, R. S. and MacKenzie, H. C. (1954) *Straight Fight* (London: Hansard Society).

Milne, R. S. and MacKenzie, H. C. (1958) *Marginal Seat* (London: Hansard Society).

Moon, N. (1999) *Opinion Polls: History, Theory and Practice* (Manchester: Manchester University Press).

Mughan, A. (1993) 'Party leaders and presidentialism in the 1992 election: a post-war perspective', in D. Denver, P. Norris, D. Broughton and C. Rallings (eds), *British Elections and Parties Yearbook 1993* (London: Frank Cass), 193–204.

Newton, K. (1993) 'Economic voting in the 1992 general election', in D. Denver, P. Norris, D. Broughton and C. Rallings (eds), *British Elections and Parties Yearbook 1993* (Hemel Hempstead: Harvester Wheatsheaf), 158–76.

Newton, K. and Brynin, M. (2001) 'The National Press and Party Voting in the UK', *Political Studies*, 49, 265–85.

Nicholas, H. G. (1951) *The British General Election of 1950* (London: Macmillan).

Niemi, R., Whitten, G. and Franklin, M. (1992) 'Constituency characteristics, individual characteristics and tactical voting in the 1987 British general election', *British Journal of Political Science*, 22, 229–54.

Nordlinger, E. (1967) *Working-Class Tories* (London: Macgibbon & Kee).

Norpoth, H. (1992) *Confidence Regained: Economics, Mrs. Thatcher and the British Voter* (Ann Arbor, MI: University of Michigan Press).

Norris, P. (1987) 'Four weeks of sound and fury? . . . the 1987 British election campaign', *Parliamentary Affairs*, 40, 458–67.

Norris, P. (1990) *British By-elections* (Oxford: Clarendon Press).

Norris, P. (1997a) *Electoral Change in Britain since 1945* (Oxford: Basil Blackwell).

Norris, P. (1997b) 'Political Communications', in P. Dunleavy, A. Gamble, I. Holliday and G. Peele (eds), *Developments in British Politics 5* (London: Macmillan), 75–88.

Norris, P. (ed.) (2001) *Britain Votes 2001* (Oxford: Oxford University Press).

Norris, P. and Wlezien, C. (eds) (2005) *Britain Votes 2005* (Oxford: Oxford University Press).

Norris, P., Curtice, J., Sanders, D., Scammell, M. and Semetko, H. (1999) *On Message: Communicating the Campaign* (London: Sage).

Norton, P. (2002) 'The Conservative Party: Is There Anyone Out There?', in A. King (ed.), *Britain at the Polls 2001* (New York: Chatham House), 68–94.

O'Leary, C. (1962) *The Elimination of Corrupt Practices in British Elections 1868–1911* (Oxford: Clarendon Press).

Paterson, L., Brown, A., Curtice, J., Hinds, K., McCrone, D., Park, A., Sproston, K. and Surridge, P. (2001) *New Scotland, New Politics?* (Edinburgh: Polygon).

Pattie, C. and Johnston, R. (1998) 'Voter Turnout at the British General Election of 1992: Rational choice, social standing or political efficacy?', *European Journal of Political Research*, 33, 263–83.

Pattie, C. and Johnston, R. (1999) 'Context, conversation and conviction: social networks and voting at the 1992 British General Election', *Political Studies*, 47, 877–99.

Pattie, C. and Johnston, R. (2001) 'Talk as a political context: conversation and electoral change in British elections, 1992–1997', *Electoral Studies*, 20, 17–40.

Pattie, C., Johnston, R. and Fieldhouse, E. (1993) 'Plus ca change? The changing electoral geography of Great Britain, 1979–92', in D. Denver, P. Norris, D. Broughton and C. Rallings (eds), *British Elections and Parties Yearbook 1993* (Hemel Hempstead: Harvester Wheatsheaf), 85–99.

Pattie, C., Johnston, R. and Fieldhouse, E. (1995) 'Winning the Local Vote: The Effectiveness of Constituency Campaign Spending in Great Britain, 1983–1992', *American Political Science Review*, 89 (4), 969–83.

Pulzer, P. G. (1967) *Political Representation and Elections in Britain* (London: George Allen & Unwin).

Quinn, T. (2006) 'Tony Blair's Second Term' in J. Bartle and A. King (eds.) *Britain at the Polls 2005* (Washington DC: CQ Press).

Rallings, C. and Thrasher, M. (1990) 'Turnout in Local Elections: An aggregate data analysis with electoral and contextual data', *Electoral Studies*, 9, 79–90.

Rallings, C. and Thrasher, M. (2000) *British Electoral Facts 1832–1999* (Aldershot: Ashgate).

Rallings, C. and Thrasher, M. (2005) *Election 2005: The Official Results* (Plymouth: Local Government Chronicle).

Reif, K. and Schmitt, H. (1980) 'Nine Second-Order Elections', *European Journal of Political Research*, 8, 3–45 and 145–62.

Rose, R. (1974) 'Britain: simple abstractions and complex realities', in R. Rose (ed.), *Electoral Behaviour* (New York: Free Press).

Rose, R. and McAllister, I. (1986) *Voters Begin to Choose* (London: Sage).

Rose, R. and McAllister, I. (1990) *The Loyalties of Voters* (London: Sage).

Rose, D. and Sullivan, O. (1996) *Introducing Data Analysis for Social Scientists*, 2nd edn (Buckingham: Open University Press).

Rosenbaum, M. (1997) *From Soapbox to Soundbite: Party Political Campaigning in Britain since 1945* (London: Macmillan).

Saggar, S. (1998) *The General Election 1997: Ethnic Minorities and Electoral Politics* (London: Commission for Racial Equality).

Sanders, D. (1991) 'Government popularity and the next general election', *Political Quarterly*, LXII, 235–61.

Sanders, D. (1992) 'Why the Conservatives won – again', in A. King (ed.), *Britain at the Polls 1992* (New York: Chatham House), 171–222.

Sanders, D. (1993) 'Forecasting the 1992 British general election outcome: the performance of an economic model', in D. Denver, P. Norris, D. Broughton and C. Rallings (eds), *British Elections and Parties Yearbook 1993* (Hemel Hempstead: Harvester Wheatsheaf), 100–15.

Sanders, D. (1995) 'It's the Economy, Stupid: The Economy and Support for the Conservative Party, 1979–1994', *Talking Politics*, 7, 158–67.

Sanders, D. (1999) 'The Impact of Left–Right Ideology' in G. Evans and P. Norris (eds) *Critical Elections* (London: Sage), 181–206.

Sanders, D. (2005) 'The Political Economy of UK Party Support, 1997–2004: Forecasts for the 2005 General Election' *Journal of Elections, Public Opinion and Parties*, 15 (1), 47–71.

Sanders, D., Ward, H. and Marsh, D. (1987) 'Government popularity and the Falklands war: a reassessment', *British Journal of Political Science*, 17, 281–313.

Sanders, D., Clarke, H., Stewart, M. and Whiteley, P. (2001) 'The economy and voting', in P. Norris (ed.), *Britain Votes 2001* (Oxford: Oxford University Press), 223–38.

Sarlvik, B. and Crewe, I. (1983) *Decade of Dealignment* (Cambridge: Cambridge University Press).

Scammell, M. (1995) *Designer Politics: How Elections are Won* (London: Macmillan).

Scammell, M. and Harrop, M. (1997) 'The Press', in D. Butler and D. Kavanagh, *The British General Election of 1997* (London: Macmillan), 156–85.

218   *References*

Seymour-Ure, C. (2002) 'New Labour and the Media', in A. King (ed.), *Britain at the Polls 2001* (New York: Chatham House), 117–42.

Shaw, E. (1994) *The Labour Party since 1979* (London: Routledge).

Steed, M. (1986) 'The core-periphery dimension of British politics', *Political Geography Quarterly,* 5, 91–103.

Stokes, D. (1992) 'Valence politics', in D. Kavanagh (ed.), *Electoral Politics* (Oxford: Clarendon Press).

Swaddle, K. and Heath, A. (1989) 'Official and reported turnout in the British general election of 1987', *British Journal of Political Science,* 19, 537–51.

Teer, F. and Spence, J.D. (1973) *Political Opinion Polls* (London: Hutchinson).

Trenaman, J. and McQuail, D. (1961) *Television and the Political Image* (London: Methuen).

Wallas, G. (1910) *Human Nature in Politics* (London: Constable).

Whiteley, P. (1986) 'The accuracy and influence of the polls in the 1983 general election', in I. Crewe and M. Harrop (eds), *Political Communications: The 1983 Election Campaign* (Cambridge: Cambridge University Press), 312–24.

Whiteley, P. and Seyd, P. (1994) 'Local Party Campaigning and Voting Behaviour in Britain', *Journal of Politics,* 56, 242–51.

Worcester, R. and Mortimore, R. (1999) *Explaining Labour's Landslide* (London: Politico's).

Worcester, R. and Mortimore, R. (2001) *Explaining Labour's Second Landslide* (London: Politico's).

Worcester, R., Mortimore, R. and Baines, P. (2005) *Explaining Labour's Landslip: The 2005 General Election* (London: Methuen).

Name index

Subject index